# Human Relationship Skills

*Human Relationship Skills: Coaching and Self-Coaching* presents a practical 'how to' guide to relationship skills, showing how readers can improve and, where necessary, repair relationships. This thoroughly revised and updated 4th edition reflects the increased interest in coaching, showing how it can be applied to everyday life.

In this essential book, Richard Nelson-Jones takes a cognitive-behavioural approach to coaching people in relationship skills. These skills are viewed as sequences of choices that people can make well or poorly. Covering a range of skill areas the book assists readers to make affirming rather than destructive choices in their relationships. It begins by addressing the questions of 'What are relationship skills?' and 'What are coaching skills?', and follows with a series of chapters which thoroughly detail and illuminate various relationship skills including:

- Listening and showing understanding.
- Managing shyness.
- Intimacy and companionship.
- Assertiveness and managing anger.
- Managing relationship problems and ending relationships.

The book concludes with a chapter on how users can maintain and improve their skills by coaching themselves.

Accessibly written and using activities, the book is appropriate for those involved in 'life coaching' as well as general counselling and therapy. It will be essential reading for lecturers, coaches and trainers as well as students and anyone who wishes to improve their relationship skills.

**Richard Nelson-Jones** is a leading international author whose books have helped train many thousands of psychotherapists, counsellors and helpers worldwide. He has held university appointments in Britain and Australia, and is a Fellow of the British and Australian Psychological Societies and of the British Association for Counselling and Psychotherapy.

'Many people do not possess the needed skills for positive interpersonal relationships. This pragmatic handbook will allow you to help yourself and others to gain mental health and happiness. I highly recommend this book and hope that it is widely read.'

Jon Carlson, Distinguished Professor, Governors State University, Illinois

'This excellent book comprehensively covers key human relationship skills. During my workshops and lectures often I would recommend the earlier version of this book as an aid to practitioners and their clients. This new revised 4th edition is even better, especially with its coaching and self-coaching approach.'

Stephen Palmer, Director of the Centre for Coaching

'Richard Nelson-Jones's 4th edition will be my recommended text in my roles as (tertiary education) lecturer, counsellor, and supervisor of mental health professionals. His comprehensive skills training enables mastery and self-reliance in this essential field.'

Meredith Fuller, Counselling Psychologist, Lecturer, and
Supervisor of Mental Health Professionals

'Richard Nelson-Jones has produced another of his excellent skills manuals – this time inviting us to self-examine and self-improve on all the dimensions of relationships. Richard's writing is enriched with significant breadth of knowledge of the wisdom of the field, but he offers his own special brand of invitation to think of skills, and to reflect and work on ways to improve those skills. With extraordinary attention to detail he uncovers many aspects of relationships – shyness, assertiveness, sexuality among others. The exercises for self-examination are demanding, intriguing, and enlightening. Very worthwhile for counsellors, life coaches, and indeed for anyone who would like to reflect on and improve their relationship skills.'

Ron Perry, Director, Institute of Counselling, Sydney

# Human Relationship Skills

## COACHING AND SELF-COACHING

**4th edition**

**Richard Nelson-Jones**

Routledge
Taylor & Francis Group

LONDON AND NEW YORK

First published 1986 as *Human Relationship Skills: Training and Self-help* by Cassell, London and by Holt Rinehart and Winston, Sydney

Second edition published 1990 as *Human Relationship Skills: Training and Self-help* by Cassell, London and 1991 as *Human Relationship Skills* by Holt Rinehart and Winston, Sydney

Third edition published 1996 as *Relating Skills: A Practicle Guide to Effective Personal Relationships* by Continuum, London and as *Human Relating Skills* by Harcourt Brace, Sydney

Fourth edition published 2006
by Routledge
27 Church Road, Hove, East Sussex BN3 2FA

Simultaneously published in the USA and Canada
by Routledge
711 Third Avenue, New York, NY 10017

*Routledge is an imprint of the Taylor & Francis Group, an Informa business*

Copyright © 2006 Richard Nelson-Jones

Typeset in Goudy by RefineCatch Limited, Bungay, Suffolk
Paperback cover by Hybert Design

This publication has been produced with paper manufactured to strict environmental standards and with pulp derived from sustainable forests.

*British Library Cataloguing in Publication Data*
A catalogue record for this book is available from the British Library

*Library of Congress Cataloging-in-Publication Data*
Nelson-Jones, Richard.
    Human relationship skills : coaching and self-coaching / Richard Nelson-Jones. – 4th ed.
        p. cm.
    Previously published: Relating skills: a practical guide to effective personal relationships. London : Continuum, 1996.
    Includes bibliographical references and index.
    ISBN 0-415-38586-5 – ISBN 0-415-38587-3    1. Interpersonal relations.
2. Social skills.    3. Personal coaching.    I. Title.
    HM1106.N45 2006
    158.2–dc22                                                          2005027114

ISBN13: 978-0-415-38586-2
ISBN13: 978-0-415-38587-9

# Contents

# Activities

# Preface

Welcome to the fourth edition of *Human Relationship Skills: Coaching and Self-Coaching*. The following are answers to some questions you may have about the book.

## WHAT IS THIS BOOK'S PURPOSE?

This is a practical 'how to' book on coaching relationship skills. Written for lecturers, trainers and coaches and those being lectured, trained and coached, the book aims to show you how to improve and, where necessary, to repair relationships. I aim to help you to gain greater relationship satisfaction and prevent unnecessary distress and pain. Relationship skills are viewed as sequences of choices in various skills areas that you can make well or poorly. You can either support or oppress yourself and one another by the choices you make. This book coaches you in how to make affirming rather than destructive choices in your relationships.

## FOR WHOM IS THIS BOOK INTENDED?

This book is intended for the following audiences.

- Lecturers, trainers and coaches running relationship training and coaching courses in colleges and universities, schools, adult education centres and in non-educational settings. Such courses may be run in psychology departments – as an applied change from academic teaching – and in personnel work, social work, education, nursing, personnel work, pastoral care and as part of college general education programmes.
- Students training for the helping services: for instance, as psychologists, counsellors, social workers, nurses, personnel officers, teachers and pastoral care workers.
- Students in colleges, universities and adult education centres taking human relations and human communication courses.

- Staff and individual clients and groups of clients in college counselling centres. Many counselling centres run courses on aspects of human relationship skills.
- Trainers and participants on marriage preparation and relationship coaching courses run by voluntary and church-related agencies.
- Students in the final years of secondary school.
- Helping service professionals and voluntary agency counsellors for reference and for recommending to clients.
- Singles and couples interested in improving their relationship skills by means of self-help.

Though strongly supporting family values, I do not intend this book for those wishing to learn more about family and parenting skills. Nevertheless, I hope the book indirectly results in happier families and children.

## WHAT ARE THIS BOOK'S CONTENTS?

The first chapter introduces the idea of people possessing a repertoire of relationship skills, each of which is composed of communication skills and mind skills. The second chapter is the only one in the book written mainly for those coaching and describes some central skills of being an effective coach. There then follow 11 chapters to support the coaching of various important relationship skills: listening, show understanding, manage shyness, choose a relationship, intimacy, companionship, sexual relationship, assertiveness, manage anger, manage relationship problems, and end a relationship skills. The final chapter addresses the issue of coaching yourself and getting assistance in so doing. I have put skills-building activities throughout the book.

## WHAT FEATURES DOES THIS BOOK POSSESS?

- *Lifeskills emphasis.* Human relationship skills are important lifeskills that you can be coached in and learn well or poorly. Fortunately, you can keep improving your skills. Throughout the book, I use the term relationship skills rather than lifeskills.
- *Comprehensiveness.* I offer a comprehensive coverage of the skills you require for effective personal relationships. I break the sexual silence of most texts on relationship skills by devoting a chapter to this important topic.
- *Emphasis on mental cultivation.* The book emphasizes personal responsibility, courage and mental discipline. Nowhere do I encourage you to think that relating well is always easy.
- *Anglo-Australian emphasis.* Unlike most relationship coaching and education texts which are American, this book draws on British and Australian demographic data, books, articles and research findings.
- *Practical activities.* The book includes numerous practical activities to

help you as singles, partners or in groups develop your knowledge and skills.

- *User-friendly format*. Each chapter follows the same user-friendly format: chapter outcomes, text and activities.
- *Readability*. I have endeavoured to write the book in clear and simple English.

## A FINAL WORD

I hope the book articulates a vision of how to relate that resonates with you. Good luck and, above all, good skills!

Richard Nelson-Jones

# What are human relationship skills?

**Chapter outcomes**
By studying and doing the activities in this chapter you should:

- gain some knowledge into what are relationships
- understand more about changing patterns of relationships
- be introduced to a skills approach to relationships
- be introduced to communication skills
- be introduced to mind skills
- understand the role of feelings and physical reactions.

Human relationship skills are the skills involved in human connection. All human beings are biologically programmed to need other people, both for the acts of conception and birth and then throughout their lives. Relationships come with no guarantee of happiness and can be for good or ill, for pleasure or pain. However, the more skilled you are at relating, the greater the likelihood that you will maximize your own and others' happiness and contribute less to the sum of human misery and pain. We all like our relationships to be rewarding. The following are examples of people who relate in *rewarding* ways.

Whenever Jim and Tricia come home from work, they may rest for a short time, but then they always check with interest how each other's day has gone.

Chloe and Paul do not just enjoy their sexual relationship, they also enjoy the companionship that comes from regularly kissing, hugging, putting an arm over each other's shoulders and holding hands.

Though initially Lucy did not like visiting her partner Tony's parents regularly, she now goes over with him every other week-end and gets along well with them. Tony greatly appreciates the effort she has made.

The following are examples of people relating in *unrewarding* ways.

Tom gets jealous because his wife Emma is having an animated discussion with their friend Pete at a party. Later Tom angrily accuses Emma of flirting with Pete, despite this not being the case.

Often when Susan wants to make a point with Joe, she comes on very strong which has the effect of making him withdraw from any real discussion of situations.

Dave and Sophie rarely listen properly to each other any more, even when one of them is trying to say something important in a reasonable way.

In each of these examples, people used varying degrees of relationship skills. Those who were giving and getting rewards in their relationships used their relationship skills effectively to attain these ends. Those behaving in unrewarding ways failed to use good skills. In reality, people often use a mixture of good and poor skills, though in good relationships skilled behaviour predominates.

## WHAT ARE RELATIONSHIPS?

Connection is the essential characteristic of relationships. People in relationships exist in some connection with one another, be it marriage, kinship, friendship or acquaintance. Isolation or being placed apart from others is very different from relationship, though even in isolation people can mentally relate to others. John Donne, the Elizabethan, wrote in his *Devotions upon Emergent Occasions* (1624: 17): 'No man is an Island, entire of it self; every man is a piece of the Continent, a part of the main'. In short, humans are social animals who cannot avoid relationships. We are condemned not only to exist, but to relate. However, in an existential sense, humans are also condemned to isolation: for example, no one can die another's death for them. Out of their human separateness, humans strive to relate.

Though relationships can be very brief, the term can imply a broader time frame. Personal relationships are often long term and contain the expectation that they will continue into the future. Feelings of attachment, commitment and obligation, as well as of hatred and despair, can run very deep in such relationships.

Inevitably relationships involve change. Over time, all people change in varying ways and degrees. For instance, they age and develop different interests. Furthermore, how partners relate can contribute to changes in each of them, such as greater or less self-confidence. In addition, change can be deliberately initiated in relationships, for example, getting married, buying a flat and having a baby. Sometimes external circumstances precipitate change, for instance, unemployment or an inheritance. Relationships need to accommodate changes. Given the imperative in life of change and challenge, relationships can grow and strengthen or wither and die.

## Levels of relationships

When two people relate, they do so on differing levels. First, there is the *intrapersonal* level. Each individual is in a relationship with herself or himself. As a simple illustration, shut your eyes for 30 seconds and try to think of nothing. Most people will soon become aware that they are talking to themselves and possibly getting visual images as well. Your relationship to yourself can be of varying levels of psychological wellness. For instance, some people may be quite isolated from themselves. Such isolation may stem from a mixture of their biological make-up and unfortunate early learning experiences that psychologically they have not moved beyond. The results of this can include insufficient sense of identity and poor access to feelings and thoughts. You also relate to yourself not just in terms of your past, but also in terms of your present and future: for instance, you think and feel about current and future relationships with others. The inner game of relating is another expression for the intrapersonal level of relationships.

Second, there is the *interpersonal* level of relationships. This is the level of relationships alluded to in the previous discussion on connection. People outwardly relate to others in terms of their thoughts, feelings, physical reactions and how they communicate and act. In all relationships, people have roles, for instance, spouse, partner, parent and child. A distinction may be made between role relationships and person relationships. Role relationships tend to be heavily influenced by traditional expectations of behaviour for the role. Person relationships allow for spontaneity. Though a simplification, as relationships progress, people move beyond relating as they should be (their roles) to relating as they are and choose to become (as persons).

Third, there is the *social context* level of relationships. All relationships take place within social contexts. For instance, the social contexts of two people contemplating marriage include their families, friends, acquaintances, cultures, social class, race, religion, and so on. The arenas in which relationships take place provide important social contexts: for instance, homes, schools, workplaces and recreational facilities. An important aspect of such social contexts is that they provide rules and expectations about appropriate and inappropriate behaviour.

## Relationships as perceptions

All individuals exist in the subjective world of their perceptions (Rogers, 1951, 1975). Your perceptions are your reality. A Chinese proverb states: 'Two-thirds of what we see is behind our eyes.' Relationships do not exist independent of people's perceptions of them. Two people in the same relationship perceive and experience it differently. Thus within a marital relationship, there are *her* and *his* relationships as well as *our* relationship. Your perceptions influence all aspects of your relationships: intrapersonal – for instance, not seeing some negative attribute you possess; interpersonal – seeing only good qualities in someone to whom you are attracted; and social context – the importance you attach to behaving in accordance with your culture.

Two of you in a relationship do not just relate to each other. Instead you relate to your perceptions of yourselves, each other and your relationship. These perceptions are of varying degrees of accuracy. Another way of stating this is that each of you develops a personification of yourself and the other (Sullivan, 1953). These personifications – literally making up or fabricating a person – are the mental maps that guide your relationship journeys. In distressed relationships, misunderstandings can begin and be maintained by partners developing and holding on to distorted pictures or personifications of each other and of themselves (Beck, 1988, 1999).

# SOME FACTS ABOUT RELATIONSHIPS

## Marriage and cohabitation

In 2002 the population of the United Kingdom was 59,229 people. Over the past 30 years or so there has been a distinct trend towards a decline in marriages and an increase in cohabitation. In 1976 there were 406,000 marriages in the United Kingdom, whereas in 2001 there were 286,100 marriages. Of the 2001 marriages, approximately 176,000 were first marriages. There is also a trend among those who do get married to marry later: for instance, the median (mid-point in a set of scores) ages for first marriages in 1976 were 25.1 for men and 22.8 for women respectively, whereas these figures in 2001 were 30.8 for men and 28.4 for women (Office for National Statistics, 2003a).

In the early 1990s, approximately 70 of first marriages were preceded by premarital cohabitation compared with approximately 10 per cent in the early 1970s. For those marrying in the 1990s and 1970s, the median duration of premarital cohabitation was about two years and one year respectively. In 1993, over 20 per cent of non-married men and women were cohabiting, compared with under 15 per cent in the mid-1980s (Haskey, 1995). This trend towards cohabitation appears not only to have continued but to have increased. In addition, growing proportions of men and women are living outside a partnership. The younger age groups, particularly those in their twenties, show the greatest changes in patterns of marriage and cohabitation.

In Australia, the population has been growing rapidly: 3.4 million in 1901,

6.6 million in 1942, 10.7 million in 1962 and 19.7 million in 2002 (Trewin, 2004). In 1971, the marriage rate was 9.3 per thousand, with the median age at first marriage for men being 23.8 years and the median age for women 21.4 years. By 2001 the marriage rate to 5.3 per thousand, with the median ages 30.6 and 28.6 for men and women, respectively. The crude marriage rate has been declining since 1970 and this can be mainly attributed to changes in attitudes to marriage and living arrangements that have occurred since then. In 2002, there were nearly one million people in de facto relationships. The rate of premarital cohabitation has risen from below 2 per cent in the 1950s to 71 per cent in 2001 (De Vaus *et al.*, 2003). There is some evidence from Australia that premarital cohabitation does not pose any greater risk of subsequent marriage breakdown than not living together.

## Relationship distress

In the last 30 years in Australia, marriage 'rates have declined, there is less pressure to marry, it is easier to end a damaging relationship, fertility has sharply declined, women can more easily control their fertility, and the participation of women in the (part-time) workforce has steadily increased' (De Vaus, 2002). The same is true for Britain. Though the proportion of cohabiting people has been rising, most people still get married and expect it to be permanent. However, as Shakespeare wrote: 'The course of true love never does run smooth.' In both Britain and Australia the divorce rates are high. In England and Wales, in 1991, there were 306,800 marriages and 158,700 divorces. In 2002, there were 249,200 marriages and 143,800 divorces (Office for National Statistics, 2003b). For both 1991 and 2002, when examining the ratio between marriage and divorce, the falling marriage rate needs to be taken into account, thus making the proportion of divorces seem higher than was the case.

In Australia, the percentage of marriages ending in divorce has greatly increased since the Family Law Act of 1975. This Act stated that there was only one ground for divorce, namely the irretrievable breakdown of the marriage measured as separation of the spouses for at least one year. By 1991, about 40 per cent of Australian marriages ended in divorce (Australian Institute of Family Studies, 1993) and this figure has probably risen to over 45 per cent since then.

The divorce figures underestimate the extent of marital distress and break-down. If figures for the separated population were added to those of the divorced population to form a 'dissolution index', the statistics for marital breakdown would be considerably higher. Moreover, for numerous reasons – including concern for children, financial insecurity, fear of going it alone and religious beliefs – many couples remain unhappily married. Add these people to the 'dissolution index' and it could be that more marriages end up being unhappy than happy.

Frequently partners leaving marital relationships have numerous painful experiences. Some may end up wishing that they had never left (Litvinoff, 1993). Most will suffer a loss of confidence and self-esteem. Many will experience financial hardship and loneliness. All are either building or will need to build new lives.

Divorce and relationship breakup also involve children. The vast majority of single-parent families are headed by lone mothers. Though divorce may be better than living with a high level of conflict, it can negatively affect children. However, the child's relationship with each parent may be a more critical factor in their adjustment than the parents' relationship to each other. Negative effects of divorce on children can show up in increased depression, self-blame for the parental split, conflicting loyalties and anxiety over their future (Goldenberg and Goldenberg, 1990, 2005). Children with divorced parents may need to make more adjustments than children from intact families: for example, to moving house, moving school, visiting a non-custodial parent, mother starting a new job and either or both parents remarrying.

## Reasons for marital breakdown

The reasons for marital breakdown are both personal and social. Some American evidence exists that people whose parents were divorced are more likely to become divorced themselves than people whose parents stayed together (Segin *et al.*, 2005). Partner alcoholism and violence are mainly women's reasons for wanting to separate. Other reasons are more evenly divided among the sexes: for instance, relationship problems, infidelity, perceptions that 'things won't change', and growing apart through external pressures such as those caused by work and in-laws (Australian Institute of Family Studies, 1993). In addition, poor relationship skills increase the chance of marital breakdown.

Social reasons for marital breakdown include the fact that obtaining a divorce is easier and less socially stigmatized than in the past. In addition, there has been a rise in expectations regarding marital happiness and these higher expectations have an increased chance of not being fulfilled. The greater participation of women in the workforce and the fact the modern marriages involve fewer children than in the past means that women may be less dependent on their husband's income and so freer to leave. Furthermore, the decline in the influence of the church lowers another psychological barrier to divorce.

## A RELATIONSHIP SKILLS APPROACH

### Universal human being skills

Are there universal human being skills that underlie and transcend cultural diversity? By universal human being skills I mean skills that characterize the good or effective person regardless of the culture or country in which they live (Nelson-Jones, 2002). The survival of the human species depends on the existence of sufficient good or skilled human beings to protect the interests of future generations.

A way of thinking of human being skills is in terms of level of functioning or developing human potential. Here a distinction exists between possessing subnormal, normal and supranormal skills. For genetic, social learning and economic reasons, some humans function at below the norm for the human race. The vast majority of people possess a mixture of good and poor human being skills that place them within the range of normal functioning. However, some people develop their human being skills to the point where their level of functioning is clearly superior. Though not using the word skills, Maslow, in his study of self-actualizing people, tried to identify some of the characteristics of supranormalcy (Maslow, 1970).

What are some advantages of using a skills framework or skills language? First, attempts can be made to identify and define the skills human beings require if they are to function effectively. Second, the concept of skills provides a focus for training people in human being skills. Already much successful training takes place without using the concept of skills. For example, children reared in loving and nurturing environments are more likely to possess the skills of relating to other people warmly than those children who are emotionally abused or deprived. Nevertheless identifying, articulating and training people in what are desirable human being skills might lead to better child-rearing practices. Third, the concept of skills provides human beings with a self-help framework for monitoring, improving and, where necessary, self-correcting how well they use their mind skills and communication/action skills.

A starting point for discussing the issue of universality in human being skills is that of the biological basis of human nature. Over thousands of years, humans have evolved as a distinct species whose behaviour is influenced by their thoughts rather than solely determined by instinct. Nevertheless the role of instinct remains strong: for instance, in regard to meeting biological needs, reproducing the species, nurturing the young and caring for the sick.

Every individual has a biologically based inner nature comprised of elements that are common to the species and those that are unique to that individual. Charles Darwin referred to humans possessing an 'instinct of sympathy' and this would appear to be an important survival instinct for the species (Dalai Lama and Cutler, 1998). However, much of western thinking sees human nature as egoistic, selfish and destructive, summed up in one of Freud's favourite quotes, which came from the Roman writer Plautus: 'Man is a wolf to man.' This 'bad animal' view of humans might be seen as based on humans who are not at a high level rather than on the healthiest human beings (Maslow, 1971). Furthermore, it ignores the ample evidence that humans can be cooperative and caring as well as hostile and uncaring (Argyle, 1991; Beck, 1999). How people act appears to be largely a matter of training and of how much their animal nature is lovingly nourished or frustrated.

Much research points to the conclusion that humans across the world share many common or universal characteristics. For example, Ekman and Friesen (1971) have identified seven main facial expressions for emotion across cultures: happiness, interest, surprise, fear, sadness, anger and disgust or contempt. Another example is that of Schwartz (1992) who classified values into ten types: power, achievement, hedonism, stimulation, self-direction, universalism, benevolence, tradition, conformity and security. Based on information from

20 countries in 6 continents, he confirmed that each of the 10 values was found in at least 90 per cent of the countries he surveyed, suggesting that his value types were near universal.

Alongside universality, there is also diversity. Humans across the world have had to face the tasks involved in human existence within the contexts of different physical environmental circumstances, such as climate, topography and natural resources. Throughout history, people in different locations have been in a constant process of evolving their cultures. Though some of the distinctiveness of individual cultures increasingly risks being eroded by globalization resulting from technological advances (Hermans and Kempen, 1998), a huge range of cultural diversity still exists.

Maslow was cautiously optimistic about the biological nature of human beings. However, he thought that positive instinctual aspects of human nature, such as altruistic concern for others, were frequently weak, needed a benign culture for their appearance, and could be inhibited or shattered by bad cultural conditions (1971). The noted anthropologist Ruth Benedict used the notion of *synergy* to describe the healthy interaction between individual and society (Benedict, 1942). Probably there is a reciprocal interaction between the development or lack of development of individuals and the cultures or societies to which they belong.

Viewing human functioning in skills terms is important. At present there are many different psychological theories about how human beings function, but they tend not to be couched in skills terms. Currently humans in their dealings with one another are not nearly as skilled as they should be to make the world a happier and safer place. Not to apply the concept of skills to human functioning leaves a huge gap in thinking about how to improve the human condition. Almost certainly there are universal human being skills. Furthermore, humans have the potential to develop such skills to a high level. Though family and social environments differ across cultures, certain characteristics or skills of the good person almost certainly transcend culture. One possible reason for this is that such skills are ultimately grounded in human biology and evolutionary requirement of survival of the species.

Diversity within universality is desirable. Positive cultural diversity, reflecting life-affirming variations of universal human being skills, requires nurturing and encouraging. Much more effort needs to be put into identifying what are universal human being skills before it is too late. This book, which is based on the work of numerous others such as Albert Ellis and Aaron Beck, is an attempt to identify and to provide training material for some universal relationship skills, though they are approached within a western context.

## Skills language

To talk about how to relate requires a common language in which to do so. Skills language provides such a framework.

## *What are skills?*

One meaning of the word skills pertains to *areas* of skill. For instance, albeit overlapping, broad areas of skills include: work skills, study skills, leisure skills, health skills and relationship skills. As demonstrated in subsequent chapters, relationship skills can be further broken down into areas such as rewarding listening, overcoming shyness, caring, assertion, managing anger and solving relationship problems. A second meaning of the word skills refers to *level of competence* or expertise. For instance, in a specific skills area you can be skilled, unskilled or a mixture of the two.

The third meaning of the word skills is less common. This meaning relates to the knowledge and *sequence of choices* entailed in implementing a skill. The main way that I can help you to acquire, develop and maintain satisfactory levels of competence in specific skills areas is by training you in their required sequences of choices.

The concept of relating skills is best viewed not in either/or terms in which you either possess or do not possess a skill. Rather, in any skills area it is preferable to think of yourself as possessing *skills strengths* or *skills weaknesses*, or a mixture of the two. If you make good choices in a skills area, for instance, either in listening or in talking about yourself, this is a skills strength. If you make poor choices in a skills area, this is a skills weakness. In all relationship skills areas, in varying degrees you are likely to possess both strengths and weaknesses. For instance, in the skills area of listening, you may be good at understanding talkers but poor at showing them you actually have understood. The object of working on your relationship skills is, in one or more areas, to help you shift the balance of your strengths and weaknesses more in the direction of strengths. Put another way it is to help you affirm yourself and others more by becoming a *better chooser*.

## *What is skills language?*

Skills language means consistently using the concept of skills to describe and analyse people's behaviour. In regard to relationships, skills language means, when necessary, thinking about how you relate in terms of skills strengths and weaknesses. A distinction exists between everyday or descriptive language and skills language. Below is an example of Tim who shows caring to his wife Anna by massaging her shoulders when she is stressed. Anna likes this very much.

> **Tim thinking in everyday language:** 'When I notice that Anna is stressed I sometimes massage her shoulders.'

> **Tim thinking in skills language:** 'I use my noticing when Anna is stressed skills and then, if she seems stressed, I sometimes use my massaging skills on her shoulders.'

The above is a simple example of the use of skills language. More sophisticated uses of skills language involve identifying specific mind skills and communication skills strengths that help people deal with relationship problems. You may consider it artificial to translate how you relate into skills terms. Many people are brought up to think in skills language when learning how to drive a car or play a sport. However, probably you have not learned to apply skills language to how you relate.

Why, then, do I advocate thinking about relationships in skills language? First, skills language requires you to identify the specific skills you require for your relationships. Second, skills language provides you with a relatively simple way that you can analyse and work on problems. You now have the tools with which to break problems down into the skills weaknesses that contribute to maintaining them. Third, many of you may find it less threatening to look at your problems in terms of the skills you need to work on them rather than having to admit personal inadequacy or blame. Fourth, my assumption is that many of your relationship problems repeat themselves. Consequently you may need not only to deal with current problems, but to prevent future similar problems. Skills language lends itself to self-instructing not only now but in future. As such, it provides a practical language for continuing self-helping.

Learning and implementing specific relationship skills can involve three steps: public use of skills language between trainers and learners; aware private use of skills language self-talk on the part of learners; and automatic use of skills language self-talk as learners gain fluency in using the skill. An analogy is that of learning to drive a car. First the instructor tells you what to do, then you are aware of instructing yourself, and lastly your self-instructions become automatic. During this process, your use of driving skills moves from feeling awkward to feeling natural. The same feelings can occur as you learn and then gain fluency in implementing specific relationship skills. Activity 1.1 gives you practice at translating everyday into skills language.

---

**ACTIVITY 1.1**          **Translate everyday into skills language** |

---

This activity may be performed in relation to either a specific partner or another close relationship. Either way, first do the activity on your own. Then, if appropriate discuss your answers with your partner, another or others.

1. Using your usual everyday language, list ways that you show caring to your partner/close friend.
2. Using your usual everyday language, list ways that your partner/close friend shows caring to you.
3. From each of the above lists, translate at least one way of showing caring from everyday language to skills language:

   (a) Me to my partner or close other
   (b) My partner or close other to me.

As a guide, here is the example of Tim and Anna used in the text.

> **Tim's everyday language:** 'When I notice that Anna is stressed I sometimes massage her shoulders.'

> **Tim's skills language:** 'I use my noticing when Anna is stressed skills and then, if she seems stressed, I sometimes use my massaging skills on her shoulders.'

4. How positively or negatively do you react to the idea of using skills language? Provide reasons for your answer.

---

## Repertoire of relationship skills

For your various relationships you require a *repertoire* of relationship skills. Sometimes you may not have a particular skill in your repertoire: for instance, the ability to say no to an unreasonable request. Other times you may want to strengthen a particular skill: for instance, expressing appreciation to a loved one. With some skills, you may also want to strike a more appropriate balance: for example, neither depending too much nor too little on others. Some relationship skills weaknesses you should eliminate altogether: for instance, physical or sexual abuse. Your repertoire of relationship skills comprises your strengths and weaknesses in each skills area.

## A framework for relationship skills

If you are to control how you relate, you need to think and communicate effectively. A simple way to highlight the distinction is to talk about the inner and outer games of relating. The inner game refers to what goes on inside you, how you think and feel, or your mind skills and feelings. The outer game refers to what goes on outside you, how you communicate and act, or your communication/action skills. Thinking and feeling are covert, communicating and acting are overt.

## Your communication and action skills

Communication and action skills involve observable behaviours. Communication skills refer to what you do and how you do it rather than what and how you feel and think. These skills vary by area of application: for instance, in personal relationships or at work. There are five main ways that you can send relationship skills, and indeed any other communication and action messages:

1. *Verbal messages.* Messages that you send with words: for example, saying 'I love you' or 'I hate you.'
2. *Vocal messages.* Messages that you send through your voice for instance, through your volume, articulation, pitch, emphasis and speech rate.
3. *Body messages.* Messages that you send with your body for instance, through your gaze, eye contact, facial expression, posture, gestures, physical proximity and clothes and grooming.
4. *Touch messages.* A special category of body messages that you send with your touch: for instance, through what part of the body you use, what part of another's body you touch, how gentle or firm you are, and whether or not you have permission.
5. *Taking action messages.* Messages that you send when you are not face to face with others: for example, sending flowers or a legal writ.

Activity 1.2 helps you to understand the ideas in this section.

**ACTIVITY 1.2**                    **Send communication/action skills messages**

This activity may be done in relation to either a specific partner or another close relationship. Either way, first do the activity on your own. Then, if appropriate, discuss your answers with your partner, another or others.

1. In each of the categories below, identify specific communication and action skills messages by means of which you show caring to your partner/close friend.

   (a) Verbal messages
   (b) Vocal messages
   (c) Body messages
   (d) Touch messages
   (e) Taking action messages.

2. In each of the categories below, identify specific communication and action skills messages by means of which your partner/close friend shows caring to you. In particular, emphasize caring messages that are different to the messages you send.

   (a) Verbal messages
   (b) Vocal messages
   (c) Body messages
   (d) Touch messages
   (e) Taking action messages.

3. Think of a communication and action skills message that you could send to improve the relationship with your partner/close friend and, if appropriate, enact it.

---

*Your mind skills*

You can use how you think to support yourself and others or to oppress yourself and others. Below are brief descriptions of six of the main mind skills areas derived from the work of leading psychiatrists and psychologists such as Aaron Beck and Albert Ellis. Rather than describe the skills in detail here, I illustrate their use throughout this book.

1. *Creating rules.* Your unrealistic rules make irrational demands on yourself, others and the environment: for instance, 'I must be liked by everyone', 'Others must not make mistakes', and 'Life must be fair'. Instead you can develop realistic rules: for instance, 'I prefer to be liked, but its unrealistic to expect this from everyone.'
2. *Creating perceptions.* You avoid perceiving yourself and others either too negatively or too positively. You distinguish between fact and inference and make your inferences as accurate as possible.
3. *Creating self-talk.* Instead of talking to your self negatively before, during and after specific situations, you can make coping self-statements that calm you down, coach you in what to do, and affirm the skills, strengths and support factors you possess.
4. *Creating visual images.* You use visual images in ways that calm you down, assist you in acting competently to attain your goals and help you to resist giving in to bad habits.
5. *Creating explanations.* You explain the causes of events accurately. You avoid assuming too much responsibility by internalizing, 'It's all my fault', or externalizing, 'It's all your fault'.
6. *Creating expectations.* You are realistic about the risks and rewards of future actions. You assess threats and dangers accurately. You avoid distorting relevant evidence with unwarranted optimism or pessimism. Your expectations about how well you can relate are accurate.

Activity 1.3 gives you the chance to assess your mind skills.

---

**ACTIVITY 1.3**                    **Assess my mind skills** ▮

---

First do the exercise on your own. Then, if appropriate, discuss your answers with your partner, another or others. Using the rating scale below, assess how skilled you are at using each of the following mind skills in a relationship of particular importance to you.

5  Extremely skilled
4  Very skilled
3  Skilled
2  Moderately skilled
1  Slightly skilled
0  Unskilled.

### Your rating

_____ creating rules
_____ creating perceptions
_____ creating self-talk
_____ creating visual images
_____ creating explanations
_____ creating expectations

Summarize your main mind skills strengths and weaknesses in this relationship. To what extent is how you think harming or helping you to relate effectively?

## Your feelings and physical reactions

To relate effectively, you require the ability to experience, express and manage your feelings and physical reactions. Though fundamental to relationships, feelings represent your animal nature and are not skills in themselves. Dictionary definitions of feelings tend to use words like 'physical sensation', 'emotions' and 'awareness'. All three of these works illustrate a dimension of feelings. Feeling as *physical sensations or reactions* represent your underlying biological nature. People are animals first, persons second. As such you need to learn to value and live with your underlying biological nature and to get it working for rather than against you. The word *emotions* implies movement. Feelings are processes. You are subject to a continuous flow of biological experiencing. *Awareness* implies that you can be conscious of your feelings. Illustrative feelings are happiness, sadness and anger. Illustrative physical reactions, which accompany feelings, include tightness in the stomach, staring and smiling.

Three areas in relationships, albeit overlapping, where feelings are important are experiencing feelings, expressing feelings and managing feelings. Below I illustrate each area with a brief example.

### Experiencing feelings

Robyn, 19, finds it very difficult to experience feelings of anger in her relationship with her boyfriend Russell.

*Expressing feelings*

Sandy, 39, is in a marriage heading for the rocks. He has always had great difficulty expressing his positive feelings towards his wife, Brittany. She sees him as far too negative and critical.

*Managing feelings*

Daphne, 28, is very jealous of her husband Geoff. She gets upset and angry when he talks to other women and afterwards picks fights with him. She has no evidence that Geoff has ever been unfaithful.

In the above examples, Robyn, Sandy and Daphne need to experience, express and manage their feelings more effectively. To do this, they need to identify the mind skills and communication skills that contribute to maintaining their feelings difficulties and work on them. For instance, Robyn may inhibit her angry feelings because of mind skills weaknesses such as: 'Women must never show anger' (unrealistic rule) or 'If I show anger, I will automatically be abandoned' (unrealistic expectation). She may also inhibit her feelings of anger because she lacks the communication skills to express her anger assertively and to cope with Russell if he returns her anger.

Sandy may have difficulty expressing positive feelings because of thinking skills deficits such as: 'Brittany should know that I love her' (unrealistic rule) and insufficiently acknowledging what Brittany does for him (perceiving inaccurately). Sandy may also need to develop the communication skills of how to show appreciation to Brittany with his verbal, vocal, body, touch and taking action messages.

Daphne may have difficulty managing her feelings of jealousy because of thinking skills weaknesses such as: 'I'm insufficiently lovable' (perceiving inaccurately) and 'If Jim talks to another woman, it means that he doesn't love me' (explaining cause inaccurately). She may need to develop the communication skills of sharing her self-doubts tactfully with Geoff and avoid coming on too strong.

Feelings are crucial to relationships. However, the way to influence feelings is by working on the appropriate mind skills and communication skills. In sound relationships, partners cooperate to build not only their own but one another's relationship skills. In the above examples, Robyn and Russell, Sandy and Brittany, and Daphne and Geoff could help with what the problems are not only for themselves but for their relationship together.

Many chapters in this book, like this one, end with a group activity relevant to the chapter's content (Activity 1.4).

## ACTIVITY 1.4     Group discussion: a relationship skills approach |

This is intended as a group exercise, though it may be done individually or in pairs.
For each part:

1. Spend 10–15 minutes answering the question in groups of three or four,
2. Each group shares its answers with the whole group.
3. The whole group ranks the three most important points in each category from the most important to the least important.

## Part A  Disadvantages of a relationship skills approach

List the three most important actual or potential disadvantages of viewing relationships and how you relate in relationship skills terms.

...............................................................................................................................

...............................................................................................................................

...............................................................................................................................

## Part B  Advantages of a relationship skills approach

List the three most important advantages of viewing relationships and how you relate in relationship skills terms.

...............................................................................................................................

...............................................................................................................................

...............................................................................................................................

# 2

# *What are coaching skills?*

**Chapter outcomes**
By studying and doing the activities in this chapter you should:

- understand what are levels of wellbeing
- know about what is coaching
- know about coaching relationship skills
- know about speaking skills
- know about demonstration skills
- know about guided practice skills
- know about negotiating homework skills
- be introduced to self-coaching.

## LEVELS OF WELLBEING

Leaving aside major areas of psychiatric disturbance, people can be viewed as possessing relationship skills on three main levels of wellbeing: remedial, normal and growth. Another way of stating this threefold distinction is subnormal, normal and supranormal. Coaching can also take place on each of these levels, though with variations. At the remedial level, people have either never learned or else are having difficulty enacting one or more relationship skills. For example, they may listen poorly, say little about themselves, get angry easily and be weak at solving relationship problems. Usually such people lack confidence, which partly results from their poor skills. This lack of confidence can also have the effect of adversely influencing how they perform many skills. In addition, it is still possible for a reasonably confident person to need remedial help in one or more skills areas: for instance, listening or managing conflict.

Some underconfident and even some reasonably confident people are best helped by undergoing supportive counselling prior to learning specific relationship skills by being coached in them. When they do receive coaching, this can be part of either a counselling process or a process that more clearly emphasizes training, though the distinction may be unclear. For example, some counselling approaches, such as cognitive therapy and rational emotive behaviour therapy, have a heavy training or coaching component. Consequently, coaching takes place in counselling as well as in situations that are labelled as training.

The vast majority of people, who are not severely disturbed, possess both good and poor relationship skills. They require help in lessening their poor skills improving their good ones. At the moment, most people mainly learn their relationship skills in their home environments where they get exposed to people with varying levels of skills. People also learn skills at school and in the homes of friends. The fortunate mostly get exposed to skilled people, whereas others get models of varying degrees of unskilfulness. People also differ in how vulnerable they are to having their poor rather than their good skills brought out in their relationships, especially close ones. For instance, it is possible for a skilled partner to help a relatively unskilled one to become more skilled. Other relationships can be much more destructive. Arguably, this normal grouping of people acts considerately much of the time to those within their family, social and cultural group and probably even to those outside it, although less so. Nevertheless, such people could avoid much unhappiness and gain greater happiness if they received coaching in good relationship skills early in life. Normal people and their counsellors and coaches are the main audience of this book.

There is a small group of people who are functioning at a growth or supranormal level of wellbeing (Nelson-Jones, 2004). Such people's hearts are awakened in that they acknowledge that all humans belong to the same species and have an innate potential for goodness that provides the basis for developing humanistic consciences. These superior functioning people are largely able to curb anger and aversion. Instead they cultivate goodwill, sympathetic joy at others' good fortune, gratitude, compassion and equanimity. In addition, they are genuinely concerned with being generous and with helping and serving others. Those with remedial and normal skills possess the potential for and can show such superior qualities too, but not nearly to the same extent.

# WHAT IS COACHING?

## Defining life coaching

Dictionary definitions of coaching use words like instruct, train, teach and tutor. Life coaching is coaching that focuses on improving people's personal or working lives. Though a relatively recent phenomenon, it is undoubtedly here to stay. In the USA, since the 1990s, there has been a huge increase in attention to life coaching. In 1996, the International Coach Federation, founded in 1992, had its first US convention. Life coaching is spreading worldwide, including in Britain and Australia. For instance, in 2002 the Association for Coaching was established in Britain and in 2005 the British Psychological Society set up a Coaching Psychology Section. In 2002, the Interest Group Coaching Psychology (IGCP) was established in the Australian Psychological Society and by 2004 it was the second largest interest group in the Society (Elliott, 2004). Nevertheless, even in the USA the profession of coaching is not clearly known by the public. Prior (2003), who was co-chair of the ICF Ethics and Standards Committee, writes that more often than not coaching is incorrectly understood by an unknowing public to be a virtual version of modern therapy.

Life coaching has numerous facets and is conducted in many different ways. The definition of life coaching on which the remainder of this book is based is the following:

> Life coaching involves coaches using their skills to help generally adequately functioning people learn to improve and maintain their mind skills and communication/action skills and so lead happier, more productive and ful-filled lives. The ultimate aim of life coaching is to help clients to become skilled at self-coaching.

Relationship skills coaching is one area of life coaching. It may be performed with different goals, by people with different training and backgrounds, and in different ways. The issue of relationship skills coaching is now discussed in relation to such differences.

## Goals of relationship skills coaching

Already I have stated that there are three levels of wellbeing: remedial or sub-normal, normal and growth or supranormal. The clienteles of counselling and psychotherapy tend to be those seeking remedial help. Nevertheless, counselling clients are often coached, albeit not always very systematically, to obtain one or more better relationship skills. Such coaching within the context of counselling may take place individually, in couples and families, and in counselling groups. Ideally, coaching does not end with counselling, but continues as self-coaching by clients.

As indicated in Chapter 1 by the relationship breakdown figures, there is a huge need for effective coaching in relationship skills for the vast majority of the population. Such coaching can be about attaining happiness and not just about overcoming hardships. Seligman believes that 'the strengths and the virtues are just as basic to human nature as the negative traits' (Seligman, 2003: 127). Diener and Seligman (2002) conducted research on American undergraduates that showed that happy people had stronger romantic and social relationships than did the less happy groups. Seligman advocates a positive psychology that is about helping people become happier. The goals for coaching for normal people – normal here meaning having a normal amount of relationship problems – should be both about overcoming the tendency to behave in ways that lead to negative outcomes as well as about releasing people's potential to think and communicate in ways likely to lead to positive outcomes. Coaching normal people in relationship skills can be conducted individually, in couples and training groups, and ultimately by self-coaching. Such coaching can have a preventive function as well as helping those already facing relationship difficulties (Bradley, 2002).

Though not the major focus of this book, there is also a need to coach people who are already functioning well on how to attain supranormal relationship skills. Such well-functioning people may be able to do much coaching for themselves. Nevertheless they can still require access to coaches and good coaching material if they are to attain and maintain their highest potential for relating well.

## Relationship skills coaches

Much coaching in human relationship skills gets performed by counsellors and psychotherapists. Carroll (2003) observes that while coaching made its way into counselling life counsellors failed to notice how much counselling was becoming like coaching. Especially with the continued rise of cognitive behavioural approaches, there has been an increasing emphasis on psychological education or coaching. However, leading writers in cognitive behavioural counselling and therapy rarely use the term coaching, nor do they directly specify coaching skills as part of their approaches. Neenan and Dryden (2002) are exceptions. They have written that they call the psychoeducational aspects of their work with non-clinical groups cognitive behavioural coaching, but here they emphasize the audiences for an approach as much as its content. However, coaching can be used with clinical as well as non-clinical clients.

Coaching in relationship skills is also performed outside of clinical and counselling settings. Such coaching may be performed with individuals or groups of various sizes. Often the coaches are counsellors and therapists, but this is frequently not the case. Coaches can be business people in business settings, teachers in educational settings, health workers in health settings and so on. People with a wide variety of training and backgrounds are engaging in relationship skills coaching. Sometimes the word coaching is directly used, but on other occasions this is not the case. For instance, a coaching programme might go by the name of relationship education and an individual coaching course might be titled by its objective, for instance, an assertion skills course or a listening skills course.

## Ways of coaching

The individual face-to-face interview is probably the way most relationship coaching is provided by counsellors and psychotherapists. Such coaching may be part of short-term treatment or may go on for 20 or more sessions. Counsellors and therapists also work on people's relationships in face-to-face couple counselling, family counselling and group counselling. Sometimes, counsellors will indicate that they are going to take a coaching approach to a relationship skills group, though they may not do so directly. For instance, it may often be assumed that a group on solving differences in relationships will involve coaching clients in one or more skills rather than group discussion alone.

Outside of counselling and therapy, individual face-to-face coaching also takes place. However, partly for cost reasons, providing relationship coaching for groups of people is common and likely to become increasingly so. For example, an organization such as a bank, police force or telephone company cannot afford to train its employees individually in various relationship skills for dealing with customers, the public and other employees. However, individual training may be conducted as part of regular supervision. In addition, for people who still experience difficulty adapting the skills in real life settings, individual contact with coaches may be encouraged after coaching or training courses are finished. However, such contact is not always possible.

Though not a major focus of this book, some coaches use the telephone as the major way of meeting with their clients. In their book *Therapist as Life Coach*, Williams and Davis (2002) state that they do the majority of what they call life coaching on the telephone. They emphasize that for busy clients working over the phone has the advantage of saving them travel time to the therapist's office. However, phone coaching in the relationship skills area has the disadvantage of the coach not being able to experience fully how a client relates other than on the phone. Tony Grant, Director of the Coaching Psychology Department at the University of Sydney, also advocates using the telephone though he says that increasingly 'sessions' are conducted by email, in keeping with clients' ever-busy lifestyle (Drever, 2002). Until a person has a thorough grounding in the relationship skills concerned, coaching over the phone or internet should be kept mainly for emergencies.

Relationship skills coaching may also be achieved through reading books and by watching television programmes and movies. Some relationship skills books, such as this one, assume that most readers will either be coaching clients or members of properly conducted relationship skills groups. Other relationship skills books are more of the self-help variety. Norcross (2000) states that there is a self-help revolution going on and advocates that mental health professionals cease devaluing self-help, encourage sophisticated self-change efforts, and conduct more research into self-help and self-change.

## COACHING SKILLS

### Being a coach

Despite many counselling approaches either explicitly or implicitly imparting skills to clients, to date there has been relatively little emphasis on how to impart skills systematically to clients. Indeed, often counsellors and those coaching independent of counselling have received little training in coaching skills. Skilled coaches possess good facilitation and good training skills and know how to combine them to best effect. Especially when conducted as part of counselling, facilitation skills provide the foundation for coaching. In addition, counsellors and coaches require training skills such as speaking, demonstrating and rehearsing.

In combining training with facilitation skills, remember that you are assisting clients and trainees to acquire and improve applied 'how to' skills, not academic knowledge. Clients' and trainees' emotions are often heavily involved and they may need to calm down before they are willing to work systematically on improving skills. Keeping the emotional climate human and personal, you then need to train thoroughly at the same time as avoiding trying to do too much. You can respect clients and trainees by allowing them to have the final say in whether and how best to use the targeted skills in addressing difficulties that they may face.

## The coaching relationship

When coaching people in improving how they communicate, act and think, it is important that you allow them to retain ownership of their problems and problem situations. Furthermore, always strive to maintain good collaborative working relationships. Avoid the urge just to teach and instruct which can sometimes override respect for clients' and trainees' potentials to lead their own lives and make the decisions that work best for them.

A useful distinction is that between counsellor/coach-centred coaching and client/trainee-centred coaching. Counsellor/coach-centred coaching essentially takes the jug and mug approach: the counsellors and coaches are the jugs pouring knowledge and skills into clients' and trainees' mugs. Counsellors and coaches are in control and their comments take the form of 'First you do this, then you do that, then you do that', and so on. Clients and trainees are passive receptacles who are allowed to assume little responsibility for the pace and direction of their learning. In reality, very few readers would work as crudely as this depiction.

Client/trainee-centred coaching respects clients and trainees as autonomous human beings. Where possible, counsellors and coaches develop plans to attain goals in conjunction with clients and trainees and draw out and build upon their existing knowledge and skills. Furthermore, they allow clients and trainees to participate in decisions about the pace and direction of learning, and also assist them to improve their knowledge and skills in such ways that they can help themselves after terminating contact.

Take the example of providing feedback about someone's performance when rehearsing how to improve their verbal, vocal and body messages in a specific situation. Cousellor/coach-centred coaches provide the feedback themselves as though they are the experts. Client/trainee-centred coaches try to develop the expertise of clients and trainees by asking them to evaluate their own performances before providing feedback themselves. Even when they do provide feedback, where possible client/trainee-centred coaches are prepared to discuss it and leave clients and trainees with the final say regarding its validity for them.

Since the skills of being a good listener are covered in Chapters 5 and 6, albeit from the viewpoint of coaching others in them, they are not covered here. It is essential, however, that coaches possess good listening and showing understanding skills. Possessing these skills is both useful for coaching itself as well as providing a powerful model from which client and trainees can learn. Within the context of collaborative working relationships, counsellors and coaches can impart applied skills by focusing on the three dimensions of 'Tell', 'Show' and 'Do'.

## Speaking skills

One approach to assisting clients and trainees to change is to facilitate them and allow them to come to their own conclusions as to how they might think and communicate better. A more active approach is being advocated here in which there are many occasions when you require speaking skills while assisting clients and trainees to develop their relationship skills. Such situations include the following:

- when offering reasons for developing skills
- when initially describing the component parts of skills
- when providing commentaries for skills demonstrations
- when coaching clients/trainees as they rehearse skills
- when answering client/trainee questions about skills
- when negotiating homework assignments.

Speaking skills for training are somewhat different from those for active listening. Some people experience difficulty switching from the more passive role of active listening to the more active role of imparting information where they are unable to feed off clients' most recent utterances. Without overwhelming clients, you can communicate information as clearly and as interestingly as possible. Furthermore, you can remain conscious that the best learning requires clients and trainees to develop their own capacity for self-talk about how to implement skills.

### *Prepare clear content*

Clients and trainees cannot be expected to comprehend poorly presented skills, let alone know them well enough to instruct themselves once counselling or a coaching group ends. You may experience difficulty in explaining skills clearly. Some readers are aware that they have this difficulty, others may be less so. In some cases, anxiety is a factor. Unfortunately, all too often those coaching do not properly understand skills they present. Consequently, their explanations are either muddled or clearly inaccurate. On other occasions, they may understand the skills, but communicate them insufficiently clearly.

You require the skills of introducing and describing the key points of any relationship skills that you impart. Systematic preparation is desirable, especially for beginners. Such preparation should not lead to rigid presentations. Rather, when clear in your own mind often you can better address the needs and learning rates of either the individuals or groups whom you coach.

Your presentations can focus on the mechanics of how to perform a skill or subskill. They are not academic discourses. You should use simple language: for instance, *active listening* is better than *empathic listening*. In addition, you should be concise and specific aiming to describe skills as clearly as possible so that clients and trainees can easily describe the skills to themselves. You should also avoid long sentences. The language of speech uses shorter sentences than written language. Furthermore, the longer the sentences become, the fewer are the people who can comprehend them.

## *Develop delivery skills*

Preparation of clear content is only part of the way to introducing and describing skills effectively. You still need to put your message across. Your voice and body are delivery tools for holding interest, emphasizing points and enlisting motivation. You should consider using visual as well as aural presentation. Audiovisual aids, for instance, the whiteboard, may help you to present information more clearly than if you just talk about it. However, think carefully about how to integrate audiovisual aids into your presentations so that they are not disruptive.

### SEND EFFECTIVE VOCAL MESSAGES

Let us now take the VAPER acronym and suggest how you may use volume, articulation, pitch, emphasis and rate when you deliver content. This usage may be rather different than when responding to others.

- *Volume*. When presenting skills you are under less obligation to adjust your volume to reflect that of others than when responding as a listener. Without being overwhelming, you need to speak reasonably loudly, possibly louder than when you respond. Some of you may be better at being gentle listeners rather than outgoing talkers. If so you may need to project your voice when presenting skills, whether in individual coaching or in coaching groups.
- *Articulation*. Clear articulation may be even more important when presenting information than when responding. If you enunciate poorly when sending listening responses, people at least are able to put what you say in the context of their previous utterances. They do not have this opportunity when you present information for the first time. Instead they may be struggling to understand both delivery and content. Furthermore, the longer speakers talk, the more poor enunciation distracts.
- *Pitch*. Pitch errors that you possess – for instance, uncomfortable highness, lowness or narrowness of range – may be more pronounced when you present information than when you respond. One reason is that, when responding, you may modify your pitch to match another's pitch. Another reason is that, when presenting information, you may be less conscious of pitch because you are thinking of what to say. Furthermore, you have

more scope for pitch errors since you are likely to speak for longer when presenting material than when responding.

- *Emphasis.* When using reflections in response as a listener, you emphasize the same words and phrases that the speaker emphasizes. As presenters of information you emphasize words and phrases highlighting your own main points. Your use of emphasis should convey interest and commitment.
- *Rate.* When describing skills you should speak fairly slowly. A slow but comfortable speech rate gives you time to think and listeners time to comprehend. Effective use of pauses can both clarify and emphasize what you say and also allows others to ask questions. Pause errors include too many, too few, too long, too short, and making extraneous sounds such as 'uhms' and 'ers'.

### SEND EFFECTIVE BODY MESSAGES

Sending effective body messages when describing a relationship skill is partly a matter of avoiding interfering messages and partly a matter of sending good messages. Many body messages for attending to clients when listening are still appropriate when delivering coaching content: for instance, relaxed body posture, physical openness, sensitivity to physical proximity and height, appropriate clothing and grooming, and appropriate facial expressions. The following are some additional suggestions for using effective body messages when presenting skills during coaching:

- *Gestures.* You should use gestures economically to help explain what is being said. Fischer (1972) states there are three kinds main types of gestures: *emphatic* gestures, such as pointing the finger, designed to make it clear that what is being said is important; *descriptive* gestures, for instance, stretching out one's arms when saying that marital partners are poles apart, designed to help illustrate points; and *symbolic* gestures to which a commonly understood meaning has been ascribed, for instance, shaking the head to say no. Another broad category of gestures is that of *distracting* gestures: touching one's head, scratching one's nose, pulling lint off one's cuff, waving arms around, tugging hair, and so on. You can learn to use gestures to work for rather than against sending your coaching messages.
- *Gaze and eye contact.* Talkers tend to use much less gaze and eye contact than listeners. Nevertheless, when presenting relationship skills you require an adequate gaze level to read listeners' reactions. You can present skills almost as though you are conversing with clients and trainees rather than talking at them. Use of gaze and eye contact is a most important way of relating directly to others when making learning points. Gaze and eye contact errors include looking down too much and keeping turned away when writing on whiteboards rather than checking listeners' reactions.

## Put content and delivery together

Counselling skills students may practise long and hard to develop active listening skills so that clients want to talk to them. The same conscientiousness is required for coaches, be they counsellors or others, developing the sender skills of imparting information so that clients and trainees want to hear it. An analogy may be made with effective parenting: parents not only need to listen so that their kids will talk, but they also need to talk so that their kids will listen (Gordon, 1970). Probably you will need to rehearse and practise gaining fluency in describing different relationship skills to others. Furthermore, you will need to learn to combine talking and listening skills in such a way that others feel valued parts of the training process and not just receptacles of your knowledge.

You can use speaking skills to help clients and trainees to develop self-instruction skills. Ideally, when learning new skills, learners start by being receptive to the instructor's voice in their heads. However, they then need to replace the instructor's voice with their own voices.

# Demonstrating

One of the main ways in which people learn is from observational learning or learning from models (Bandura, 1986). In real life, much modelling is unintentional. However, you can consciously promote observational learning of desired skills and subskills. Here the more everyday word demonstrating is preferred to modelling. You can use demonstrations to assist others to develop different and better ways of communicating and thinking. Furthermore, you can then demonstrate how to accompany communicating and thinking differently with appropriate self-talk.

## Methods of demonstration

The following are some ways in which you can use demonstrations of improved ways of communicating and thinking.

### LIVE DEMONSTRATION

Probably most demonstrations of relationship skills are live. You may demonstrate live when initially presenting skills, when coaching afterwards, and when working with current material that clients and trainees bring into later sessions. Live demonstrations have the advantage of here-and-now communication. Clients and trainees can receive verbal, vocal and body messages as they occur. In addition, you can interact with clients and, if appropriate, show different or simpler ways to enact skills.

Live demonstrations have limitations as well as advantages. Unless demonstrations are recorded, clients and trainees have no copies to listen to or watch on their own. Another limitation is that in live demonstrations it can be difficult to portray scenes involving more than one or two persons.

A variation of live demonstration is to encourage clients and trainees to observe good and poor demonstrators of targeted skills in their everyday lives. For instance, those with difficulty initiating contact with others can look out for how socially skilled people do this. Those with poor parenting skills can be asked to observe parents they admire.

Written demonstrations are more appropriate for helping people to change how they think than to change how they communicate and act. However, written demonstrations that contain visual images, such as cartoon characters, can convey desirable communications and actions. It is possible for you to demonstrate mind skills either on a whiteboard or with a notepad during sessions. Skills can also be demonstrated through the written page – either from handouts or from passages in books and training manuals. Written demonstrations can be used as examples for homework assignments. Furthermore, they can often be easily stored and retrieved.

Recorded demonstrations can use audiocassettes and videotapes. Audiocassettes and videotapes can either be integral parts of initial skills demonstrations or used for homework assignments. Advantages of audiocassette and videotape demonstrations include that they can be reproduced, loaned and used independently by clients and trainees, and that that they lend themselves to playback and to repeated viewing.

Audiocassettes are particularly useful for demonstrating mind skills. With audiocassettes as contrasted to videotapes, listeners can be taken through the sequences of choices entailed in targeted skills without visual distractions. Clients and trainees probably require repeated listening to demonstrations for the mind skills to become part of their everyday repertoires (Ellis, 1987). Disadvantages of audiocassette demonstrations are that they are not always as spontaneous as live demonstrations and that they may be insufficiently geared to individual needs.

A major advantage of videotape over audiocassette demonstration is that viewers observe body messages. During sessions videotapes may be used to demonstrate communication skills: for instance, excerpts of how either to make an assertive request for a behaviour change or to manage a difficulty with another person better. Clients and trainees may also self-administer demonstration videotapes as part of homework.

Many training audiocassettes and videotapes are already on the market. However, commercial videotapes may be neither available nor suitable. Readers who make demonstration videotapes have the choice of whether or not to bring in outside resources.

VISUALIZED DEMONSTRATION

You can ask clients and trainees to visualize or imagine the demonstration scenes that you describe. They can be asked to visualize either themselves or someone else performing the targeted communications. Visualized demonstrations are only appropriate for those who can imagine scenes adequately. A potential drawback is that, even when instructions are given well, there may be important differences between what is described and what gets imagined. In general people visualize best when relaxed.

## Demonstrator skills

Beyond speaking well, following are some demonstrator skills. Even live demonstrations require adequate preparation. You must know the material well to integrate good demonstrations into skills presentations. You also need to pay attention to characteristics of the demonstration. One issue is whether to demonstrate incorrect as well as correct behaviours. You may plan briefly to demonstrate negative behaviours as a way of highlighting positive ones. However, you should make sure not to confuse people and always have the major emphasis on correct rather than incorrect skills.

You should take care how you introduce demonstrations. Your initial demonstration of a skill is likely to be part of a 'tell', 'show', 'do' sequence. You may increase observers' attention by telling them what to look out for and also informing them that afterwards they will perform demonstrated behaviours.

During and at the end of demonstrations you may ask observers whether they understand the points demonstrated. In addition, you can ask observers to summarize the main points of demonstrations. Research suggests that observers actively summarizing the main points of demonstrations are better able to learn and retain this information (Perry and Furukawa, 1986). Probably the best way to check learning is to observe and coach clients or trainees as they perform the demonstrated behaviours.

Activity 2.1 gives the reader practice in using demonstrator skills. Some readers may want to go through the chapters on the different human relationship skills before performing this chapter's activities.

## ACTIVITY 2.1                    **Use demonstration skills** ▐

Work with a partner with one of you taking the role of counsellor/coach and the other taking the role of client/trainee. Client/counsellor or trainee/coach hold a discussion to choose a specific human relationship skill that requires improving. Do not attempt too much. The counsellor/coach then goes through the following steps in a demonstration.

1. Cuing the client/trainee what to observe.
2. Demonstrating each of the verbal, vocal and body message components

of the targeted skill to the client/trainee and then demonstrating all three together (your partner is the client/trainee as you demonstrate).
3. Asking the client/trainee to summarize the main points of the demonstration.

Afterwards hold a sharing and discussion session focused on the counsellor/coach's use of demonstration skills. If necessary repeat the demonstration until the counsellor/coach feels she/he has obtained some degree of competence in using demonstration skills. Then reverse roles.

---

## Rehearsing

Rehearsing is a possibly less threatening expression than role playing. Some people become uncomfortable at the idea of role playing. Feeling shy and vulnerable already, they think they will further expose themselves in role plays. You may need to explain to clients and trainees that rehearsing can help them by allowing them to try out communicating differently in an environment where mistakes do not really matter. As such, rehearsing can provide knowledge and confidence for communicating effectively in actual problem situations.

### *Skills for assisting rehearsing*

The following are some skills for conducting rehearsals.

#### EXPLAIN REASONS FOR REHEARSAL

Some people find the idea of rehearsal off-putting. For example, they may be self-conscious about their acting skills, especially if this involves performing in front of a group. Explain the reasons for rehearsals to ease participants' anxieties and help motivate them. Here is a rationale for using a managing anger role play rehearsal with a client, Doug, who gets excessively angry when his teenage daughter, Angie, comes home late.

> Doug, I think it would be helpful if we rehearsed how you might use your new skills to cope better with Angie next time she comes home late. I realize that it may seem artificial acting the scene here. However, role playing gives us the chance to rehearse different ways you might behave – your words, vocal messages, and body messages – so that you are better prepared for the real event. It is safer to make mistakes here where it doesn't count for real. There is no substitute for learning by doing. What do you think about this approach?

Elicit information about the physical setting of proposed scenes, what other characters are involved, and how they behave. If you are to rehearse a client or trainee in how to deal with someone – for instance, Angie – collect sufficient information about Angie's verbal, vocal and body messages for you or someone else to get into her role. Depending on what sort of office or training area you are using, furniture may be moved around to create a 'stage', for instance, a family living room.

## ASSESS CURRENT SKILLS

Sometimes time is well spent if initial role plays are conducted in which people demonstrate how they currently communicate in problem situations. For instance, much relevant information may be elicited about non-verbal communication that may not be apparent if they only talk about how they act. Assessment role plays can also reveal how people think in situations.

## FORMULATE CHANGED COMMUNICATION

You can cooperate with clients and trainees to formulate new and better ways of communicating that both use targeted skills and yet feel 'comfortable'. You should facilitate their contributions to the discussion prior to making suggestions. As part of this process you can demonstrate the different verbal, vocal and body message components of appropriate relationship skills. In addition, you can explore how clients and trainees can cope with different responses by others.

## REHEARSE CHANGED SKILLS

Once clients or trainees are reasonably clear about their new roles and you or one or more other trainees understand your 'part' or 'parts', trial enactments or rehearsals take place. Avoid trying to do too much or anything too difficult too soon. You may allow rehearsals to run their course. Alternatively, you may intervene at one or more points along the way to provide feedback and coaching. Role-play rehearsals are dry runs of how to use communication skills in specific situations. Video feedback may be used as part of coaching both during and after rehearsals. A number of rehearsals may be needed to build skills. Some of these rehearsals may involve people in responding to different situations. For example, people asking for dates may get accepted, postponed or rejected in separate rehearsals.

Role reversal and mirroring are psychodrama techniques that you may use (Moreno, 1959; Blatner, 2005). In role reversal, you get clients or trainees to play the other person during interactions. Role reversals force them to get some way into another's internal frame of reference. With mirroring, you 'mirror back' clients' or trainees' verbal, vocal and body messages. They then have a chance to see themselves as others experience them.

Clients and trainees may also rehearse changing their mind skills along with their communication skills. For example, they may learn to use the calming and coaching dimensions of self-talk to accompany new communication skills. In addition, you can rehearse them in other mind skills relevant to targeted communication skills.

PROCESS REHEARSALS

Processing involves spending time dealing with the thoughts and feelings gener-ated by rehearsals. Together you and those with whom you are working can discuss learnings from the rehearsals and then make plans to transfer rehearsed skills to daily life. Clients and trainees can be asked processing questions like: 'How were you feeling in that rehearsal?' 'How well do you think you used your skills in that rehearsal?' 'What have you learned in that role play that is useful for real life?' and 'What difficulties do you anticipate in implementing your changed behaviour and how can you overcome them?' In counselling, after processing the previous rehearsal, you can move on to the next one either regarding the same or with another problem situation. If you are running a coaching group, you may work with other trainees in relation to a similar or to different situations (see Activity 2.2).

## ACTIVITY 2.2                                **Use rehearsing skills**  |

Work with a partner with one of you taking the role of counsellor/coach and the other taking the role of client/trainee. Either for a specific human relationship skill that was demonstrated in Activity 2.1 or for another specific relationship skill that the client wants to improve, go through the following sequence.

1. Cuing the client what to observe.
2. Demonstrating each of the verbal, vocal and body message com-ponents of the relationship skill and then demonstrating all three together (your partner is the client/trainee as you demonstrate).
3. Asking the client/trainee to summarize the main points of the demonstration.
4. Introducing the idea of rehearsing the relationship skill.
5. Rehearsing and coaching the client/trainee to the point where, within the limits of this activity, she/he feels competent to perform the relationship skill in real life competently. Audiocassette or videotape playback may be used as part of the rehearsing process.

Afterwards hold a sharing and discussion session focused on the counsel-lor/coach's use of rehearsing skills. If necessary, allow the counsellor/coach to rehearse some more until she/he feels she/he has obtained some degree of competence in using rehearsing skills. Then reverse roles.

# Case study: Example of coaching

*Phil, 20, initially comes to see a counsellor at university, Margaret, because he finds himself getting very depressed and this is adversely affecting his studying and ability to get good grades. One of Phil's issues is that he has a very poor social life, partly because he feels extremely shy about asking women out. With Phil's permission, Margaret has placed him in an overcoming shyness group that she coaches.*

*After a brief presentation by Margaret on starting relationships, she asks the group if anyone is willing to share a difficulty in the area of getting started. Phil volunteers and says that in his economics class there is a student called Mary, 19, with whom he sits at times and talks with a little. Phil likes Mary very much and thinks that the feeling may be mutual. However, to date he has been far too scared to make a move towards Mary that might allow their relationship to develop. Phil asks Margaret and the group if they can help him. Together Phil, Margaret and the group discuss how Phil might find out whether Mary would like a closer relationship with him. Phil decides that as a first step he will ask Mary whether she would like to have a coffee with him after class ends. With the help of the group, Phil develops the following verbal request for Mary to have coffee: 'Mary, would you like to have a coffee with me after class one day this week?' Phil decides that his voice should be calm and clear. Regarding his body messages, Phil decides he will make sure to sit next to her in class and smile pleasantly at her when he asks her to spend time with him. Margaret then demonstrates how Phil might ask Mary for coffee.*

*Next, Margaret suggests that Phil rehearses asking Mary the question with another group member role playing Mary. Before the group member plays her part, she is helped to find out more about how Mary communicates. At the first rehearsal, Phil sounds very stilted and fails to smile pleasantly and make 'Mary' feel at ease. When Margaret asks Phil how he thought the rehearsal went, he replies that he felt he came over very nervous and 'Mary' and the group agreed. Margaret then suggests that Phil put more emphasis into his voice and demonstrates again how to do this. She also reminds him to smile. Phil then rehearses with 'Mary' again. Margaret lets Phil evaluate how he did and afterwards 'Mary' acknowledges that she felt more comfortable this time with his question. Phil has a further rehearsal and gets more feedback so that he performs more competently in the session. Margaret gets Phil to write down his verbal, vocal and body messages and suggests that he might practise again, either on his own or with a friend, before asking Mary.*

## Negotiating homework

Homework is an important part of coaching in relationship skills, whether it takes place as part of counselling or in a coaching group. Homework assignments include practising and then trying changed behaviours in real life settings and filling out self-monitoring sheets and worksheets for developing mind skills. One of the central problems in assigning homework activities is that of getting clients and trainees to do them. The following are some guidelines for negotiating and setting homework.

- *Make homework assignments clearly relevant.* Homework assignments must be client/trainee centred in the sense that they are clearly seen by clients and trainees as being central to attaining their goals. It is a waste of time to set assignments to people unless they are cooperative, see their relevance and hence are motivated to complete them.
- *Collaborate with clients/trainees in formulating assignments.* Clients and trainees need to be involved in formulating homework assignments to perform outside of formal sessions. They can make suggestions as to what specific communications, actions and thoughts they may change. Furthermore, once they understand the concepts of mind skills and communication/action skills they can also suggest which ones they need work on and at what rate.
- *Keep assignments manageable.* Homework assignments need to be manageable in a number of ways. They should be of a size that people are likely to do them. Furthermore, they should be of a difficulty that they can be clearly understood. You can discuss with clients and trainees what seems reasonable. Especially at first, small and simple may be the way to go.
- *Graduate the difficulty of homework assignments.* You can both set tasks within the clients' and trainees' skills levels at the same time as making them progressively more difficult. It is important to experience success in achieving assignments, so setting manageable yet progressively difficult tasks needs to be taken very seriously. Sometimes, changing a way of thinking, communicating or acting requires giving up long-established habits. Here, it can be especially important not to agree on too difficult an activity too soon. Where possible try to build in some early successes to encourage clients and trainees to persist in working on their skills.
- *Make sure that clients/trainees have a written summary of any instructions.* You can protect clients and trainees if you ensure that they are clear what to do and that they have a record of what is required. You can design your own homework assignment forms and hand out tailor-made instructions as occasion arises. If you want clients or trainees to fill out forms such as monitoring logs, provide these forms yourself.
- *Begin homework assignments during sessions.* Where possible it can be important to begin homework assignments during sessions since it cannot be assumed that clients or trainees understand them. You can check both the clarity of the instructions and how well they are understood. Checking understanding saves time in the long run because otherwise people may not

do assignments properly, if at all. Further difficulties in understanding and doing assignments need to be dealt with as they occur.

- *Anticipate difficulties in completing homework assignments.* When asked, clients and trainees often have a good idea of what might get in the way of their doing homework assignments. For example, some prefer to indicate definite times when they undertake to do tasks rather than leave them to chance. Those who are inclined to forget homework tasks can put up reminder notices in prominent places. Clients and trainees can also be helped to deal with unsuccessful attempts at homework tasks. For example, after a seemingly negative attempt at performing a task, they can explore how well they used specific targeted skills. If they did not do as well as they would have liked, options include trying to do the same task better in ways they have identified or trying an easier task. They need to be helped to realize that it can take time to build good skills. In addition, you can assist them to identify people who can support their efforts at change.
- *Emphasize learning.* You can assist clients and trainees to view their attempts at homework as learning experiences. For example, some return to negative if not downright hostile environments. If so, you may need to prepare them more thoroughly prior to suggesting that they implement their improved communication and actions outside their sessions. Such preparation may include devising strategies for dealing with negative feedback. You may also conduct rehearsals with those who may face difficult people as they apply their changed skills.

  Clients and trainees can learn that there are numerous reasons that they might not get the results they want right away. For example, it can take time to learn a skill, so at first they may not be as successful as they would like because they are still learners. Sometimes, they may use good skills, but still not get positive results, so here it can be important to distinguish between process and outcome. You can also assist them to learn even from tasks that they do not do properly or fail to do at all. For instance, they may need further assistance in understanding how to implement skills like assertion or sharing intimacy. Where they do not perform homework tasks, they can be assisted in understanding the feelings or other circumstances that they have allowed to interfere with progress. You can also check that the homework assignments were clear and appropriate.
- *Show interest and follow-up in the next session.* You should signal a joint progress review by letting clients and trainees know that when you next meet you will ask them how they fared in their homework assignments. People who know that those assisting them are interested in and supportive of their attempts to complete homework assignments are more likely to be motivated to do so. However, this assumes that you avoid becoming controlling and judgemental (see Activity 2.3).

**ACTIVITY 2.3**                    **Use negotiating homework skills**

Work as a counsellor/coach with a partner acting as client/trainee who selects a problem situation in which she or he wants to use a human relationship skill better (possibly, a skill that you worked on in Activity 2.1 and 2.2). If you work with a new relationship skill, collaborate with your partner to identify some key verbal, vocal and body messages in need of improvement. Using speaking, demonstrating and rehearsing assist your partner to improve her/his skills. Then rehearse and practise how to negotiate one or more homework assignments so that your partner can use the time (assume a week) before you next meet to good effect. To increase the chances of compliance, observe the following guidelines:

- Make homework assignment(s) clearly relevant.
- Collaborate with the client/trainee in formulating the assignment (s).
- Keep assignment(s) manageable.
- Graduate the difficulty of homework assignment(s).
- Make sure that the client/trainee has a writing summary of any instructions.
- Begin homework assignment(s) during sessions.
- Anticipate difficulties in completing homework assignment(s).
- Emphasize learning.
- Show interest and follow-up in the next session (where possible).

Afterwards hold a sharing and discussion session focused on the counsellor/coach's use of negotiating homework skills. If necessary, allow her/him to practise some more until she/he feels reasonably confident in negotiating homework assignments. Then, if feasible, reverse roles.

## Self-coaching

The topic of self-coaching is addressed in this book's final chapter and so is only briefly mentioned here. Ultimately all human relationship skills training is performed to enable former clients and trainees to coach themselves once they are on their own. Initially material needs to be presented clearly and learned thoroughly, if possible. Former clients and trainees need to develop the skills of monitoring themselves and, where necessary, correcting their behaviour. They can improve targeted human relationship skills when they are on their own through repeated practice. Furthermore, as they keep using the skills many are also able to teach themselves how to improve them.

# 3

# Listening skills

**Chapter outcomes**
By studying and doing the activities in this chapter you should:

- know what rewarding listening is and why it is important
- understand what it means to possess and attitude of respect and acceptance
- know how you can tune into another's internal frame of reference
- know how you can send good vocal messages
- know how you can send good body messages
- understand how you can use opening remarks, small rewards and open-ended questions.

Whereas the last chapter on coaching skills was directed more at counsellors and coaches, the remaining chapters of the book are written so that they may be used by clients and trainees as well as by those helping and coaching them.

Zeno of Citium said: 'The reason why we have two ears and only one mouth is that we may listen the more and talk the less.' In distressed relationships, common crys are 'You don't understand me' and 'You never listen.' The next two chapters focus on rewarding listening skills. Listening is one of the most powerful psychological rewards that you can give. However, with how many people can you be open and share the secrets of your heart? Some readers may answer none. Most people are short of confidants who genuinely listen. Varying degrees of unrewarding listening are widespread. Occasionally not being listened to may create mild psychological pain; often not being listened to, moderate pain; and mostly not being listened to, severe pain. Never being listened to would be like a psychological death penalty.

# REWARDING LISTENING

A distinction may be made between hearing and listening. *Hearing* involves the capacity to be aware of and to receive sound. *Listening* involves not only receiving sounds but, as much as possible, accurately understanding their meaning. However, you can listen accurately without being a rewarding listener. *Rewarding listening* entails not only accurately understanding speakers' communications, but showing and, where necessary, clarifying your understanding. As such, rewarding listening involves both receiver and sender skills.

Four kinds of listening take place in any two-person conversation. Listening takes place both between persons and within each of them. Indeed the quality of your inner listening, or being appropriately sensitive to your own thoughts and feelings, may be vital to the quality of your outer listening. If you listen either poorly or too much to yourself, you listen less well to others. Conversely, if you listen well to others, this may help the quality of their inner listening. Following is a saying of Lao-tsu that beautifully illustrates this point.

> It is as though he/she listened
> and such listening as his/hers enfolds us in a silence
> in which at last we begin to hear
> what we are meant to be.

## Importance of rewarding listening

The following are some reasons why it is important that you work to develop and maintain your rewarding listening skills.

### *Making contact*

Often the people you meet are shy and anxious. Trust may not come easily. If you listen well to them, you increase the chances that they will feel comfortable, safe and understood by you. Your skills help them to disclose personal information and share their thoughts and feelings. If you use poor listening skills, you set up blocks to starting relationships. Perhaps the major finding from research into self-disclosure is that intimacy levels of disclosures tend to be matched. Your gradually telling me your secrets and my gradually telling you mine is a process that depends on us being willing to listen to each other as well as to disclose. Trust is built as much from acceptance of our disclosures as from our willingness to disclose.

### *Knowing another*

Erich Fromm in *The Art of Loving* states that there are common elements in all forms of love: care, responsibility, respect and knowledge. Relating closely to another person involves knowing their separateness and prizing it. You know them on their terms. In close relationships such knowledge 'does not stay at the periphery, but penetrates to the core' (Fromm, 1957: 27). Rewarding listening allows another to feel safe and to strip away the social masks that they wear for protection. You no longer need make so many assumptions about what they think and feel since they tell you anyway. Furthermore, no one can know the weight of another's burden unless told.

## Knowing yourself

Listening effectively to others provides you with valuable information about yourself. Though you may not always like what you hear, remaining open to feedback gives you the opportunity to change. Furthermore, if others listen well to you, it gives you the opportunity to experience and explore your thoughts and feelings.

## Maintaining relationships

Once you start a relationship, skilled listening and disclosing helps to maintain it. Relationships are ongoing conversations. Happy couples are skilled at taking an interest in one another's lives. They use their listening skills to transcend their narcissism and show their respect and concern for each other. Many of their conversations are mutually satisfying. In addition, rewarding listening builds trust and stability by helping partners prevent and manage problems. If partners are able to say what they think and feel, misunderstandings are less likely to occur. Furthermore, if partners listen well to each other, they stand a much better chance of resolving difficulties to their mutual satisfaction.

Poor listening skills interfere with maintaining relationships. Defensiveness or tuning out to information that clashes with your picture of yourself corrodes a relationship as does switching off to your partner. You and your partner may replace an *open* communication system, in which you share what you think and feel, with a *closed* communication system. Here you may tiptoe around each other's fragile egos at the expense of honesty. During this process, you can become progressively alienated from yourselves and one another through not having the courage to provide and listen to feedback.

## Bridging differences

Every person has a potential set of blinkers depending upon her or his circumstances. How can you know what it is like to be old, dying, female, male, gay, physically disabled, an immigrant, white, black, Asian, Aboriginal or Maori . . . if the description does not fit you? However, if you relate to someone with a different set of life's circumstances, she or he can greatly assist you to understand them if you use good listening skills. Similarly, if she or he listens skilfully to you, together you build bridges and not walls.

## Rewarding listening: A ten-skills approach

The remainder of this chapter and the next chapter describe ten key skills of being a rewarding listener. Some of the skills overlap. Each of these skills requires you to make choices.

*Skills of rewarding listening*

- *Skill 1.* Possess an attitude of respect and acceptance.
- *Skill 2.* Understand the speaker's internal viewpoint.
- *Skill 3.* Send good vocal messages.
- *Skill 4.* Send good body messages.
- *Skill 5.* Use opening remarks, small rewards and open-ended questions.
- *Skill 6.* Paraphrase.
- *Skill 7.* Reflect feelings.
- *Skill 8.* Clarify by questions.
- *Skill 9.* Clarify by challenges.
- *Skill 10.* Use mind skills.

## SKILL 1 POSSESS AN ATTITUDE OF RESPECT AND ACCEPTANCE

An accepting attitude involves respecting yourself and others as separate human beings with rights to one's own thoughts and feelings. Fromm (1957) notes that respect comes from the Latin word *respicere* meaning to look at. Respect means the ability to look at yourself and others as you are and to prize your unique individuality. Respect also means allowing oneself and other people to grow and develop without exploitation and control.

Ellis and Crawford (2000) write that good communication starts with acceptance. The first of their seven guidelines for great relationships and better communication is to accept your partner 'as is'. They state that there are three possible roles in a relationship: one-up, one-down, or a peer partnership. The goal of having a good relationship is to move to having a 'peer' or 'equal' partnership. Such a partnership, however, not only involves accepting your partner, but accepting yourself 'as is'.

Noted relationship researchers Jacobson and Christensen (1996) also strongly recommend acceptance. Partners require assistance in letting go of the struggle to change one another in terms of their idealized image of a husband or wife. However, an acceptance versus change dichotomy is false because acceptance techniques can often be one of the most effective ways of generating change. Gottman and Silver (1999) consider certain kinds of negativity in relationships so lethal that they can 'clip-clop' into the heart of a marriage. These kinds of negativity, which are the opposite of acceptance, are criticism, contempt, defensiveness and stonewalling, which involves tuning out to another person.

The extent to which you are able to respect and accept yourself is reflected in the level of acceptance and respect, and hence the listening skills, you can offer another. In close personal relationships you will be put to the test when in conflict. Unless you discipline yourself, the acceptance that underlies skilful listening can be the first casualty of an angry conflict. Consequently, self-acceptance should be extended to mean accepting yourself enough to control your temper and stay tuned in to another when the going gets rough.

## Barriers to an accepting attitude

An accepting attitude involves respecting oneself and others as separate and unique human beings. Regarding accepting others, this does not mean that you agree with everything they say. However, you are secure enough in yourself to respect what they say as their versions of reality. You do not need to use barriers and filters to protect you from listening to the full range of their messages. These barriers can be internal and external. Internal barriers operate on, distort and filter out certain elements of the messages you receive. At worst you may deny or block out the whole message. External barriers manifest themselves in subtle and not so subtle voice and body cues to others that they should edit what they say.

What are some of the main barriers and filters that act as sources of interference to your receiving another loud and clear? All of them are related to your sense of worth and to how much debilitating anxiety you possess. The stronger you are emotionally, the less need is there for you to use barriers and filters, so the more open you are to others. Barriers to possessing an accepting attitude include the following.

### *Strong feelings*

Experiencing strong positive or negative feelings can interfere with your listening. Think how hard it can be to stay open to another when in an angry conflict. Strong positive feelings can also contribute to your not adequately hearing another. Sexual harassment and date rape are instances where negative messages are not heeded.

> Kathryn, 23, was very attracted to Roger, 22, whom she had just met. After their first dinner date, Kathryn drove him home and accepted his invitation to come up for a coffee. During coffee, despite Roger's feedback, Kathryn came on increasingly strongly about wanting sex with him. Roger ended up reluctantly asking Kathryn to leave.

## Unfinished business

You may have unfinished emotional business that interferes with your listening skills. For instance, if you come home after a row with someone at work you may be less ready to listen to your partner who wants to discuss his or her day. If you have strong feelings about a past occurrence in your relationship, until you have processed this you may listen less well. In addition, you may transfer unfinished business from previous relationships into present ones.

> Jennifer and Sam are a couple in their late twenties. Jennifer has just come out of a relationship with Gerry. At times she finds herself getting upset with Sam as though he were Gerry, even though Sam treats her much better.

## Trigger words and phrases

Trigger or 'red flag' words and phrases are those that you perceive to be emotionally charged 'put-downs'. Each individual has their own triggers. Many of these are 'you' messages: for example, 'You're weak', 'You stuffed it up', 'Can't you do anything right?' Children can switch off when adults make comments starting with 'When I was your age' or 'Grow up'. Adjectives like 'thoughtless', 'clumsy' and 'effeminate' can also act as trigger words. Much of the power of trigger words and phrases comes from the negative voice and body messages that accompany them.

> Matt, 39, and Elaine, 38, argue a lot about how much time to spend with his mother, Joyce, 66. When Elaine shouts 'You care for Joyce more than me', Matt thinks 'What's the use!' and tells Elaine to 'F . . . off.'

Positive words and phrases can also trigger feelings that interfere with your listening. For example, flattery like 'Gee, you're wonderful Mr/Ms Murgatroyd, I really admire you' may contribute to your not hearing other less flattering feedback.

## Anxiety-evoking people

There may be specific people or categories of people with whom you feel anxious and hence do not listen to them well. These may include your parents, your relatives, friends of the same or other sex, strangers and authority figures.

> Ted, 17, tends to get anxious when older males in authority give him instructions. He is afraid that he will not be able follow the

instructions adequately and thus creates a 'self-fulfilling prophesy'. However, Ted does not get nearly so anxious when older females, people his own age or younger people of either sex give him instructions.

## Anxiety-evoking topics

For reasons connected with how you were brought up, certain topic areas may be anxiety evoking. You may either not like discussing them at all or get defensive when others state different opinions.

Katie, 19, was brought up in a home where sex was not openly discussed. Katie gets very nervous when in a group of women who share details of their sex lives.

## Anxiety-evoking situations

Anxiety and threat are present to a greater or lesser degree in all situations. Below are some common situations where people may feel vulnerable and hence their own agendas may preclude fully listening to others:

- Going on your first date with a different person.
- Going to a party where you do not know anyone.
- Meeting for the first time your girlfriend/boyfriend's parents.
- Having to answer questions after a public talk you have given.
- Going for a job interview.
- Being teased on a sensitive topic.
- Making love for the first time.

Many of the above illustrations involve coping with new situations. However, even when you have either been for a number of job interviews or fielded questions after a number of talks, you may still experience some debilitating anxiety that interferes with your listening skills.

## Prejudices

Again for reasons connected with your upbringing, you may tune out to people who are different to you by reasons of, amongst others, their age, sex, sexual orientation, culture, race, social class, physical disability and intelligence level.

Tricia, 26, dislikes lesbian and gay people. She does not seem to realize that they have thoughts and feelings that merit respect just as much as her own. She treats anyone she suspects of being lesbian or gay coldly and maintains her distance from them.

## Information differing from your self-picture

You may find it hard to keep assuming an accepting attitude when the information you receive differs from your picture of yourself. People differ in their thresholds for being open to such information. Positive as well as negative information can be denied and distorted.

Kevin, 43, is a powerful and narcissistic primary school headmaster. He is quick to notice others' failings. He discourages honest feedback about himself and dismisses any seemingly negative remarks, however constructive they may be, as 'trouble making'.

Sue tells Alan she finds him very intelligent. Alan looks shy and replies, 'Oh, not really.'

## Physical barriers

Physical considerations may contribute to your being less accepting of others than you might be. For instance, fatigue, illness, the discomfort of being too hot or too cold and external noise may all affect how well you listen. The stresses of your life may contribute to your being depressed, irritable and tense. None of these feelings are conducive to your being open and accepting of another person (see Activity 3.1).

Joe, 36, and Carol, 34, live in a small flat with three children under the age of ten. Due to fatigue, constant noise and interruptions, they find it hard to create the physical and psychological space required to discuss important 'you–me' issues in their relationship.

---

**ACTIVITY 3.1          Assess my barriers to an accepting attitude                                when I listen** |

---

First do this exercise on your own. Then, if appropriate, discuss your answers with your partner, another or others.

1. Assess yourself in terms of how much each of the following barriers interferes with your possessing an attitude of respect and acceptance when you listen.

| Barrier | My assessment |
|---------|---------------|
| Strong feelings | |
| Unfinished business | |
| Trigger words and phrases | |
| Anxiety-evoking people | |
| Anxiety-evoking topics | |
| Anxiety-evoking situations | |
| Prejudices | |
| Information differing from my self-picture | |
| Physical barriers | |
| Other(s) | |

2. Summarize the extent to which you see yourself possessing an attitude of respect and acceptance when you listen to:

   (a) your spouse/partner/girlfriend/boyfriend
   (b) your friends.

---

## SKILL 2 UNDERSTAND THE SPEAKER'S INTERNAL VIEWPOINT

The Native American proverb states: 'Don't judge any man/woman until you have walked two moons in his/her moccasins.' If the people are to feel that you receive them loud and clear, you need the skills to 'get inside their skins' and 'see the world through their eyes'. At the heart of rewarding listening is a basic distinction between 'you' and 'me', between 'your view of you' and 'my view of you' and between 'your view of me' and 'my view of me.' Now 'your view of you' and 'my view of me' are inside or internal viewpoints, whereas 'your view of me' and 'my view of you' are outside or external viewpoints. Rewarding listening is based on your choosing to acknowledge the separateness between 'me' and 'you' by getting into another's internal viewpoint rather than remaining in your own external viewpoint.

If I respond to what you say in a way that shows an accurate understanding of your viewpoint, I am responding *as if* I am inside your internal viewpoint. If, however, I chose not to show an understanding of your viewpoint, or lack the skills to do so, I respond from my external viewpoint. In short, if I respond to you as if inside your internal viewpoint, I respond to you from where you are. If I step outside your internal viewpoint, I respond in an external way that reflects more where I am or think you should be than where you are. The following are examples of responses by listeners from their *external* viewpoints.

- Don't talk to me like that.
- Stop crying. You shouldn't let yourself get so upset.
- Let me tell you about a similar experience to yours.
- You're not still going on about that, are you?

Tuning into speakers' internal viewpoints involves understanding them on their terms. You listen carefully and allow them the psychological space to say what they want. In addition, you need to decode their messages, taking into account vocal and body as well as verbal messages (see Activity 3.2). The following are examples of responses by listeners as if in speakers' *internal* viewpoints:

- You feel betrayed by her/him.
- You have mixed feelings about continuing to see her/him.
- You're annoyed that he phoned.
- You're pleased that she/he has finally started to share in keeping the garden tidy.

---

**ACTIVITY 3.2**                    **Tune into another's internal viewpoint**

---

## Part A  Identify another's internal viewpoint

Part A of this activity asks you to identify whether the listener has responded as if from the speaker's internal viewpoint. Some responses may seem artificial since they have been devised to make the point of the exercise clear. Answers for the exercise are provided at the end of the chapter. Below are some statement–response excerpts from different relationships. Three responses have been provided for each statement. Write IN or EX by each response according to whether it represents the speaker's internal viewpoint or comes from an external viewpoint.

## Example

*Girlfriend to boyfriend*

*Girlfriend:* I have been really happy since we started living together.
*Boyfriend:*

| | |
|---|---|
| EX | (a) It may not last. |
| IN | (b) You've been delighted from the time we began sharing together. |
| EX | (c) I have been wondering what you've been feeling at times. |

## Statements and responses

### 1. *Husband to wife*

*Husband:* I'm not sure we can afford such an expensive car.
*Wife:*

| | |
|---|---|
| _____ | (a) I want that car very badly. |
| _____ | (b) You are always on the stingy side. |
| _____ | (c) You're uncertain whether we have sufficient funds for such a high-priced car. |

### 2. *Friend to friend*

*Friend A:* I'm finding it difficult to stay interested in my studies.
*Friend B:*

| | |
|---|---|
| _____ | (a) You're struggling to stay motivated to study. |
| _____ | (b) What are you going to do if you drop out? |
| _____ | (c) Your course sounds pretty boring to me. |

### 3. *Partner to partner*

*Partner A:* I'm very tired after such a long day at work.
*Partner B:*

| | |
|---|---|
| _____ | (a) You shouldn't get tired so easily. |
| _____ | (b) You feel exhausted having worked for so long. |
| _____ | (c) Well, what about my hard day too? |

## Part B Summarizing another's internal viewpoint

Work with a partner.

1. Person A talks for at least two minutes about what he/she considers important in a close relationship (Person A's internal viewpoint). Person B does not interrupt.
2. When Person A finishes, Person B summarizes the main points of what Person A was saying. Person A does not interrupt.
3. When Person B finishes summarizing, Person A comments on how accurate Person B was in understanding her/his internal viewpoint. Person B can respond to this feedback.
4. Then reverse roles and repeat 2, 3 and 4 above.

---

## SKILL 3 SEND GOOD VOCAL MESSAGES

The emotional atmosphere you provide when you listen can be greatly enhanced by your voice messages. Talkers need to feel that you are responsive to their feelings. One of the main ways you can do this is by sending vocal messages that neither add nor subtract emotional meaning and emphasis.

- *Volume.* You need to respond at a level that is comfortable and easy to hear.
- *Articulation.* Poor enunciation can interrupt the speaker's train of thought. Heavy accents can be very difficult to listen to, especially if accompanied by poor use of grammar and language. Again, this may interfere with the speaker's train of thought.
- *Pitch.* High-pitched and shrill voices can disconcert. A harsh tone can threaten.
- *Emphasis.* It is important that your voice is expressive in accurately picking up the major feelings and feeling nuances of speakers. Speaking in a weak and diffident voice may indicate that you have problems and deter the speaker. Speaking too firmly overwhelms.
- *Rate.* You create a more relaxed atmosphere if you do not talk too fast when you respond. Your use of pauses and silences can enhance your capacity to be a rewarding listener. To make it easy for speakers to tell their stories, you can pause after each utterance to see if they wish to continue. Good use of silences can allow speakers more psychological space to think things through before speaking and to get in touch with their deeper feelings (see Activity 3.3).

**ACTIVITY 3.3**                     **How rewarding are my vocal messages when I listen?**

## Part A  Assess my vocal messages

First, on your own, assess your good and poor skills at sending vocal messages when you listen. Then, if appropriate, discuss your answers with your partner, another or others.

| *Vocal message* | *My assessment* |
| --- | --- |
| Volume | |
| Articulation | |
| Pitch | |
| Emphasis | |
| Rate | |

Identify specific poor skills in your vocal messages when listening and set goals for change.

## Part B  Using terrible and good vocal message skills when listening

Work with a partner and hold a conversation on a topic of mutual interest.

1. First two minutes: both of you converse normally.
2. Second two minutes: use terrible vocal message skills as you try to show your partner you are listening to her/his utterances.
3. Third two minutes: use good vocal message skills as you try to show your partner you are listening to her/his utterances.
4. Evaluation period: discuss what it felt like receiving and sending terrible and good vocal messages. Your evaluation session may be more educational and fun if you play back a cassette of your six-minute conversation.
5. Then reverse roles and repeat 2, 3 and 4 above.

## SKILL 4 SEND GOOD BODY MESSAGES

The following are some of the main body message skills that demonstrate interest and attention (Argyle, 1992; Egan, 2002; Ivey and Ivey, 2002). In varying degrees, they provide non-verbal rewards for talking.

### Availability

People who are always off to the next events in their busy lives may not find time to listen adequately to those to whom they relate. Close relationships require an investment of quality time. If this is not forthcoming, sooner rather than later either or both partners are likely to feel that they are being inadequately listened to. If you are rarely or never available to listen, you have withdrawn much of your interest and attention from the other person.

### Facial expression

A friendly relaxed facial expression, including a smile, initially demonstrates interest. However, as the other talks your facial expressions need to show that you are tuned into what they say. For instance, if another is serious, weeping or angry, adjust your facial expression to indicate that you observe and hear what they communicate.

### Gaze and eye contact

Good gaze skills indicate your interest and enable you to receive important facial messages. In addition, gaze can give you cues about when to stop listening and start responding. However, the main cues used in synchronizing conversations are verbal and vocal messages rather than body messages (Argyle, 1994). Good eye contact skills involve looking in the other's direction so that you allow the possibility of your eyes meeting reasonably often. There is an equilibrium level for eye contact in any relationship depending upon cultural and social rules, the degree of anxiety in each partner, the nature and state of development of the relationship, and the degree of attraction involved. Staring at another threatens. Looking down or away too often may indicate that you are tense or uninterested.

### Gestures

The head nod is perhaps the most common gesture in listening 'small ones to show continued attention, larger and repeated ones to indicate agreement' (Argyle, 1992: 11). Head nods can be viewed as rewards to talkers. On the negative side, head nods can also be powerful ways of controlling speakers. Then unconditional acceptance becomes conditional acceptance. Arm and hand gestures can also be used to show responsiveness to speakers. However, listeners who gesture either too little or too much with their heads and arms can discourage. Other negative gestures include tightly crossed arms and legs that act as barriers, hands clenched together, finger drumming, fiddling with your hair, your hand over your mouth, ear tugging and scratching yourself, to mention but some.

## Posture

Postural skills include physical openness, being relaxed, degree of trunk lean and postural similarity. Physical openness means facing the speaker not only with your face, but with your body. You need to be sufficiently turned towards the other person so that you can receive all their significant facial and body messages. A relaxed body posture, provided you do not sprawl, conveys the message that you are emotionally accessible. If you sit in a tense and uptight fashion, the listener may either consciously consider or intuitively feel that you are too bound up with your personal agenda and unfinished business to be fully accessible to them.

Your trunk lean may be forwards, backwards or sideways. If you lean too far forward you look odd and others may consider that you invade their personal space. If you lean far back others may find this distancing. A slight forward trunk lean can both encourage talkers and avoid threat, especially at the start of relationships. Some research suggests that postural similarity, where two people take up mirror-image postures, is perceived as a sign of liking (Argyle, 1992).

## Proximity

There are various zones of intimacy for different kinds of conversations. Rewarding listening entails respecting these zones. If you move too quickly into another's personal space, they may feel uncomfortable and move away. If you are physically too far away, not only do they have to talk louder, but they may perceive you as emotionally distant. The most comfortable height for conversations is if your heads are at the same level. If you persist in standing when someone seated talks to you, this is likely to feel awkward for them. When seated, listener's and speaker's chairs should be at the same level, though this becomes less important when people become comfortable with each other.

## Touch

When people date there may be high levels of touch as they listen to and get to know one another. Their body contact may include holding hands, a semi-embrace and sitting close so that their legs touch. In many relationships, touch can be an effective way of showing concern for someone who is hurting and in pain. Demonstrations of concern include touching another's hands, arms, shoulders and upper back. The intensity and duration of touch should be sufficient to establish contact and yet avoid creating discomfort. Part of being a rewarding listener includes picking up messages about the limits and desirability of your use of touch.

Both *within* your body messages and also *between* your body messages and your vocal and verbal messages, consistency increases the chances of your being perceived as a rewarding listener. For instance, you may be smiling and at the same time either fidgeting or tapping your fist. Your smile may indicate interest, your foot tapping impatience, and your overall message may appear insincere (see Activity 3.4).

| ACTIVITY 3.4 | How rewarding are my body messages when I listen? |

## Part A  Assess my body messages

First, on your own, assess your good and poor skills at sending body messages when you listen. Then, if appropriate, discuss your answers with your partner, another or others.

| *Body message* | *My assessment* |
|---|---|
| Availability | |
| Facial expression | |
| Gaze and eye contact | |
| Gestures | |
| Posture | |
| Proximity | |
| Touch | |

Identify specific poor skills in your body messages when listening and set goals for change.

## Part B  Using terrible and good body message skills when listening

Work with a partner and hold a conversation on a topic of mutual interest.

1. First two minutes: both of you converse normally.
2. Second two minutes: remaining silent, use terrible body message skills when listening as your partner talks.
3. Third two minutes: still remaining silent, use good body message skills when listening as your partner talks.
4. Evaluation period: discuss what it felt like receiving and sending terrible and good body messages. Your evaluation session may be more educational and fun if you play back a video of your six-minute conversation.
5. Then reverse roles and repeat 2, 3 and 4 above.

---

## SKILL 5  USE OPENING REMARKS, SMALL REWARDS AND OPEN-ENDED QUESTIONS

Opening remarks, small rewards and open-ended questions all require the use of a few words as well as of good voice and body messages. They each make it easier for the speaker to talk.

### Opening remarks

Opening remarks, openers or permissions to talk are brief statements indicating that you are prepared to listen. Such remarks can occur at any time in a relationship. The message contained in all opening remarks is: 'I'm interested and prepared to listen. I'm giving you the opportunity to share what you think and feel.' A good time to use an opening remark can be when you sense something is bothering another and she or he requires encouragement to share it. Such an opener may be a response to another's body messages. Here are some examples of opening remarks.

| | |
|---|---|
| How are you? | How was your day? |
| You look really happy. | You seem tense today. |
| What's the matter? | Is there something on your mind? |
| Would you like to talk about it? | I'd like to know what you think? |

When using opening remarks, you must be sensitive to others' reactions. They may not be ready to talk or consider you are not the right person to talk to. They probably do not want information dragged out of them. However, sometimes you rightly sense that others want to talk, but have difficulty doing so. In such situations follow-up remarks, for instance, 'It's pretty hard to get started' or

'Take your time', may further help the speaker open up. Poor body messages can totally destroy the impact of an opening remark. For example, a husband who looks up and says 'What's on your mind dear?' and then continues reading the newspaper discourages his wife from telling him.

## Small rewards

Small rewards are brief verbal expressions of interest designed to encourage speakers. The message they convey is: 'I am with you. Please go on.' Small rewards can be used for good or ill. On the one hand they can reward people for talking to you from their internal viewpoint. On the other hand, they may range from crude to subtle attempts to take others out of their internal viewpoint by shaping what they say. For instance, you may say 'Tell me more' whenever someone says what you want to hear, yet remain silent when they do not. Below are some examples of verbal small rewards, though perhaps the most frequently used 'Um-hmm' is more vocal than verbal.

| | |
|---|---|
| Um-hmm | Sure |
| Please continue | Indeed |
| Tell me more | And |
| Go on | So |
| I see | Really |
| Oh | Right |
| Interesting | Ah |
| Then | Yes |
| I hear you | |

Another kind of small reward is to repeat the last word someone has said:

*Speaker*:   I'm feeling anxious.
*Listener*:   Anxious.

## Open-ended questions

You may use questions in ways that either help speakers to elaborate their internal viewpoints or lead them out of their viewpoints, possibly into yours. Open-ended questions allow speakers to share their internal viewpoints without curtailing their options. Open-ended questions include 'Tell me about it?', 'Please elaborate' and, slightly less open ended, 'How do you feel about that?' Open-ended questions may be contrasted with closed questions that curtail speakers' options. Indeed they often give only two options, 'yes' or 'no'.

*Open-ended question*:   How do you feel about your relationship?
*Closed question*:   Is your relationship good or bad?

Closed questions may have various negative outcomes. You may be perceived as leading and controlling the conversation. You may block another from getting in touch with and listening to themselves and responding from their internal viewpoint rather than to your external viewpoint. You may set the stage for an interrogation. Since closed questions can be disincentives to talking, they can create silences in which the stage is set for further closed questions. I do not mean to imply that you never use closed questions. It depends on the goals of your listening. They are useful if you wish to collect information. However, show restraint if you wish to help others to share their worlds. You may also need to use open-ended questions sparingly (see Activity 3.5).

## ACTIVITY 3.5                    Group discussion: listening skills |

This is intended as a group exercise, though it may be done individually or in pairs.

For each part:

1.  Spend five to ten minutes answering the questions in groups of three or four.
2.  Each group shares its answers with the whole group.
3.  The whole group ranks the four most important points or skills from the most important to the least important.

## Part A  Advantages of rewarding listening

List the four main advantages of rewarding listening in personal relationships.

## Part B  Vocal message skills

List the four main vocal message skills for rewarding listening in personal relationships.

## Part C  Body message skills

List the four main body message skills for rewarding listening in personal relationships.

## ANSWERS TO ACTIVITY 3.2 (PART A)

1     (a) EX   (b) EX   (c) IN
2     (a) IN    (b) EX   (c) EX
3     (a) EX   (b) IN    (c) EX

# Show understanding skills

**Chapter outcomes**
By studying and doing the activities in this chapter you should:

- know what is active understanding
- be able to use paraphrasing skills
- begin being able to use reflecting feelings skills
- know how to use questions
- know how to use challenges
- know about using some mind skills when listening and showing understanding.

The first part of this chapter presents some skills of actively showing understanding of another's internal viewpoint. The second part of the chapter looks at clarifying understanding by using questioning and challenging skills. The chapter ends by examining some mind skills that you may use for good or ill when listening and showing understanding.

## SHOWING UNDERSTANDING

You can show understanding by responding as if in the speaker's internal viewpoint. Showing understanding entails tuning in to and reflecting with your verbal, vocal and body messages the crux of the meaning contained in the verbal, vocal and body messages of another. Here is an example:

*Friend to friend*
> *Friend A:* When I first realized that I'd lost my girlfriend/ boyfriend, my world fell apart. I'm still pretty shaken and do not really understand why we've broken up.

> *Friend B:*     You felt flabbergasted when you realized that she/he was ending your relationship. You are still reeling and can't fully explain why it's over.

When assessing a showing understanding response, think of a three-link chain: first statement – show understanding response – second statement. Good responses allow the opportunity for another's second statement to be a continuation of the train of thought contained in their first statement. Bad responses do not.

## Uses of showing understanding

When people are first introduced to the skills of showing understanding they frequently express reservations: for instance, 'It's so unnatural', 'People will just think I'm repeating everything they say' or 'It gets in the way of my being spontaneous.' When learning any new skill, from driving a car to driving a golfball, there is a period where you are likely to have to concentrate extra hard on selecting the correct sequence of choices that make up the skill. Showing understanding is no exception. If you work and practise a skill, you are ultimately likely to own it as a 'natural' part of you. It is natural to the extent that it feels natural. Showing understanding skills should not be used all the time, but flexibly incorporated into your repertoire of responses. Following are some occasions where using showing understanding skills may help you to relate more effectively:

- When another struggles to understand herself or himself.
- When another requires help in expressing thoughts and feelings.
- When another is trying to manage a personal problem or make a decision.
- When you need to be clear about another's position in a disagreement.
- When you wish to ensure that the responsibility for a decision or course of action in her or his life rests with the other person.

However, on other occasions in relationships you may gain from either not using showing understanding skills or using them sparingly:

- When you consider someone talks too much and it is time communication became more two-way.
- When you wish to match the level of intimacy of another's disclosures.
- When you are aware that you are listening as a means of avoiding defining and asserting yourself.
- When you feel too tired or hassled to listen properly.
- When you consider another's solution might damage either yourself and/or her or him.

## SKILL 6 PARAPHRASE

Along with reflecting feelings, paraphrasing is one of the component skills of showing understanding. It is important that you paraphrase because you drive people crazy if you parrot them. As a frustrated husband once said to his wife, 'If I had wanted someone to repeat everything I said after me, I would have married a parrot.' Paraphrasing means rewording speakers' verbal utterances. However, it excludes showing understanding of their vocal and body messages. When you paraphrase, you may sometimes use the speaker's words, but sparingly. You try to stay close to the kind of language they have used. Here are a few basic examples:

*Wife to husband*
> *Wife:*         Go to hell.
> *Husband:*   You're mad at me.

*Partner to partner*
> *First partner:*        I've got the blues.
> *Second partner:*   You feel really low.

*Divorcee to friend*
> *Divorcee:*   It's painful for me that all the friends we knew as a couple now seem to want to see only Jim [her ex-husband].
> *Friend:*       You're hurt that your mutual friends now appear interested only in keeping in contact with Jim.

A good paraphrase can provide a response that is often clearer and more succinct than the original utterance. If so, speakers may comment 'That's it' or 'You've got me.' A simple tip for paraphrasing is to start your responses with the personal pronoun 'you' to indicate that you reflect the speaker's internal viewpoints. Another tip is not to speak too quickly – this gives you more time to think. A good memory and a large vocabulary also help. To become confident, flexible and fluent in paraphrasing and reflecting feelings skills requires much practice (see Activity 4.1).

**ACTIVITY 4.1**                      **Develop my paraphrasing skills**

## Part A On your own

1. Paraphrase once the content of each of the following statements into clear and simple language. Use 'you' or 'your' where the speaker uses 'I' or 'me'. Remember there is no single correct answer.

   (a) It bothers me when you don't respond.

(b) I appreciate the help you've given me.

(c) I shall miss my girlfriend when she's away.

(d) I couldn't help laughing when he screwed up.

(e) You're having me on.

2. Think of at least three different ways of paraphrasing the following statements:

(a) I've always been shy in social situations.

(b) I feel shut out by her and don't know why.

Possible answers to Part A are at the end of this chapter.

## Part B  Practice in pairs and in a group

1. *In pairs.* You 'feed' each other statements. Listeners paraphrase speakers' statements and speakers provide feedback on their reactions to each paraphrase.

2. *In a group.* Members take turns in making statements. They may write them on whiteboards or blackboards. After each statement all group members formulate a paraphrase and then share them with the group.

---

# SKILL 7  REFLECT FEELINGS

Reflecting feelings is the main skill of actively showing understanding. Reflecting feelings entails responding to the speaker's music and not just to their words. It may be viewed as feeling with a speaker's flow of emotions and experiencing and being able to communicate this back. When you reflect feelings, you give another the opportunity to listen more deeply to their own feelings.

There is a risk that if you constantly reflect the speaker's feelings you can just encourage self-pity. For instance, Mark may persist in feeling sorry for himself when discussing his relationship with Tricia, which is not going well. You need to use your judgement in how much and when to reflect feelings. For instance, you might use reflecting feelings responses to allow Mark to express his feelings and to show that you understand them. Then, possibly, you could ask a question like 'Well, is there anything you can do to improve the situation?'

## Pick up feelings words and phrases

Let's start with the obvious. A good but not infallible way to discuss what another feels is to listen to their feelings words and phrases. Sometimes people ask 'Well, what did you feel?' just after they have already been told. Sometimes feelings words are not the central message. For instance, Valerie may say 'It's just great' that, after the break-up of a relationship, she is living on her own again, at the same time as her voice chokes, her face looks sad and the corners of her mouth are turned down. Also, sometimes people say 'I feel' when they mean 'I think'. For example, 'I feel that equality between the sexes is essential' describes a thought rather than a feeling. On the other hand, 'I feel angry about sex discrimination' describes a feeling. It is important that you distinguish between speakers' thoughts and feelings if you wish to be skilful at picking up feelings accurately.

Feelings phrases are colloquial expressions used to describe feelings words. For instance, 'I'm over the moon' is a feelings phrase describing the emotion of joy. It is cumbersome, when reflecting feelings, always to put 'You feel' before feelings words and phrases. Sometimes 'You're' is sufficient: for example, 'You're delighted' instead of 'You feel delighted.' The following is an example of someone using feelings words and phrases that communicate clearly what she means. Ally says to Ken: 'I really enjoyed our date last night. It was just great. Even after so little time I feel there is something special between us. When can we meet again?' Ally's feelings words and phrases are 'really enjoyed', 'just great', 'something special between us' and 'can we meet again?' Skilful reflection of feelings words and phrases requires attention to the following areas.

- *Strength*. Try and understand the strength of speaker's feelings. For instance, after a row the speaker may feel 'devastated' (strong feeling), 'upset' (moderate feeling), or 'slightly upset' (weak feeling).
- *Multiple and mixed feelings*. Sometimes people use many words to describe their feelings. The words may cluster around the same theme, in which case you may choose to reflect the crux of the feeling. Alternatively, speakers may verbalize varying degrees of mixed feelings ranging from simple opposites, for instance, 'happy/sad' to more complex combinations, such as 'hurt/anger/guilt'. Good reflections pick up all key elements of feelings messages as in the following example:

> *Girlfriend:*  Most of the time, we've a great relationship, but sometimes we fight and sometimes I want my own space.
> *Friend:*  You really enjoy being with Robin, but that doesn't mean you don't also argue and sometimes just want your own company.

- *Assisting labelling of feelings*. Sometimes you can assist speakers to find the right way to express their feelings. Here reflecting feelings involves helping others choose feelings words that resonate for them:

> *Julie:*  I don't know how to express my reaction to the way my father treated me . . . possibly angry . . . upset, no that's not quite it . . . bewildered . . .
> *Helen:*  Hurt, anxious, confused . . . do any of these words strike a chord?

## Pick up vocal and body messages

Much information about speakers' feelings comes from their vocal and body messages. Frequently, people's vocal and body messages are inconsistent with their verbal messages. Speakers may struggle to express what they truly feel in face of their conditioning about what they should feel. In relationships it takes time to develop the trust that leads to more open communication.

If you are unclear about speakers' real or underlying feelings, you can check with them. For instance, you may make comments like 'I think I hear you saying (state feelings tentatively)' or 'I want to understand what your feeling, but I'm still not altogether clear.' Another option is to reflect back the mixed message: for instance, 'On the one hand you are saying you don't mind. On the other hand, you seem tearful.' After a pause you might add: 'I'm wondering if you are putting on a brave face?' A further consideration in picking up feelings is to understand whether and to what extent speakers possess insight into their feelings: for example, being able to acknowledge to themselves that they feel hurt.

## Sender skills for reflecting feelings

When you've decoded speakers' feelings messages to the best of your ability, how do you actively show that you understand them? Here are a few guidelines for reflecting feelings.

1. *Reflect the crux of the message.* Whatever else you do, communicate back the speaker's main feeling. Even though speakers may not start with their main feeling, they may feel better understood by you if you reflect their main feeling at the front of your response.

> Paul:       We just argue and argue and don't seem to get anywhere. I don't know what to do. It's so frustrating. I wish I knew the answer. I don't seem able to handle my mum.
>
> Penny:      You're extremely frustrated with constant unproductive arguments and not knowing how to improve matters with her.

2. *Keep your responses simple.* Use simple and clear language. Avoid unnecessary words and qualifications. However, be prepared to state different parts of multiple and mixed messages.
3. *Use vocal and body messages to add expressiveness to your verbal messages.* You are not just talking about feelings, you are reflecting feelings. For instance, if a hypothetical suicide-prone friend says 'I'm at the end of my tether', you can adjust your voice and facial expression to mirror, to some extent, a sense of despair.
4. *Where appropriate, reflect feelings and reasons.* Sometimes you can reflect speakers' feelings and the reasons they offer for them. A simple way of

doing this is to make a 'You feel . . . because . . .' statement that mirrors their internal viewpoint. Reflecting back reasons does not mean that you make an interpretation or offer an explanation from your external viewpoint.

> *Neil:* I'm uncertain whether to quit my job. I like the security, but want more difficulty and stimulation.
>
> *Mohammed:* You feel undecided about leaving your position because you would like more challenge and interest, but appreciate the safety of where you are.

5. *Check your understanding.* You respond to speakers' utterances with differing degrees of tentativeness depending on how clearly they have communicated and how confident you are about receiving their messages accurately. However, all your reflections of feelings should contain an element of checking the accuracy of your understanding. Sometimes you check by slight voice inflections. On other occasions, you check by asking directly: for instance, 'Do I understand you properly?' (see Activity 4.2).

---

**ACTIVITY 4.2**          **Develop my reflecting feelings skills**

---

## Part A  Identify and change feelings words and phrases

For each of the following statements: (a) identify the words the speaker has used to describe how she or he feels; (b) change these words to accurately reflect how the speaker feels.

1. *Mary to Marsha:* 'I find being without a boyfriend depressing. Right now my prospects look bleak.'

   Mary's feelings words:

   ...............................................................................................................

   ...............................................................................................................

   Your reflection of Mary's feelings:

   ...............................................................................................................

   ...............................................................................................................

2. *Arthur to Alison*: 'I'm determined to be my own man. It's exciting to think I could have a successful business.'

Arthur's feelings words:

.................................................................................................................

.................................................................................................................

Your reflection of Arthur's of feelings:

.................................................................................................................

.................................................................................................................

## Part B  Reflect feelings and reasons

For each of the following statements formulate a 'You feel ... because ...' response that reflects the speaker's main feeling or feelings and states their explanation for it/them.

1. *Joy to Kevin*: 'I hate being teased. I just hate it. I'm no different from the other girls and yet they seem to enjoy ganging up on me. It makes me feel so angry and lonely.'

You feel

.................................................................................................................

because

.................................................................................................................

.................................................................................................................

2. *Ian to Sarah*: 'I get annoyed when people don't understand my relationship with Ray. Sure we are emotionally very close, but what's wrong with that? Some people can't understand intimate friendships between guys.'

You feel

.................................................................................................................

because

.................................................................................................................

.................................................................................................................

Possible answers to Parts A and B are at the end of this chapter.

## Part C Practice in pairs and in a group

1. *In pairs.* Each of you takes turns to be speaker and listener. When listening, help your speaker to talk about her/his feelings by reflecting them accurately. Pay attention to vocal and body as well as to verbal messages.
2. *Group exercises*

   (a) The group picks a feeling. Then members identify and demonstrate the verbal, vocal and body messages required to express that feeling mildly, moderately and strongly. Repeat the exercise for other feelings.

   (b) This exercise may be done with a beach ball or tennis ball. Members sit in a circle. The member holding the ball (the speaker) expresses a feeling by means of verbal, vocal and body messages. She/he pauses to allow all members to formulate a reflection of feeling response and then throws the ball to one member (the listener) who attempts to reflect the feeling accurately. Then the listener becomes the speaker and so on.

   (c) One member sits in front and acts as a speaker who is trying to share and explore his feelings on a topic. The remaining group members sit in a semi-circle around him/her. The speaker states a feeling to each member of group in turn. After each statement, the member who is 'listener' reflects the speaker's feeling as accurately as possible. Members take turns in being the speaker.

---

# EXPANDING UNDERSTANDING

So far I have focused on being a rewarding listener so that you make it easy for another to share their internal viewpoint. However, at times you may help to expand another's understanding by asking questions and challenging them. Questions and challenges come from your internal and the speaker's external viewpoint. You can use questioning and challenging skills to take another beyond her or his existing internal viewpoint. Depending upon how you use these skills, the focus of the conversation can remain on another or change to you.

# SKILL 8 CLARIFY BY QUESTIONS

Questions can show another person you are interested in what they say. Questions can also help or hinder another in managing problems. Let's take the example of Martina who has a problem at work that she wishes to discuss with her partner Jake. There are two extremes to how Jake might question Martina. Jake could use questions to take control of Martina's problem and come up with solutions for her. Alternatively, Jake could use questions to help Martina to arrive at her own solutions. Underlying these two ways of questioning is the issue of who owns the problem, Jake or Martina? When Jake asks controlling questions for his purposes, he owns Martina's problem. However, if Jake asks questions that help Martiina to cope with the problem on her terms, he allows the ownership of the problem to remain with her (Gordon, 1970). If Jake uses good questioning skills he can help Martina to explore, clarify and enlarge her internal viewpoint.

## Types of questions

Listeners need to choose from among various types of questions, including the following:

1. *Open-ended versus closed questions.* Open-ended questions give speakers considerable choice in how to respond, whereas closed questions restrict choice (see Chapter 3, pp. 53–54).
2. *Specific detail questions.* You can use specific detail questions to collect concrete information about an issue or problem:
   - How did you actually behave?
   - When did it start?
   - Where does it happen?
   - Describe a specific instance of her/his doing that?
3. *Elaboration questions.* Elaboration questions are open questions that give speakers the opportunity to expand on what they have said:
   - Would you care to elaborate?
   - Tell me more.
4. *Eliciting personal meanings questions.* The information that speakers provide often has personal or symbolic meaning for them. For example, whenever her husband would come home late without having called her, his wife would think he did not care about her (Beck, 1988). Eliciting personal meaning questions should be tentative, since speakers may need to think before answering:
   - I'm wondering about the meaning of . . . for you?
   - What do you make of that?
   - Why is it so important for you?
5. *Checking understanding questions.* These questions seek information about and clarify the speaker's words and phrases, for example:
   - When you say . . . what do you mean?
   - Sounds to me you're saying . . .
   - Can I check that I've understood you properly?
6. *Solution-focused questions.* Solution-focused questions ask about the various alternatives that may exist:
   - What are your options?
   - What are you planning to do?
   - How might you change your behaviour?

# Enlarging another's internal viewpoint

I do not advocate that you always ask questions for another's benefit and not yours. However, since this is a chapter on rewarding listening, I focus on questioning that helps speakers to understand themselves better. Below are some skills of collaborating with another when asking questions.

1. *Intersperse active understanding with questions.* Speakers feel interrogated if you ask a series of questions in quick succession. You can soften your questioning if you pause to see if another wants to continue responding and then reflect each response before asking another question. Following are two brief conversations between Jake and Martina about her work problem:

   Jake owning the problem:
   | | |
   |---|---|
   | *Martina:* | I'm having difficulty getting on with my boss. |
   | *Jake:* | Why do you always seem to have problems with people at work? |
   | *Martina:* | I have this large project to finish and she refuses to let me have more help. |
   | *Jake:* | Why aren't you being more assertive with her? |
   | *Martina:* | I've tried to talk to her, but I don't seem to make any impression. |
   | *Jake:* | If I were you, I'd tell her to stop making unrealistic demands and realize how hard you work. |

   Jake allowing Martina to own the problem:
   | | |
   |---|---|
   | *Martina:* | I'm having difficulty getting on with my boss. |
   | *Jake:* | You're worried about this conflict. What do you think is going on? |
   | *Martina:* | I have this large project to finish and she refuses to let me have more help. |
   | *Jake:* | You feel stressed because she's not backing you up. Is there anything you think you can do about it?' |
   | *Martina:* | Last time I talked with her, I did not explain clearly how many different angles there are to the project. Perhaps, I could sit down with her and try to negotiate some limits on it. |

   Though these are only short excerpts, in the first one Jake dominates Martina, whereas in the second Jake uses questions to help Martina enlarge her internal viewpoint and do her own work. In the second excerpt Jake also shows active understanding of Martina's feelings.

2. *Ask follow-on questions.* Avoid jack-rabbiting in which you quickly hop from one topic to another. Listen carefully to what another has just said. Frequently, your next question follows on from and encourages the speaker to enlarge upon their last response. Questions linked logically to the speaker's previous responses help to show your understanding.

3. *Carefully observe how questions are answered.* Much of the skill of questioning lies in decoding another's answers. Speakers send messages by what is left unsaid or only partially said and by vocal and body messages. Skilled listeners tune in finely to subtle messages. They sensitively pick up another's anxieties, confusions and vulnerabilities and take them into account in whether and how they ask their next question (see Activity 4.3).

## ACTIVITY 4.3                    Develop my questioning skills

## Part A  Different types of questions

Provide an example of each of the following types of questions:

Open-ended question

..................................................................................................................

..................................................................................................................

Specific detail question

..................................................................................................................

..................................................................................................................

Elaboration question

..................................................................................................................

..................................................................................................................

Eliciting personal meaning question

..................................................................................................................

..................................................................................................................

Checking understanding question

..................................................................................................................

..................................................................................................................

Solution focused question

..................................................................................................................

..................................................................................................................

## Part B  Practice in pairs and in a group

1. *In pairs.* Work with a partner who discusses a problem with you. Help your partner to understand her/his problem more clearly by using the listening skills of paraphrasing, reflecting feelings and questioning. Throughout, pay attention to your verbal vocal and body messages. End by asking your partner to summarize the 'session'. Afterwards, discuss and reverse roles.
2. *In a group.* One person acts as speaker who presents a problem to the group who sit in a semi-circle facing her/him. Each member takes turns in responding to the speaker first by reflecting what she/he has just said and then by asking a question. When finished, the speaker provides feedback on the 'session'. Members take turns as speakers.

---

# SKILL 9  CLARIFY BY CHALLENGES

The skill of challenging is sometimes called confronting. My emphasis here is on using challenging, when listening, to help another expand and explore their perceptions (Egan, 2002). The starting point is his or her internal viewpoint rather than yours. There may be other occasions in your relationships, for instance, confronting a conflict, when the starting point may be your viewpoint.

You can challenge another's existing perceptions so that they can work with more and better information. Each of you lives in the world of your own perceptions. Sometimes a challenge or confrontation from an external viewpoint can broaden and deepen the speaker's internal viewpoint. In relationships, challenges can be invitations to consider other ways of viewing matters. Needless to say, the skills you use when challenging are very important. Challenging inconsistencies and possible distortions of reality are two of the main skills of challenging that you can include in your repertoire of relationship skills.

## Challenging inconsistencies

When someone talks to you, you can experience inconsistencies in the messages they send you. Such inconsistencies may include the following:

- *Inconsistency between verbal, voice and body messages.* 'On the one hand you say that you are fine, but on the other I catch a note of pain in your voice and see you looking tearful.'
- *Inconsistency between words and actions.* 'You say you love your mother, but you rarely spend time with her even though she lives quite close.'
- *Inconsistency between past and present statements.* 'You now say you love her, but a week ago you were saying how much you hated her.'
- *Inconsistency between your view of you and my view of you.* 'You say that you see yourself as uninteresting, but I genuinely do not see you that way.'

- *Inconsistency between your view of you and others' views of you.* 'You see your-self as rather unpopular in the group, but you seem to be getting a lot of messages that other members of the group like you.'

How do you challenge inconsistencies? A common response here is: 'On the one hand you say . . . but on the other hand . . .' – for example, 'On the one hand you say that you are fine, but on the other hand I catch a note of pain in your voice.' This response is often shortened to 'You say . . . but . . .' – for example, 'You say that you are fine, but I catch a note of pain in your voice.'

## Challenging possible distortions of reality

When another person talks to you he or she may make statements like the following: 'I have no friends', 'I'm a poor father', 'I'm no good with women/men', 'She/he doesn't love me any more', 'I'm no good at anything', 'They made me do it', and 'She/he never says anything positive.' All these statements are possibly faulty perceptions that harm rather than help. One way you could respond is to reflect the speaker's internal viewpoint. Another way is to chal-lenge the speaker's version of reality. People often jump to conclusions on insufficient evidence and then treat their conclusions as facts (Beck and Weishaar, 2005). You require judgement as to whether you continue listening within the internal viewpoint or you challenge possible distortions of reality.

How do you challenge possible distortions of reality? A good response for challenging distortions is 'You say . . . but where's the evidence?' – for example, 'You say that you have no friends, but where's the evidence?' Such a response reflects the speaker's internal viewpoint and then invites them to produce evi-dence to support it. The speaker may then make a remark like: 'Well, Ron never phones me up any more?' Then you may challenge them again with a question such as 'Is there any other way of looking at that?' With the questions 'Where's the evidence?' and 'Is their any other way of looking at that?' you invite speakers to produce their own evidence to confirm or negate their versions of reality rather than doing it for them. On other occasions you may suggest that they consider some evidence from your viewpoint.

## Some guidelines for challenging

The following are some guidelines on how to challenge:

1. *Start with active understanding.* Always start your response by showing that you have heard and understood the speaker's message. Then build on this with your challenging response. This way you are more likely to keep the speaker's ears open to what comes from your viewpoint.
2. *Where possible, help speakers to challenge themselves.* By reflecting inconsisten-cies, you allow speakers to draw their own conclusions about them. Simi-larly, by asking speakers to search for evidence to back their statements, you

help them to challenge themselves. Often assisting speakers to challenge themselves leads to less resistance than if you challenge them directly from your external viewpoint.

3.  *Do not talk down.* Keep your challenges at a democratic level. Make your challenges invitations for exploration rather than papal pronouncements. Avoid 'You' messages. A major risk in challenging others is that they perceive you as putting them down rather than being helpful.

4.  *Use the minimum amount of 'muscle'.* Only challenge as strongly as required to achieve your goal. Heavy challenges can create resistances. Though sometimes necessary, they are generally to be avoided.

5.  *Avoid threatening vocal and body messages.* Try to avoid threatening vocal and body messages like raising your voice and glaring.

6.  *Leave the ultimate responsibility with the speaker.* Allow speakers to decide whether your challenges actually help them to move forward in their exploration. Many of your challenges, if well timed and tactfully worded, should not elicit much defensiveness.

7.  *Do not overdo it.* No one likes being challenged persistently. With constant challenges, you create unsafe emotional climates for speakers. You can help others move forward with skilled challenges, but you can block them and harm your relationship if you challenge too often and too clumsily (see Activity 4.4).

## ACTIVITY 4.4            Develop my challenging skills

## Part A   Examples of challenges

Provide a tactful challenging response in each of the following areas.

1.  *Challenge inconsistencies*
    Inconsistency between verbal, vocal and body messages

.............................................................................................................................

.............................................................................................................................

Inconsistency between words and actions

.............................................................................................................................

.............................................................................................................................

Inconsistency between past and present statements

.............................................................................................................................

.............................................................................................................................

2. *Challenge possible distortions of reality*
   Give two examples
   Example 1:

...............................................................................................................

...............................................................................................................

   Example 2:

...............................................................................................................

...............................................................................................................

## Part B  Practice in pairs and in a group

1. *In pairs.* Work with a partner who 'feeds' you inconsistencies on which you can develop your challenging skills. Afterwards, reverse roles.
2. *In a group.* Members of the group take it in turns to provide stimulus statements involving inconsistencies to the whole group. After each statement, each member shares their challenging response.

---

## SKILL 10  USE MIND SKILLS

## Think about how you think

How you think is vital to how well you listen to and understand others. Everyone is at risk of not listening properly because of weaknesses in one or more mind skills. Most people are especially likely to use their weaknesses when situations get heated. Mind skills weaknesses can contribute to creating as well as maintaining misunderstandings. On the other hand, using mind skills strengths can help you avoid some misunderstandings and deal better with those that occur. Here are some things to look out for.

*Creating rules*

You may have unrealistic rules about how you and others must be that interfere with how well you listen. For example, your sensitivity to criticism might be caused by a rule like 'I must be perfect'. Possessing such an unrealistic rule makes you vulnerable if and when you receive negative feedback. Sometimes, you may even turn neutral or positive remarks into negative ones when you think this way. Your emotions get aroused and you then fail to listen adequately to what is being said. Much better is to change your demanding perfectionist rule into a preference: for example, 'I would prefer not to make mistakes, but some mistakes are inevitable and what is important is to learn from them.'

Related to unrealistic rules about yourself are unrealistic rules that you hold about others. For example, you may think that 'Everybody must like me' and then get greatly upset and listen poorly when someone appears not to like you. Again, you can change an unrealistic rule into a more realistic preference: for instance, 'I would prefer to be liked, but sometimes this may not be possible and I can handle it if I have to.' Developing your skills of creating preferential rather than demanding rules will help you to listen to and understand yourself and others better.

## Creating perceptions

Your perceptions of yourself and other people may be of varying degrees of accuracy. For example, you may perceive that 'I am a good listener' and so remain unaware of the times when you fail to pick up others accurately. This failure may cause difficulty in your relationships. Instead, you can ask yourself questions like 'Where is the evidence that I am a good listener?' and 'I heard her/him saying this, but is there another way of viewing what has been said?' In relationships it is also very easy to perceive other people inaccurately and so not listen to them and understand them properly. You may become aware of specific people or situations where your listening may be less good than you would like it to be, so you can improve your performance.

## Creating self-talk

You can create self-talk that helps you to listen and understand another. For example, you can calm yourself down with statements like 'Relax', 'Calm down' and 'Take it easy.' You can coach yourself with statements like 'Really try and understand her/his viewpoint – I don't have to agree with it', 'I can check with her/him whether I have understood properly' and 'I will get my chance to speak, so just listen for now.' You can also make affirming self-talk statements such as 'It helps me to listen well and understand her/his position' and 'I'm learning to hold off and not interrupt.' You can put calming, coaching and affirming self-talk together: for instance, 'Calm down, listen carefully. I'm getting better at understanding where she/he is coming from.'

## Creating visual images

You can imagine yourself listening well if it helps you to do so. One way to do this is to visualize yourself listening calmly. Another way is to clear your mind of any irrelevant bad images concerning the speaker. You can also try to picture accurately what another person is trying to convey to you.

## *Creating explanations*

It is important that you assume responsibility for developing and using your listening and understanding skills. Many if not most people possess the illusion that they listen and understand others better than is actually the case. When living with another on a daily basis, there is a tendency to think that you know your partner well and can often therefore accurately explain both their behaviour towards you and your behaviour towards them. The result of such explanations may be that you stop listening properly to each other. In relationships it is easy to blame others when things go wrong. You may both be trying hard to make your points, but failing to hear and therefore adequately understand one another. Listening to and understanding another person, especially when in conflict, requires much discipline.

## *Creating expectations*

At the start of relationships people often expect the best of themselves and of one another. At this time there is a risk of not listening and understanding properly and so allowing too rosy a picture of one another to develop. Towards the end of a relationship, the reverse process may take place and your expectations of each other may become worse than is justified. Such negative expectations adversely affect your ability to listen to and understand what is happening in your relationship. Sometimes it is possible that, had your expectations not been so negative, you might have spent more time really understanding the other person in a way that might have strengthened the relationship. People fail to bring up issues in relationships because they fear that they will not be adequately listened to. The more you can create in your partner the expectation that, however sensitive the issue, you will try very hard to listen and understand them, the greater the likelihood of your relationship remaining strong (see Activity 4.5).

---

**ACTIVITY 4.5**                           **Develop my mind skills** |

---

### Part A  On your own

Provide an example for each of the following mind skills of using a poor skill and changing it to using a good skill.

(a) Creating rules
    poor skill
    good skill
(b) Creating perceptions
    poor skill
    good skill

(c) Creating self-talk
  poor skill
  good skill
(d) Creating visual images
  poor skill
  good skill
(e) Creating explanations
  poor skill
  good skill
(f) Creating expectations
  poor skill
  good skill

## Part B  Practice in pairs and in a group

1. *In pairs.* Work together to provide examples in each of the six categories of mind skills of:
   poor skills
   good skills
2. *In a group.* Work as a group to provide examples in each of the six
   categories of mind skills of:
   poor skills
   good skills

---

## ANSWERS TO ACTIVITIES

**ACTIVITY 4.1**                    **Develop my paraphrasing skills**    |

The following are suggestions, though other answers might also be
appropriate.

## Part A  On your own

Question 1
(a) You feel upset when I don't reply.
(b) You're grateful for my assistance.
(c) You're going to be lonely when [name of girlfriend] isn't around.
(d) You couldn't control your mirth at his mistake.
(e) You feel I'm making a fool of you.

Question 2
(a) You've always been bashful in company.
    You've always been timid when socializing.
    You've always been anxious with people.
(b) I feel excluded by her and can't find the reason.
    I feel pushed away by her and can't understand it.
    I feel rejected by her and have no explanation for it.

---

**ACTIVITY 4.2**                    **Develop my reflecting feelings skills**  |

---

## Part A  Identify and reflect feelings words and phrases

Other reflections than those suggested below may also be appropriate.

1. Mary's feelings words and phrases: 'depressing', 'bleak'.
   A reflection of Mary's feelings: You feel low not having a boyfriend and think your prospects of getting one are not good right now.
2. Arthur's findings words and phrases: 'determined', 'exciting', and possibly 'successful'.
   A reflection of Arthur's feelings: You feel great thinking you could have a going business and very much want to make your own decisions.

## Part B  Reflect feelings and reasons

1. You feel mad and isolated because you loathe being treated and picked on as though you're different.
2. You feel angry because people think your feelings for Ray are gay.

# 5

# Manage shyness skills

**Chapter outcomes**
By studying and doing the activities in this chapter you should:

- know what is shyness
- understand how shyness can be defined in relationship skills terms
- know what verbal, vocal and body messages do you require to intro-duce yourself effectively
- know about some skills for starting conversations
- know about some skills for holding conversations
- know about some skills for ending conversations
- know about some skills for making a date
- understand the relationship between situations, thoughts and consequences
- understand some mind skills for managing shyness.

Ovid reportedly said that 'Venus favours the bold.' An essential relationship skill is the ability to make initial contact with others. Below are two young men, Denis and Khalid, who go to the same party where neither knows anybody else well. Unlike Khalid, Denis suffers from shyness.

Denis, 19, goes to the party having made a big effort to overcome his nerves. Though attractive, he thinks that people do not find him so. On arrival he is given a drink and introduced to a group of people. He listens to them politely, but contributes very little to the discussion. He appears tense and lacking in warmth and vitality. He does not move around much and waits for people to talk to him.

Khalid, 18, goes to the party excited and determined to do his best to have a good time. He is not afraid to go up to people whom he thinks look attractive and introduce himself. When conversing he appears interested in what others say and participates in a lively and relaxed way. Since he wants to meet new people he moves around. He enjoys himself and helps others to do likewise.

## WHAT IS SHYNESS?

Dictionary definitions of shyness emphasize words like bashful and timid. Shyness is a problem for children, adolescents and adults alike. Based on a large-scale shyness survey mainly conducted on American college students, Zimbardo (1977) found that more than 80 per cent reported that they were shy at some points in their lives. Of these, over 40 per cent considered themselves to be presently shy. Zimbardo's findings focus on people who admit their shyness. In varying degrees, anxiety is always present in social situations, though much of it goes unacknowledged.

## Describing shyness

When people feel shy, how do they describe their experience? You can feel, think and communicate shyly. However, some who feel and think shy are very good at covering it up by not communicating as though they are shy. Such people are privately rather than publicly shy. Timing is another dimension of shyness. People can worry about social situations beforehand, be shy in them, and then think about them in recurrent and intrusive ways afterwards (Rachman *et al.*, 2000).

### *Feeling shy*

Words that people associate with feeling shy include timid, anxious, insecure, bashful, lonely, confused, mistrustful, embarrassed, ashamed, afraid, tense, humiliated and vulnerable. Physical reactions that can accompany shy feelings include blushing, nausea, faintness, perspiring, knotted stomach, pounding heart, shaking, dry mouth and shallow breathing.

### *Thinking shy*

Shy people tend to have negative thoughts about both themselves and about what others think of them. Examples of negative thoughts about themselves include: 'I am uninteresting' 'I lack confidence' and 'I lack social skills.' Examples of negative thoughts about what others think include 'They think less of me because I am shy', 'They are very concerned about my behaviour', 'They may reject me.' For a person who thinks shy, the world is a dangerous place. As John Powell (1969: 12) writes: 'I am afraid to tell you who I am, because, if I tell you who I am, you may not like who I am, and it's all that I have.'

## Communicating shy

Illustrative verbal messages associated with shyness include staying silent or speaking only when spoken to, disclosing little about yourself, and being too ready to agree. Illustrative vocal messages include speaking softly, stammering and, sometimes, loudness masking insecurity. Illustrative body messages include avoiding situations, averting gaze, smiling too much and a tight body posture. Many shy people handle their social anxieties by wearing masks or acting out defensive roles (Powell, 1969). These roles include aggression, clowning, conforming, cynicism, inappropriate flirting, monopolizing, self-disparagement and playing the strong silent type.

Some people are shy with all people in all situations. However, others vary in how shy they feel, think and act depending on whom they are with and in what situations they find themselves. For example, Zimbardo's (1977) shy students were shy with the following categories of people in descending order: strangers, the opposite sex, authorities by virtue of their knowledge, authorities by virtue of their role, relatives, elderly people, friends, children and parents.

There is a range of situations in which people experience shyness. Conversing with strangers, dating, requesting help, going to a party, situations requiring assertiveness (for example, returning something to a shop), going to a dance/disco, showing your body in either non-sexual or sexual situations, starting to go out again after the break-up of a relationship are each situations that may generate shyness. Activity 5.1 asks you to assess how shy you are.

## ACTIVITY 5.1                    Assess how shy I am |

First, do the activity on your own. Then, if appropriate, discuss with your partner, another or others. Fill in the worksheet below by assessing your current experience of shyness in each of the dimensions listed. Give specific illustrations where possible. Consult the text if in doubt about the meaning of a dimension.

| Dimension | My assessment |
|---|---|
| Feelings | |
| Physical reactions | |
| Thoughts | |
| Verbal messages | |
| Vocal messages | |
| Body messages | |

| Dimension | My assessment |
|---|---|
| People with whom I'm shy | |
| Situations in which I'm shy | |

1. To what extent do you see that any shyness you possess is influenced by considerations relating to your biological sex and to your culture? If so, please explain.
2. Summarize how shy you currently perceive yourself to be. What are the consequences for you and for others?

---

## Defining shyness in relationship skills terms

If you are shy, what can you do about it? People differ in the degree to which they are extroverted or introverted. Nevertheless, there is a large learned component in how shyness is both acquired and maintained. Some people who are seriously underconfident may need long-term counselling to help rebuild their shattered self-esteem. Most shy people can gain from either counselling or from coaching focused on managing their shyness. Those who have access to neither need to rely on self-help, including reading material such as this chapter.

As stated above, you can feel, think and communicate shyly. Your feelings and physical reactions are influenced by your mind skills and communication skills. The six main mind skills covered in this book are each common among shy people: namely they experience difficulty in one or more of creating rules, perceptions, self-talk, visual images, explanations and expectations. Shy people also often have poor communication skills in areas such as introducing themselves, starting conversations, holding conversations and making a date. I do not imply that all the poor skills are equally present or important for all shy people. You have to work with the weaknesses that are relevant to sustaining your shyness. Once you have identified your personal weaknesses, you can then state them in the positive as goals. As the chapter progresses I describe how to make progress in overcoming each weakness and attaining each goal.

When thinking of goals, distinguish between coping and mastery. Coping means better management of the situations and people associated with your shyness. Mastery means not being shy at all. Try to think in terms of progressively coping better. If you focus on mastery, you will put additional pressure on yourself that could be counterproductive. If mastery ends up as a byproduct of coping, that is wonderful! If not, you can still be proud of your progress.

# DEVELOP MORE CONFIDENT COMMUNICATION SKILLS

There are different stages in starting relationships. Here the main focus is on helping you to make effective choices when first meeting people. This is the important time in which you make and receive first impressions. During this period you may plant the seeds for relationships to grow later. Alternatively, you may curtail opportunities either by choice or by mistake. When meeting people for the first time try to communicate:

- a sense of relaxed competence
- liking and interest
- absence of threat
- an initial definition of yourself
- that you are a rewarding person to get to know.

## Introduce yourself

I attach great importance to introducing yourself skills. If competent in meeting and greeting people, you get off to a good start. However, the reverse is also true. If you give others a limp handshake and avert your gaze, they may feel uncomfortable. If you crush their hands and seem overbearing, they may instantly dislike you. There are many different contexts in which you meet people – colleges, homes, discos, business venues, and so on. You may be meeting one other person or a group of people. The following are some central verbal, vocal and body message skills for introducing yourself in a range of situations:

- *Verbal messages*. Give a brief greeting and clearly state who you are: for example, 'Hello. I'm John/Jane Smith.' If others have not introduced themselves already, now they will probably do so without your needing to ask their name. If somebody else is introducing you to a third party, you can say 'Hello' followed by the third party's name. Saying another person's name makes remembering it easier for future use.
- *Vocal messages*. Speak at a comfortable volume, clearly and fairly slowly, so others can hear you first time. Be careful to avoid being monotonous by using emphasis in appropriate places. Speak with some enthusiasm and do not let your voice trail away at the end of sentences.
- *Body messages*. When you are standing, pull your shoulders back and do not slouch. Adopt an open position to the speaker. Do not get too close. Hold out your hand in a relaxed way and give a moderately firm handshake. Smile and look the other person in the eye.

How can you develop good skills at introducing yourself? First, you can observe how other people introduce themselves to you and to others. Identify some good role models and note their verbal, vocal and body message skills and the effect they have on others. Second, specify the skills you want to develop. Third, rehearse your skills. You can rehearse at home on your own, for instance, in front of the mirror or with another person. You can also use visualized rehearsal. Fourth, practise your skills in real life, evaluate their impact, and make changes as necessary. When practising your skills in real life, use coping self-talk to calm you down and coach you in what to do. Acknowledge your successes and keep working on your skills so that you maintain and develop rather than lose them.

## Start conversations

Getting started and breaking the ice is easier if you have developed a repertoire of appropriate opening remarks. You can then choose conversational openers and icebreakers appropriate to the different situations in which you find yourself. Making initial contact is usually done by way of small talk as you 'feel' each other out psychologically to see if you want the contact to continue and on what level. Safe talk is another way of describing small talk. The level of disclosure is usually low in terms of intimacy. You have yet to establish trust and mutual acceptability. However, in situations where you are unlikely to meet again, a 'strangers on the train' phenomenon can occur in which disclosures may be surprisingly intimate (Derlega and Chaikin, 1975).

Often shy people insufficiently acknowledge that the process of starting conversations with new people involves uncertainty on both sides. You can place yourself under unnecessary pressure to be fluent. Some of you may have your favorite opening gambits that have worked well for you in the past. If so, why change? Others of you may wish to build up your repertoire. For instance, you can exchange basic information: 'What brings you here?' 'Where do you live?' 'What line of work are you in?' Another suggestion is to pass comments relevant to the occasion, perhaps following them up with a question: 'It's a great party. Do you agree?' 'I've just arrived. What's happening?' You can also bring up topical events, again perhaps following them up with a question: 'I like this hot weather. Do you?' 'What do you think of the election?' If you are nervous, sometimes it is best to admit it: for instance, 'I feel nervous because this is the first time I've been here.' You can also encourage others' attempts to make conversation with small rewards like 'That's interesting', 'Really?' and with head nods.

Vocal messages are very important. Good speech is easy to hear and relaxed. Shy people often need to work on speaking louder. For instance, Adrian is a shy student who talks very softly so as not to draw attention to himself. Sometimes, without being fully aware, you may show your nervousness by speaking very quickly or by slurring your words. Even those without obvious impediments may need to work on the quality of their speech.

## Hold conversations

Argyle (1992) lists six types of rewarding verbal utterances that are conducive to developing friendships. First, you can pay compliments, for instance, 'I like your tie' or 'I like your dress.' Second, you can engage in 'pleasure talk'. You stick to cheerful, pleasant topics of conversation. There are a number of obvious ways in which you can keep yourself informed about various topics: reading newspapers and magazines, looking at the televion news, and keeping up to date on the latest developments in your specific areas of interest such as by watching your local football team or the latest movies. Third, in the interests of furthering the relationship, you can agree. Fourth, you can use the other person's name and also use 'we' to signal shared activities and group membership. Fifth, you can be helpful, for instance, with information, sympathy or practical help. Sixth, you can use humour to break down barriers and increase mutual enjoyment. However, you may need to rehearse your jokes in advance so as not to blow the punchline.

Meeting new people involves searching for common ground. This is partly to find safe talk with which to fill or structure time. In general, people find silences awkward when they do not know each other well. However, this searching for common ground is also part of the exploration of whether you later wish to become friends, lovers or marital partners. You can find out specific information, for instance, a shared hobby, a mutual friend, or similarity of interests and beliefs. When asking questions, respect another's privacy by not probing too deeply. When talking about yourself, a general rule is that you should match or even go slightly beyond the intimacy level of the speaker's disclosures.

A basic conversational sequence involves three steps: speaking–switching–listening. Use your listening, showing understanding and disclosing skills. When switching, you coordinate who has the floor by sending and receiving vocal, body and verbal cues (Argyle, 1991, 1992). When speakers finish they often use a prolonged gaze and stop gesturing with their hands. When not asking questions, the pitch of their voice may fall at the end of sentences. Politeness requires that listeners wait for speakers to finish sentences. When listeners wish to discourage speakers from continuing, they may avert their gaze, stop making 'uh hums' and verbal listening responses, and even raise their hands.

Often shy people are weak when it comes to taking turns. They leave others to do most of the work in bringing up topics and keeping conversations going. Shy people also often reveal too little about themselves. Low self-disclosure, as well as interfering with the search for common ground, can leave speakers with the feeling that they are the only ones willing to risk sharing themselves. The giving of personal information is too one-way.

## End conversations

All people need to develop exit skills – the skills of ending conversations tactfully. Often, shy people, and even those not so shy, have trouble ending conversations. There are numerous reasons why you may choose to end a conversation, ranging from boredom or heeding a call of nature to having to go when you would really rather stay conversing with someone you find attractive. Breaking eye contact, starting to edge away, making your body orientation less open, holding out your hand are all body messages that you wish to go.

How you end the conversation can have positive or negative consequences for your subsequent relationship. If you wish to meet again, you can show appreciation: for example, 'I very much enjoyed talking with you' said with a smile and with vocal messages that indicate you are sincere about it. You could also reinforce this with a comment like 'I hope we meet again.' If your feelings are even more positive you might ask 'I wonder if we could get together again some time?'

If your feelings are negative, your disengaging body messages can become more pronounced, even to the extent of holding out the palm of your hand as a stop signal. You can make closure comments like 'Well, that's about the sum of it' and 'I must be off now' said in a firm voice. You can also avoid smiling too much. If nothing else works, just leave (see Activity 5.2).

---

### ACTIVITY 5.2         Develop my conversation skills

---

Where possible, when doing these activities work with a partner or in a group. You may find it useful to video-record your rehearsals to obtain feedback.

## Part A  Introduce yourself skills

1. Assess how good you currently are at introducing yourself. Pay attention to your vocal and body as well as to your verbal messages. Also, observe other people's skills at introducing themselves.
2. Specify the introducing yourself skills you want to develop.
3. Rehearse with a partner introducing yourself skills and give each other feedback.
4. If in a group, members can go around practising their introducing themselves skills on each other.
5. Practise your introducing yourself skills in real life, evaluate their impact, and make changes as necessary.

## Part B  Start conversations skills

1. List comments and topics that you could use when starting conversations.
2. Take turns at demonstrating specific starting conversation comments to your partner, including focusing on vocal and body messages. Provide each other with feedback.

3. Rehearse starting a conversation with your partner focusing both on initiating topics and on responding to her/his agendas. Afterwards, hold a feedback session.
4. If in a group, circulate and use your starting conversation skills as you start brief conversations in pairs.

## Part C  Hold conversations skills

1. List ways that you can be rewarding during conversations.
2. Hold a conversation with your partner in which each of you takes turns in listening-switching-talking and vice versa. Make sure that both of you take responsibility for keeping the conversation going.
3. Now, without interrogating each other, both of you ask questions as you search for common ground. Remember actively to show understanding. Where appropriate, respond to a disclosure by your partner with a relevant disclosure of your own. Afterwards, hold a feedback session.
4. If in a group, you can rehearse holding conversations in threes, fours or even more.

## Part D  End conversations skills

1. Assess how good you are currently at ending conversations. Pay attention to your vocal and body as well as to your verbal messages. Also, observe other people's skills at ending conversations.
2. Specify the ending conversations skills you want to develop.
3. Rehearse with a partner your ending conversations skills and give each other feedback.
4. If in a group, members can go around practising their ending conversations skills on each other.
5. Practise your introducing yourself, and starting, holding and ending conversation skills in real life, evaluate their impact, and make changes as necessary.

---

## Make a date

Since the position in this book is that of equality between the sexes, both females and males are encouraged to initiate when they want to meet somebody again. Receiving messages from another that they might be interested in dating involves using your decoding skills. Even then you may get it wrong. Males especially may be too ready to read sexual messages into the friendliness of females. Verbal messages that convey interest in dating include compliments, making it clear that you have noticed the other in the past, reflecting the other's feelings, being helpful, and asking the other questions about themselves (Muehlenhard *et al.*, 1986). Body messages include eye contact, absence of arm and leg barriers, smiling and laughing, and light touching – for instance on the hand, arm or upper back. Vocal messages can include animated speech and variations in emphasis.

Often asking for a date is done on the telephone. Some of the mind skills discussed later are highly relevant to asking someone out. Creating coping self-talk can help you calm your anxieties as well as stay focused on the task at hand. Creating realistic rules can prevent you from oppressing yourself with exaggerated fears about rejection. Creating expectations of gain as well as risk can assist you in taking the risks that may bring you the gain. Other telephone skills include the following:

- *Clearly identify yourself.* For example 'Hello, this is Jane/John Smith. We met at Julie and Don's party last week.'
- *Send I messages.* 'I'd like it if we could get together sometime' or 'I was wondering whether you would like to come out with me this weekend?'
- *Offer specific alternatives.* If the answer is favourable, be prepared to offer specific alternatives – for example, different movies or places for coffee. Make suggestions in such a way that the other person feels safe discussing them. You can also ask for their suggestions.
- *State your agreement clearly.* At the end it can be useful to summarize your agreement: 'Just to confirm, I'll pick you up at your flat at 8 pm to go see the movie at the Palace. I look forward to seeing you then.' A misunderstanding over the first meeting is not the best ways to start a relationship.
- *Take refusals politely.* Another person has a perfect right to turn down your request for a date. If so, with any luck they will use tact. The other's courage in refusing you merits respect and you should politely end the conversation. If necessary, use appropriate self-talk to cope with the refusal – it certainly is not the end of the world! (see Activity 5.3).

## ACTIVITY 5.3                    Develop my making a date skills

If possible, do this activity with a partner or in a group. You may find it useful to audio-record or video-record your rehearsals and play them back.

1. Assess how good you currently are at making dates, either in person or on the phone.
2. Specify the making a date skills that you want to develop.
3. Rehearse your making a date skills with a partner. Role play both face-to-face requests and telephone requests. Provide each other with feedback.
4. If in a group, members can demonstrate how to make a date. After each demonstration, the other group members provide feedback.

5. Where appropriate, practise your making a date skills in real life, evaluate their impact, and make changes as necessary.

---

## DEVELOP MIND SKILLS FOR MANAGING SHYNESS

If you are shy now, probably many early learnings contributed to it, including the examples set by your parents. Zimbardo (1977: 62–63) observes: 'In general, then, about 70 per cent of the time parents and children share the same shyness label; they tend to be shy together.' Any negative consequences provided by others when you reached out may have contributed. However, your present problem is how to stop sustaining your shyness if it interferes with attaining relationship goals. One of the main ways in which you sustain your shyness is by thinking shy. I now present a framework for viewing the relationship between situations, thoughts and consequences and then the six key mind skills, in each of which you can alter the balance more in the direction of self-support than self-oppression.

If you are presently shy and do not like the consequences, you can choose to change. You can empower yourself by assuming responsibility for doing something about your shyness. Admitting that you have a choice whether or not to stay shy is the first step in assuming responsibility for changing. You can choose to develop skills that will help you to feel, think and act more confidently in social situations. With the help of this book, you can identify some of your mind and communication skills weaknesses and how to change them. Then, you need to work and practise, work and practise, work and practise until you become much more fluent in the skills. Even then, you will always need to assume responsibility for maintaining and developing your skills.

## Understand the relationship between how you think, feel and communicate

Here I provide you with an STC framework for analysing the relationships between how you think, feel and communicate. In this framework, STC stand for Situation–Thoughts–Consequences, respectively. Consequences fall into three categories: feelings, physical reactions and communications. The idea is that, more often than not, how you feel, physically react and communicate in specific situations is mediated by your thoughts at T rather than the actual situation. Let's take a before and after example of Serena who becomes shy on first dates with males whom she does not know well.

**S1 – Situation**          Serena is eating in a restaurant on her first date with Pat.

**T1 – Thoughts**          Serena's thoughts include 'I must make a good impression', 'I always get tense on first dates', and 'Pat is evaluating me all the time.'

**C1 – Consequences**      Serena's feelings consequences are feeling timid and fearful. Her physical reactions include tension in her face and neck, and her mouth going dry. Serena's communication consequences include revealing little of herself and smiling nervously.

Now let's imagine that Serena has learned some more effective mind skills. She may also have learned some more effective communication skills that help her to think more confidently on first dates. Following is her revised STC, with the name of her date changed from Pat to Scott.

**S2 – Situation**         Serena is eating in a restaurant on her first date with Scott.

**T2 – Thoughts**          Serena thinks 'We're here to enjoy ourselves. Some tension is inevitable on first dates and I know I can handle it. This date gives Scott and me the opportunity to know each other better. If we don't hit it off, Scott's not the only fish in the ocean.'

**C2 – Consequences**      Serena's feelings consequences are feeling moderately relaxed and confident. She experiences no major physical discomfort. Serena's comunication consequences include participating actively in the conversation and laughing with amusement.

If you can see the relationships between how you think, feel and communicate, you are in a better position to identify and develop appropriate skills to manage your shyness. When you detect self-defeating feelings, physical reactions and communications, you can look for thoughts and poor mind skills that may contribute to them. As illustrated above, you can combat shy thinking both by directly changing how you think and also by changing how you communicate which in turn may change how you think. In the final analysis, unless you can communicate more effectively you are unlikely to maintain your improved mind skills. To take the above example, Serena requires confirmation, by behaving differently in real life, that her changed mind skills benefit her.

## Creating rules

Your rules are the dos and don'ts by which you lead your life. Each of you has an inner rulebook that guides your living and loving. If your rules are self-supporting they can motivate and help you to attain realistic goals. However, if your rules are self-oppressing they can leave you open to a triple dose of low self-esteem. For example, Carl has a rule that he must be successful on all his first dates. However, his first date with Ellie does not go well, so this activates his first dose of low self-esteem. His second dose of low self-esteem stems from his thinking that he should not be anxious and depressed about his dating ability. Carl generates his third dose of low self-esteem by moving on to devalue not just his dating ability but his whole worth as a person.

Albert Ellis (2003, 2005; Ellis and Crawford, 2000) has coined the term '*musturbation*' to refer to rigid personal rules characterized by 'musts', 'oughts' and 'shoulds'. Ellis regards any emotional and behavioural consequences as determined by your beliefs in relation to the activating event more than by the activating event itself. I prefer the term rules to beliefs. Four important unrealistic rules that contribute to people sustaining shyness are:

1. I *must* be liked and approved of by everyone I meet.
2. I *must* never reveal anything about myself that might be viewed negatively.
3. I *must* never make a mistake in social situations.
4. I *must* never have setbacks in learning to overcome my shyness.

Let's look an example of an unrealistic personal rule of Serena's regarding first dates.

**S1 – Situation**    Serena is eating in a restaurant on her first date with Pat.

**T1 – Thought**    Serena's unrealistic rule is 'I must be approved of by everyone I meet.'

**C1 – Consequences**    The consequences of holding this rule for Serena include timidity and fear, tension in her face and neck, and revealing little of herself and smiling nervously.

What skills does Serena require for dealing with her unrealistic rule? First, she requires detecting skills; second, disputing or challenging skills; third, restating unrealistic into realistic rules skills.

1. *Detecting skills.* Serena may be helped to detect her unrealistic rule by learning to analyse her thinking in STC terms. When she has unwanted feelings and communicates inappropriately, she checks for any thoughts that may contribute to her distress.

2. *Disputing skills*. Disputing means challenging the false assumptions that you hold about yourself, others and the world. Serena needs to dispute vigorously her unrealistic rule by asking searching questions. The following are questions that Serena might ask herself to dispute her self-oppressing rule that 'I must be approved of by everyone I meet'.

   - What evidence exists that supports the truth of my rule?
   - What evidence exists that reveals the falseness of my rule?
   - What are the worst possible things that might happen to me if I were not to be approved of by someone?
   - What exactly can't I stand about not being approved by Pat?
   - Do I demand the same standards of gaining approval for other people as I apply to myself?
   - How exactly might not being approved of by Pat make me worthless as a person?
   - What are the negative consequences to me of my demand that I must be approved of by everyone I meet?

3. *Restating skills*. Restating involves substituting self-supporting for self-oppressing characteristics in specific rules. The main difference is that between demanding and preferential thinking. Unrealistic rules are based on childish demandingness and focused on me, me, me. Realistic rules acknowledge the reality that the world may not always be as you would like, but nevertheless you can cope with it. Furthermore, realistic rules help you to evaluate the usefulness of specific characteristics for attaining goals rather than to rate yourself as a whole person.

Following is Serena's STC, incorporating a more realistic rule. Again, the date is with Pat.

| | |
|---|---|
| **S2 – Situation** | Serena is eating in a restaurant on her first date with Pat. |
| **T2 – Thought** | Though I might prefer to be universally approved, it is unreasonable and unnecessary to demand that this is the case. I can meet my needs for friendship and affection if I only meet some people who like me and whom I like. |
| **C2 – Consequences** | Serena feels moderately relaxed, has no major discomfort, and participates actively in conversation. |

The following are examples of restatements of the second, third and fourth unrealistic rules cited above as common among shy people.

2. Nobody's perfect. If I am to have honest and open relationships I need to reveal my vulnerabilities as well as my strengths.

3.  To err is human. Though I would prefer not to make mistakes I can use them as learning experiences.
4.  Setbacks are part of learning any new skill. They are challenges with which I can cope.

Many shy people stay shy because of what Ellis (2005) calls low frustration tolerance. Unrealistic expectations about the learning process and smoothness of life can make you vulnerable to setbacks. Sometimes your level of performance may be good, but you do not get the outcomes you wish (Bandura, 1986). You can develop skills of supporting yourself and persisting through setbacks rather than giving in to them.

## Creating perceptions

Frequently shy people both perceive themselves too negatively and jump to conclusions unfavourable to themselves in specific situations.

### *Perceive yourself more accurately*

For shy people perceiving themselves more accurately is usually a matter of reducing unrealistic negative perceptions and owning realistic strengths (Rapee, 1993; Alden and Wallace, 1995). In a study of vulnerability to depression, British researchers Teasdale and Dent (1987) selected the following self-devaluing adjectives from a list associated with depression: deficient, failure, inadequate, incompetent, inferior, pathetic, stupid, unloved, unwanted, useless, weak, worthless. Arguably, these are many of the same words that shy people use to devalue themselves. In addition, many shy people add to their sense of inferiority by perceiving others as more socially competent, witty and strong than they really are (Alden and Wallace, 1995). The following are some suggestions for perceiving yourself more positively:

1.  *Own your strengths.* List what you, not other people, consider to be your strengths, assets and resources. Modesty is out of place when doing this; probably already you are too skilled at noting your social deficiencies. Add to this list as new ideas come to mind. Then read this list regularly to affirm your strengths. You may also put your strengths either on cue cards and read through them regularly or on cassettes and listen to them regularly.
2.  *Challenge your negative perceptions.* Use your questioning skills to challenge the accuracy of your negative perceptions. Where is the evidence for them?
3.  *Use thought stopping.* When you catch yourself in an unproductive, negative train of thought, silently shout to yourself 'STOP!' Try to stifle your unrealistic negative self-perceptions as soon as you become aware of them. The thoughts are likely to return, but you can repeat the procedure as needed.

4.  *Use thought switching.* When you find yourself ruminating on your social inadequacies, replace them with positive perceptions and an appreciation of positive social experiences. For instance, if you feel lonely and inadequate, switch to thinking of your friends and possibly even contact one.
5.  *Use visualizing.* Kassorla (1984) advocates mental vacuuming. She gets her clients to imagine a tiny toy vacuum cleaner sweeping across their foreheads and vacuuming up all their negative words and images. Another image is to place all the negative words and images in a balloon that drifts off out of sight.

## *Perceive situations more accurately*

If you are shy, the way you perceive many situations is likely to sustain your discomfort. Each person carries within them some pain and insecurity. Without necessarily knowing it, you can be so influenced by your self-doubts that in specific situations you jump to unwarranted conclusions and then treat these conclusions as facts. Often people are unaware that they may jump to conclusions rather than say to themselves 'Stop . . . think . . . what are my choices in how to view this situation?' Psychiatrist Aaron Beck observes that frequently people have underlying automatic thoughts and perceptions that influence their emotions (Beck, 1988; Beck and Weishaar, 2005). Either people are not fully conscious of these thoughts and images or it does not occur to them that they warrant special scrutiny. Beck collaborates with his patients in the scientific or detective work of identifying these self-oppressing perceptions or 'what you tell yourself'. The following is an example within the STC framework.

| | |
|---|---|
| **S** | Melanie talks to Steve at the party and then circulates. |
| **T** | Steve perceives 'Melanie does not like me.' |
| **C** | Steve feels depressed and leaves the party early. |

However, Steve might have had many other perceptions at **T**, including the following.

-   Melanie is sensible in wanting to circulate at a party.
-   Melanie liked me enough to come and talk to me.
-   I need to improve my conversational skills if I am going to hold the interest of women like Melanie.
-   There are plenty of other women at the party so why keep worrying about Melanie?
-   I quite liked Melanie but I didn't find her that fascinating.

If you are like Steve and have a tendency to jump to conclusions that are negative for you, you require detecting, disputing and restating skills to combat this:

1. *Detecting skills*. Become aware of the signals with which you may be oppressing yourself. These signals include negative feelings about yourself and others without good cause and self-defeating communication that distances you from others. You can identify the kinds of people and situations associated with devaluing yourself.
2. *Disputing skills*. Monitor your thinking in specific situations and practise making the connections between upsetting feelings and upsetting perceptions. Question your perceptions by logical analysis and search for better explanations. This process involves your engaging in the following kinds of self-talk:
   - Stop . . . think . . . what are my choices in how to perceive this situation?
   - Are my perceptions based on fact or inference?
   - If they are based on inference, are there other ways of perceiving the situation that are more closely related to the factual evidence?
   - What further information do I need to collect?
3. *Restating skills*. If appropriate, you replace your initial perception with the perception that represents the best fit in relation to the factual evidence.

Let's assume that Steve has some skills in choosing the most realistic perception. He went back in his mind over his contact with Melanie and assessed the evidence for his 'She does not like me' perception. On doing this Steve discovered that there were no facts to support this conclusion and that it was an inference on his part. He generated alternative perceptions such as the five listed above. Steve decided that the most realistic perception was 'I need to improve my conversational skills if I am going to hold the interest of women like Melanie.' He did not feel devalued by this perception which left him feeling still in control of his life.

## Creating self-talk

The ability to create coping self-talk is a very useful mind skill for managing feelings of shyness (Meichenbaum, 1983, 1985; Meichenbaum and Deffenbacher, 1988). The goals of creating self-talk are to calm your anxieties and help you deal effectively with the task at hand. Creating self-talk contains three elements: calming self-talk, coaching self-talk and affirming self-talk. Contrast creating coping self-talk with creating negative self-talk. To return to the examples at the beginning of the chapter about Denis and Khalid going to the party, their self-talk was as follows:

*Denis's negative self-talk*

I know that I am going to find this party difficult. Everybody is looking at me. I feel unattractive. I don't want to make a mistake.

I'm feeling tense and, when this happens, I know it will only get worse.

*Khalid's coping self-talk*

I enjoy parties and meeting new people. Though I get a little anxious with strangers I know I can overcome this. I can use my skills of relaxing, selecting interesting people, introducing myself, conversing and, if appropriate, arranging to meet people again. I'll give it my best shot.

Let's look at calming, coaching and affirming self-statements in turn:

- *Calming.* Simple self-statements include: 'Keep calm', 'Relax' and 'Just take it easy.' In addition, you can instruct yourself to 'Breathe slowly and regularly.'
- *Coaching.* The idea of coaching self-statements is that they guide you in the specific skills you require for competent performance. You could start by telling yourself you can cope: for instance, 'I can handle this situation' or 'My anxiety is a signal for me to use my coping skills.' Then, you can instruct yourself in what you need to do: for instance, 'When I introduce myself I need to smile, say "Hello", clearly state my name and shake hands firmly.'
- *Affirming.* You can remind yourself that you have strengths in social situations. For instance, 'I can listen well', 'Remember, I get on well with many people.'
- *Calming, coaching and affirming.* Often creating self-talk consists of putting together calming, coaching and affirming self-statements: for example, 'Calm down, take turns in listening and speaking, I get on well with many people.'

You can use creating self-talk before, during and after stressful social situations. For instance, before you might say 'Calm down. Develop a plan to manage the situation.' During you might say 'Relax. Smile. Disclose as well as listen.' And after you might say 'Each time I use my creating self-talk skills it seems to get easier.'

Another area in which you can use creating self-talk is if you are prone to potentially destructive self-doubt when starting close relationships. For example, if you had a very successful date a couple of evenings ago, but have had no further contact with your date since then, you may handle your insecurity by devaluing yourself and later possibly either not making contact or, if you do, coming on too strong. Instead, tell yourself to calm down, realistically appraise the feedback you received (much of which may have been very positive), and either initiate contact or wait and see what happens. If you cannot trust yourself to remember the positive feedback, write it down.

## Creating visual images

All people think in pictures as well as in words. For some people, using visual images is their main way of interacting with the world (Lazarus, 1984, 1992, 2005). Many shy people have negative visual images of how incompetent they are going to be in social situations and how appalled others will be. British researchers Hackmann *et al.* (1998) found that socially phobic subjects were significantly more likely than control subjects to experience negative images when anxious in social situations. Furthermore, these images were significantly more likely to involve seeing oneself from an observer's viewpoint.

Instead, you can focus on the processes and outcomes of competent performance. Say you have an upcoming social situation that you fear you will handle poorly. Before going, you can take the opportunity for visualized rehearsal. Break down the tasks and focus on the skills or processes of competent performance. In addition, identify potential setbacks and develop ways of coping with them. Rehearse your creating self-talk skills along with your visualizing skills. Furthermore, visualize some realistic outcomes of skilled performance. For example, you can imagine a specific situation in which other people enjoy your company as you converse with them. Here is an example of using visualized rehearsal to help overcome shyness in a specific situation:

> James, 33, was married for nine years to Penny, but they split up about a year ago. James is just getting his confidence back after the break-up and feels very nervous about going out with women again. Last weekend, at his tennis club, James had a long conversation with Carolyn, 35, whose own marriage ended six months ago and who is also nervous about getting involved again. James asked her if she would like to have another chat with him sometime and, when she agreed, said he would phone her at home this week. Carolyn uses her visualized rehearsal skills to imagine behaving competently when James phones, for instance, sitting with the phone, being relaxed and talking calmly. She also visualizes succeeding in arranging to meet James again and James seeing her as relaxed when they meet. A side effect of Carolyn's visualized rehearsal is that she now feels less anxious about relating to James.

## Creating explanations

How you explain your shyness influences whether you work to overcome it or stay stuck. There are a number of faulty explanations for shyness that can weaken motivation for change. These explanations are often partial truths; the error is to treat them as whole truths. Below are some possibly inaccurate explanations concerning shyness:

- *'It's my genes.'* This is the opinion that you are shy by nature rather than by nurture. Though people possess different biological propensities to anxiety, a considerable part of shyness represents learned behaviour sustained by current poor mind skills and communication skills.

- *'It's my unfortunate past.'* Your unfortunate past or 'what others did to you' may have contributed to your acquiring some poor skills contributing to shyness. However, you sustain your shyness by what you do to yourself. If you have had a very unfortunate past you may require counselling to provide the nurturing and healing you never received from natural or surrogate parents. However, many people, with or without professional help, have learned to overcome poor skills contributed to by their unfortunate pasts.

- *'It's up to others.'* Some of you may play a passive rather than an active role when meeting new people. It is as though you wait for events to happen to you rather than take an active part in shaping events. You are letting others assume the responsibility for helping you out of your shell. This may not happen. Sometimes passivity is reinforced by social rules. For instance, though changing, males are still expected to take more risks in initiating contact than females. This double standard may have negative consequences for both sexes. Shy women may have insufficiently developed their initiating contact skills and shy men can feel excessively pressured to take social initiatives. A major theme of this book is that everybody must assume responsibility for making the choices that work best for them. Sitting or standing around waiting for something to happen is frequently not the best choice.

- *'It's all my fault.'* You may consider that everything that goes wrong in social situations is your fault. You may fail to take into account that when two people relate each has a responsibility for the success of the contact, not just you. Your hypersensitivity to feelings of embarrassment and willingness to blame yourself may erode rather than help you gain the confidence to work on your shyness.

The above explanations may describe not only how you became shy but also why you remain shy. Do any of them resonate with the ring of truth for you? If so, work hard at challenging the faulty thinking contained in these explanations. Some research suggests that people who explain their social successes and failures to controllable causes experience less shyness and anxiety than those who do not (Bruch and Pearl, 1995). The following are more realistic formulations of each of the above explanations:

- Though like many people I'm naturally sensitive, I've mainly learned to be shy.

- Though others undoubtedly contributed to my becoming shy, I currently sustain my shyness through some poor skills that I can work to overcome.

- It is not up to others to make the first move to help me out of my shyness since I am responsible for making the choices in life that work best for me.

- I am only responsible for my own behaviour in social situations rather than needing to accept responsibility for everything that happens.

## Creating expectations

You lead your life into the future rather than into the past. Expectations are thoughts and images about the probability of future events. A study of depressed and non-depressed students by psychologists Pietromonaco and Rook (1987) found differences in their decision-making style. Depressed students were significantly less likely to assign weight to the potential gains of acting in social situations and significantly more likely to assign weight to the potential risks. Furthermore, for decisions about initiating social contact and establishing intimacy, depressed students expressed a greater reluctance to take the target actions than did the non-depressed students. If you are shy, this does not necessarily mean that you are depressed. However, I have cited the above study because many shy people have a similar pattern of overestimating risk, underestimating gain and hence being less prepared to act. When practising counselling, I have found that I can help some shy people by building up their skills of generating and evaluating gains.

> Sean, aged 30, had little experience of dating women; his longest experience lasting three dates. In his church group, Sean was on a committee with Suzanne who had been friendly to him and whom he wondered if he should ask out. Sean questioned 'Why bother to take the risk of seeking the gain?' With Richard as his counsellor, Sean generated both the potential risks and gains of taking this initiative. He was already expert at acknowledging risks and needed to learn that 'It is in my interests to look at gains as well as risks in my decisions.' His list of potential gains for asking Suzanne out included the following:
>
> - I might have a chance of a strong relationship.
> - I might gain more experience in developing relationships.
> - This might contribute to helping me become happier.
> - I might gain confidence and a more positive self-image.
> - I might develop my ability to express my feelings more.
> - I might give myself the opportunity of Suzanne taking some of the initiative too.
>
> Sean evaluated that the gains of asking Suzanne out outweighed the risks. She later became his first steady girlfriend.

The most conclusive way of gauging the accuracy of your expectations is, like Sean, to put them to the test. Reality testing your previously negative expectations may become easier if you carefully break down tasks, take small steps before larger steps, rehearse what you are going to do and, where appropriate, seek the support of other people.

You may have tried to overcome your shyness before and been unsuccessful. Now, your prediction is: 'I've tried before. What's the use?' However, your past is not necessarily a guide to your future. Unnecessary pessimism may result from predictions that are permanent – 'I have my problem for all time' – and pervasive – 'I have my problem in every situation' (Seligman, 1991, 2002). You require realistic optimism. For instance, this time you may try harder, understand your shyness better, possess better skills at managing it, and be better at enlisting the support of others. The fact that you have tried before does not mean that you cannot now learn new and better skills to help you succeed. Following is a more optimistic expectation than 'I've tried before. What's the use?' that you might tell yourself.

> Though I've tried before, present circumstances are different and I understand better how I maintained my shyness. Now I can develop new and better skills to become more outgoing.

In the preceding pages I have taken what psychologists call a 'cognitive' or mind skills approach to managing shyness. If you are shy you may already possess the communication skills of making contact in your repertoire. You just need the confidence to use them and, if this is the case, working with mind skills can be most important. Other shy people, along with many who would not consider themselves to be shy, do not possess adequate communication skills in their relationship skills repertoire. Such people need to work on their communication skills as well as on their mind skills (see Activity 5.4).

---

## ACTIVITY 5.4          Develop my mind skills to manage shyness

First do the activity on your own. Then, if appropriate, discuss with your partner, another or others. Work on the poor mind skills that you identify as most important to managing your shyness. Consult the text if in doubt about how to complete any part.

*Understand the relationship between how I think, feel and act*

1. Put a situation in which you feel shy into the STC framework. Be specific about S1, T1, and C1.
2. Now imagine you think more effectively. Make up a revised STC, being specific about S2, T2, and C2.

*Creating rules*

1. Detect any unrealistic personal rules that contribute to maintaining your shyness.
2. Use disputing skills to question the most important unrealistic personal rule that you detected above.
3. Restate the unrealistic personal rule you disputed above into a more realistic rule.

*Creating perceptions*

## Part A  Perceive yourself more accurately

If you consider your shyness partly maintained by unnecessarily negative perceptions of yourself:

1. List what you consider to be your strengths.
2. Use questioning skills to challenge your negative perceptions.
3. Use thought stopping.
4. Use thought switching.
5. Use visualizing.

## Part B  Perceive situations more accurately

1. Detect a particular situation where you may jump to a self-devaluing conclusion.
2. Dispute your self-devaluing conclusion by generating and evaluating different conclusions that you might have drawn.
3. If appropriate, restate your initial perception with the perception that represents the best-fit perception in relation to the facts.

*Creating self-talk*

1. Identify an upcoming situation in which you expect to feel shy.
2. Identify any negative self-talk that contributes to your shyness.
3. Generate two each of calming, coaching and affirming self-statements. Then, if appropriate, develop self-talk that puts together calming, coaching and affirming self-statements.
4. Put your self-statements on cue cards or on a cassette and rehearse them daily for as long as necessary.
5. Implement your self-talk in real life and assess its consequences.

*Creating visual images*

1. Think of a specific upcoming situation in which you might feel shy.
2. Think of the verbal, vocal and body message skills you need to perform competently in the situation.
3. Visually rehearse yourself acting competently in the situation, including coping with any difficulties and setbacks that occur.
4. Accompany your visual rehearsal with appropriate self-talk.
5. Practise your visual rehearsal plus self-talk skills daily for as long as you find it helpful.

*Creating explanations*

1. What do you consider to be the explanations for how you acquired your shyness in the first place?
2. What do you consider to be the explanations for how your shyness is maintained?
3. Challenge any possibly inaccurate explanations for maintaining your shyness now and, if appropriate, either discard them or restate them more accurately.

*Creating expectations*

1. Think of a particular person with whom you would like either to initiate or to deepen a relationship and yet have felt inhibited from doing so.
2. Make up a worksheet with the following headings.

| Gains from acting | Risks from acting |
|---|---|
| | |

3. On the worksheet first list your current expectations of gain and risk. These are the ones which, on balance, may inhibit you from acting. Then draw a line under each list.
4. Now generate as many extra expectations of gain and risk as you can and list them in the appropriate columns after your underlines. Pay particular attention to generating gains.
5. Assess your revised list of gains and risks. If appropriate, set yourself goals and alter your behaviour.

---

**ACTIVITY 5.5          Group discussion: managing shyness skills          |**

This is intended as a group exercise, though it may be done individually or in pairs. For each part:

1. Spend five to ten minutes answering the question in groups of three or four.
2. Each group shares its answers with the whole group.
3. The whole group ranks the four most important points or skills from the most important to the least important.

## Part A  Negative outcomes of shyness

List four main negative outcomes stemming from being shy.

## Part B  Conversational skills

List four important skills for holding conversations when first meeting people.

## Part C  Making a date skills

List four important skills to use when making a date.

# 6

# *Choose a relationship skills*

**Chapter outcomes**
By studying and doing the activities in this chapter you should:

- start exploring yourself as a partner
- know about some communication skills for dating and courtship
- know about some mind skills for selecting a partner
- know about some criteria for choosing a partner.

On hearing that an egocentric person had fallen in love, Viennese psychiatrist Alfred Adler asked 'Against whom?' The stark fact is that most intimate relationships start in hope and end in pain. This raises the issue of whether many people might choose their relationships better and so increase their chances of achieving stability and happiness. People tend to be more demanding of relationships than previously. Carl Rogers observed: 'It is becoming increasingly clear that a man–woman relationship will have *permanence* only to the degree to which it satisfies the emotional, psychological, intellectual, and physical needs of the partners' (1973: 18). Along with rising expectations about relationships, there is increasing disillusionment. Many young people have observed the marital distress of their parents and others and want to avoid it in their lives.

## EXPLORING YOURSELF AS A PARTNER

Choosing a partner is a process of discovery in which you explore yourself, other people, and the world or relationships. The process can start in early childhood games and then, for some people, become more intense in early adolescence. By late adolescence most people have started seriously thinking about and/or engaging in relationships with the intent of ultimately choosing a long-term partner. This choosing process starts with casual dating in which partners are not identified as a couple, progresses to serious dating in which partners are identified as a couple, and ends with marriage or de facto marriage.

Another way of looking at the choosing process is that you are trying out and developing a concept of yourself as a partner as contrasted with how you are as a single person. Hopefully, you are also developing some relationship skills strengths as a partner. In choosing whom to date, during casual dating, during serious dating, and during any pre-marital cohabitation, you are learning more about yourself, not in isolation, but in relation to a partner. A critical part of this concept of self as a partner consists of the sort of person with whom you are comfortable relating closely. What kind of person can you genuinely love? What characteristics in a partner do you like and dislike? What sort of partner helps you to bring out and develop the parts of yourself that you value? As the divorce statistics show, during marriage the process of learning about yourself and about what you like or dislike in a partner continues. Furthermore, once divorced, many people choose another mate. Thus, even after marriage, you continue developing a concept of yourself as a partner.

As a single person, you are likely to date a number of people whose difference does not fit comfortably with your emerging picture of yourself as a partner. You may only date such people once or a few times. However, you may also engage in and dissolve a number of important love relationships in your quest for a stable long-term partnership (Pistole, 1995). Dissolving any close relationship can be mutually decided, decided by your partner, or decided by yourself. Pain is not restricted to ending marital relationships. Ending late adolescent and early adulthood love relationships can be very painful for both partners, leading to feelings of grief, depression, self-pity, betrayal, anger, hurt, rejection, loneliness and low self-esteem. Some partners may long for their 'ex' and find it hard to let go emotionally and in practice. However, not all feelings attached to breaking up are negative. For example, many partners are ambivalent: sad at the loss, yet relieved to have ended a relationship that was not working so they can move on. Other partners may be delighted at their newly found freedom.

An important part of finding out about your self-concept as a partner centres on issues of commitment. The word courtship is often used to describe the process of partners getting to know one another as they move towards commitment to marriage or to stable cohabitation involving financial sharing, property and, possibly, children. During successful courtship both you and your partner consolidate your concept of selves as partners in relation to one another. However, the course of courtship, whether quick or prolonged, is not always smooth. Nineteenth-century British Prime Minister Benjamin Disraeli reportedly advised people never to be so foolish as to marry for love.

## COMMUNICATION SKILLS FOR DATING AND COURTSHIP

In this section I review in some detail skills for searching and finding a potential partner. However, I only briefly discuss disclosing, listening and assertion skills you can use during dating and courtship. This brevity avoids repetition with lengthier descriptions elsewhere in the book. Often nowadays courtship includes cohabitation. The dividing lines between dating, courtship, cohabitation and marriage can be imprecise.

## Develop search and find skills

Some of you may need to develop systematic search and find plans to locate eligible partners. Here I present some suggestions for locating and making contact with eligible partners. The following brief conversation between a spectator and a famous golfer, who had just played a superb shot from a bunker, highlights how you can make your luck.

| | |
|---|---|
| *Spectator:* | Gee, you're a lucky golfer. |
| *Famous golfer:* | You know something. The more and more I practise, the luckier and luckier I get! |

### *Search skills: How to locate potential partners*

1. *Review your existing network.* Take stock of all the people you know who might be potential partners or introduce you to potential partners. Identify those people with whom you might spend more time and those with whom you should spend less time.
2. *Identify gaps in your network.* If you are a woman, you may have many girl-friends whose company you enjoy, but know few, if any eligible men. If you are a man you may spend much time in sporting, drinking and social activities with your mates, but know few, if any, eligible women. Recognize clearly any significant gaps in your existing network.
3. *Identify ways of meeting eligible partners.* Brainstorm all the different ways that you can meet eligible partners and eligible partners can meet you. Suggestions include meeting potential partners through friends, relatives and your existing network, your work contacts, sitting next to people in lecture theatres or in cafés, joining clubs, attending social events like dances, barbecues and church fetes, taking advantage of chance encounters, using introduction agencies though 'buyer beware', advertising in magazines and using the Internet.
4. *Identify ways of not putting off potential partners.* Identify any unintentional signals indicating 'I am not available' or 'I am not interested' that you may send to people whom you might like to know better. Furthermore, identify any significant poor conversation skills that you may possess.

### *Find skills: How to make contact with potential partners*

1. *Activate your network.* Without being crass about it, let appropriate people in your existing network know you are interested in meeting eligible partners. Renew contact with people who might help in your search.

2.  *Entertain your friends.* Do not expect all the invitations to go one way. Your friends are more likely to help you if you are rewarding for them. Take people out for drinks and meals, hold dinner parties, give drinks parties or whatever it takes to show clearly you are in circulation.

3.  *Spend less time or no time at all with some people.* Finding a suitable partner is every bit as important as getting a job or buying a car. You cannot afford to squander time on low level activities and acquaintanceships that interfere with attaining your goal.

4.  *Join clubs and attend social events.* Be proactive about joining clubs, going on outings, and attending social events where you may meet potential partners.

5.  *Take advantage of chance encounters.* If you find someone attractive, you can try to catch her or his eye and strike up a conversation: for instance, at a bus stop or in the supermarket. By using good judgement, tact, diplomacy, and not pushing your luck, the risks can be minimal.

6.  *Accept invitations.* Do not play too hard to get. Be prepared to accept invitations to social events and dates graciously, if this will help you achieve your objective. Give moderately eligible potential partners the benefit of the doubt, rather than turn them down too quickly. Some people improve on further acquaintance when both of you may feel more relaxed.

7.  *Give come-ons and turn-offs.* Develop and use a repertoire of verbal, vocal and body messages that encourage those whom you want to know better. Politely and firmly, if necessary, discourage the remainder.

8.  *Develop your skills of being a rewarding person.* Choosing a potential partner is a two-way process. Other people are much more likely to want to develop friendships and romances with you if you are warm, attractive and interesting to them. If necessary, seek professional counselling or coaching to identify and eliminate obvious and more subtle ways you distance yourself from potential partners (see Activity 6.1).

## ACTIVITY 6.1     Assess and implement my search and find skills  |

This activity is in two parts. Complete each part before moving on to the next. If appropriate, discuss your answers with another or others.

## Part A  Assessment

1.  Assess myself on the following planning skills for locating potential partners:

    (a) Reviewing my existing network
    (b) Identifying gaps in my network
    (c) Identifying ways of meeting eligible partners
    (d) Identifying gaps in my network
    (e) Identifying ways of meeting eligible partners

    (f) Identifying ways of not putting off potential partners

    (g) Setting goals and subgoals

    (h) Outlining the steps to attaining goals and subgoals

    (i) Stating time frames

    (j) Monitoring progress.

2. Assess myself on the following communication skills for making contact with potential partners:

    (a) Activating my network

    (b) Entertaining my friends

    (c) Spending less time or no time at all with some people

    (d) Joining clubs and attending social events

    (e) Taking advantage of chance encounters

    (f) Accepting invitations

    (g) Giving come-ons and turn-offs

    (h) Developing my skills of being a rewarding person

    (i) Other skills, not mentioned above.

## Part B Implementation

1. *Make a plan*
Develop a plan for locating and making contact with potential partners that specifies:

    (a) My goals and subgoals

    (b) The steps I intend taking to attain each goal and subgoal

    (c) A time frame

    (d) How I intend to monitor my progress.

2. *Implement a plan*
Implement my plan to locate and make contact with potential partners by:

    (a) Engaging in goal-oriented activities

    (b) Monitoring and evaluating my progress

    (c) Persisting, despite setbacks and difficulties.

*Remember.* The more and more I practise, the luckier and luckier I get!

---

## Getting to know you skills

The following are some additional skills you can use in starting a relationship.

### Disclosing skills

During the time you and your potential partner get to know one another better, the breadth and depth of your disclosure becomes greater. You express liking and affection. You disclose your daily activities, including sharing news of success. In serious dating, you show distress and anxiety in front of the other. Furthermore, as the relationship develops, you give each other feedback and reveal your commitment to the relationship. With an increase in your expression of positive and negative feelings, you increase the chances of both intimacy and conflict. You are also more prepared to ask for personal advice.

Other ways in which you can disclose include looking each other in the eye during conversation, engaging in intentional touching – for instance hugging, kissing and sexual intercourse – giving birthday cards and presents including surprise presents, repaying debts, paying compliments, standing up for the other during his or her absence, refraining from criticizing each other in public, and making an effort to like each other's friends. In addition, as your relationship deepens, you look after the other when ill.

If and when you start cohabiting, further ways in which you disclose include: sharing the household chores, informing the other about your personal schedule and sharing the costs of the house/flat.

### Listening and showing understanding skills

As your relationship develops, you make yourself more physically available to each other. You show trust and unconditional positive regard and do not break confidences. You listen with interest and express increased concern for each other's welfare. Furthermore, by disclosing yourselves you elicit disclosures from each other to which you can listen. Thus, appropriate disclosure is also a listening skill.

### Assertion skills

When choosing a partner, there are numerous instances when you may require assertion skills: for example, resisting pressures to have sex or unprotected sex, ending relationships, and coping with third parties who disapprove of your choice of girlfriend or boyfriend. As an illustration, when resisting sexual pressures, verbal messages include: 'I know you'd like to keep going, but I won't have intercourse outside a committed relationship' and 'I won't have sex without a condom, because I want to avoid pregnancy and risk of AIDS.' Such messages need to be given in a firm voice emphasizing the word 'won't'. Your body messages should include looking the other person in the eye when you speak and, possibly, holding up your hand in a pushing away gesture.

In addition to skills discussed above, as your relationship develops you use numerous other relating skills to deepen and maintain it. Such skills, all of which are described later, include those of managing anger and solving relationship problems. Choosing a partner can include opting out as well as opting in. In such circumstances, you require ending relationships skills and, very probably, starting again skills.

## MIND SKILLS FOR CHOOSING A PARTNER

Choosing an appropriate partner is a fundamental skill in both starting and maintaining successful couple relationships. How can you avoid unnecessarily landing yourself in an unhappy relationship? There are no guarantees. All relationships go through cycles of alienation and affection, with lows as well as highs. You have to steer a course between pollyannaism, 'everything will turn out for the best', and undue pessimism, 'everything will turn out for the worst'. Following are some thinking skills that may increase your chances of choosing wisely.

Because they leave choosing a partner to chance and romance, many people settle for less happiness in their lives than they might have obtained. You can assume personal responsibility by being proactive, rather than reactive, in seeking and choosing a partner. You cannot just wait around forever for Ms/Mr Right to appear. Own responsibility for your emerging concept of yourself as a partner and for how you think, feel and act towards potential partners.

### Creating rules

When choosing a relationship, my personification of me chooses my personification of you. However, I may not really know myself. Instead what I call 'I' or 'me' may be a clutter of attitudes, rules and values taken over from other people, such as my parents, as if they were my own. I may perceive you in terms of their values and not mine. You may do the same to me. The risk of this is that as either or both of us grow into more autonomous persons we may get badly out of step with each other. Instead of being built on the rock of stable yet flexible identities, our relationship has been built on the sand of unstable and possibly rigid identities.

Some people are heavily influenced to get married because they have been brought up with the rule that marriage is their main role in life. They seek to marry a role rather than a person. They get married to secure the structure and trappings of married life without paying sufficient attention to the realities of having a loving relationship with their spouse. Because of the traditional emphasis on being homemakers, women especially may feel pressure to marry and raise a family. Disparaging remarks like 'old maid' and 'on the shelf' are sometimes made about single women after a certain age. Men may also get married to present a more socially acceptable image to the world, for instance, to advance their careers.

The following are some areas in which potential partners might fruitfully explore the realism and compatibility of their own and each other's rules. Since rules are often not expressed openly, you may need to be sensitive to hints about their existence (Beck, 1988).

- *The influence of parental rules.* How do our parents' rules and values influence us now? To what degree are these rules harmful or helpful? To what extent are we selecting a partner to please our parents? Both sexes may filter out otherwise suitable partners because of their conscious or unconscious wishes to please and be like their parents. However, some people may rebel rather than conform to parental rules. Such people may be guided in their search for partners by rigid rules about how unlike their parents their partners should be. Later on, previously rebellious offspring may revert to parental rules and then be dissatisfied if their partners do not change too.
- *Rules about sex roles.* How should men and women behave? How should husbands and wives behave? How should fathers and mothers behave? To what extent do each of you subscribe to myths about sex roles: for instance 'Men must always be the major breadwinners' and 'Women must always stand by their man, no matter how badly he behaves'?
- *Rules about relationships.* How should people behave in close relationships? For example, how should they handle issues like anger, conflict, sex, in-laws and friendships? Again, to what extent do each of you subscribe to relationship myths like 'Adequacy of sex must be the main indicator of relationship satisfaction' and 'Conflicts must be avoided rather than resolved'?

Sometimes, given flexibility on both sides, you can negotiate differences in personal rules and reach mutually satisfactory solutions. On other occasions the differences may be more intractable: for instance, differences concerning family size and children's education. Where possible find out in advance if either of you feels unable or unwilling to work through a major difference. This may influence your decision about making a longstanding commitment to the relationship.

## Creating perceptions

Perceiving yourself and others accurately is difficult at the best of times. Attraction can both clarify and distort your perceptions of yourself and of potential partners.

### *Perceive yourself accurately*

There are risks in the dating and partner selection process of both underestimating and overestimating your attractiveness. You may be prone to dwelling on your 'faults' and insufficiently realize your strengths. If you underestimate your attractiveness, you may be afraid to take risks and end up settling for a less attractive partner than you might otherwise have obtained. You may be less resilient and willing to persist in overcoming reservations and difficulties with someone for whom you care and who cares for you. In addition, your low self-esteem can contribute to your filtering out positive messages and magnifying negative messages from others. Furthermore, you are more likely to give in to pressure to select a partner against your wishes. Getting into a relationship on the rebound is another risk stemming from low self-esteem. People who feel vulnerable, incomplete and unable to handle loneliness can select partners for the wrong reasons. Beware of oversimplifying the partner finding process by using polarized categories like success or failure and acceptance or rejection. What you perceive as failure or rejection may be based on another's realistic assessment of the differences between you that is in the best interests of you both.

Overestimating your attractiveness has both advantages and disadvantages. Provided your overestimation is not excessive, your added confidence may help you to be relaxed and take realistic risks in the dating and courtship process (Bandura, 1986). However, if people perceive you as conceited and pushy, you lessen their interest in you. If you overestimate your attractiveness, you may lack sufficient insight to detect others' negative reactions to you and their reasons for them.

## Perceive potential partners accurately

The following are some ways in which you may perceive potential partners inaccurately.

### INFATUATION

If you are infatuated with another you are inspired with extravagant and unreasoning passion. Physical attraction is probably the main stimulus for people starting relationships. However, albeit very important, it is only one criterion in selecting a partner. Infatuation is a state of heightened emotionality that burns itself out. Infatuation and lovesickness are part of being alive. However, where possible, protect yourself from making major commitments until you have come down to earth and made a more realistic appraisal. Where there is strong sexual attraction it is all too easy to misperceive each other and to rationalize away potential difficulties in your relationship.

### IDEALIZATION

A combination of the myth of romantic love, your own insecurities and your date's skills of impression management may lead you to idealize her or him. You see what you want to see. You may inadequately acknowledge messages that contradict your ideal picture. Furthermore, you may insufficiently realize that this wonderful person may not reciprocate the same level of interest.

### EXAGGERATING SIMILARITY

Exaggerating similarity is slightly different from idealizing a potential partner. Both involve selectively perceiving the information that you want to perceive. When you exaggerate similarity you overemphasize what you have in common and underemphasize your differences. You fuse yourself with the other and insufficiently perceive your boundaries. You may inadequately note signs of lack of commitment (Colliver, 1992).

Try to understand the templates or blueprints that you bring from former relationships to current or new ones, especially interactive patterns for giving and receiving emotional pain. In close personal relationships, consciously or unconsciously, you may react in terms of previous relationships: for instance, men to their mothers or former girlfriends; women to their fathers or former boyfriends. Transference reactions can be positive or negative. Either way they may not be a sound basis on which to make relationship choices. You need to react to others as they are, not because they remind you of someone else.

When people date they package themselves to get the other to perceive them favourably. Imagine getting ready for a new date. In varying degrees the girl is 'out to get' the guy and the guy is 'out to get' the girl. Depending on how far out of touch they are with their own valuing processes and identity, the people you date may 'sell' themselves as though they are commodities. They emphasize their assets or selling points and strictly control the flow of information about their perceived liabilities. It can be hard to get to know another person well when, both consciously and unconsciously, they put on acts for your consumption. Appearances can be deceptive. For example, conflicts may be smoothed over so as not to interfere with the goal of winning your affection. However, later on, in the routine of daily living these conflicts surface. Some people are very adept at manipulating appearances to conceal their negative points. However, others have hidden assets that become more apparent as you get to know them better.

## Creating self-talk

When thinking of starting a relationship, starting one or ending it quickly, you can use calming, coaching and affirming self-talk:

- *Calming self-talk*. You can make self-statements like 'Calm down', 'Relax' and 'Take it easy', for instance, when on a first date with someone. You can also use the same kinds of calming self-talk if and when thinking of letting them know that you would not like to see them again.
- *Coaching self-talk*. You can coach yourself in good skills of getting to know another person and not rushing into a long-term commitment. For example, you can tell yourself that 'We can take our time in getting to know each other', 'I need to really listen to what she/he is saying' and 'I can make sure to ask her/him what she/he would like to do.' You can also coach yourself in

how to end a relationship right at the start: for instance, 'Politely, yet firmly, say I do not want to meet again, if she/he contacts me again.'

- *Affirming self-talk.* You can acknowledge when you use your skills: for instance, 'Good. I'm getting better at understanding her/him' and 'I'm happy that we're taking time to develop our relationship.' You can also use affirming self-talk when you end a relationship, for example, 'Ending the relationship is the right thing to do and frees me to look for someone with whom I have much more in common.'

## Creating visual images

Especially if you have a strong imagination, you can use visualizing skills to go backwards and forwards in gaining information about a potential partner (Lazarus, 1984, 2005). Regarding the past, you can look at each other's photograph albums and use these as springboards for getting in touch both verbally and visually with how each of you experienced life before you met. Regarding the future, you can use a skill called time projection. In time projection you visualize how life will be at some point in the future. The following are questions about your future that you might try to answer visually either on your own or with a potential partner.

- How do I see our relationship working out a year from now, in five years, and in ten years from now?
- How do I see myself developing and changing as the years go by?
- How do I see my partner developing and changing as the years go by?
- How do I see us dealing with changes in each other and our relationship?
- What sort of family will we have?
- What sort of parents will we be?
- What will we be like when we are old?

## Creating explanations

You need to explain the cause of any strong feelings of attraction accurately. If you are 'swept off your feet', you are choosing to allow this to happen. If you continue seeing someone, again this is your choice rather than saying 'I had no choice but to continue seeing her/him.' Assuming no coercion is involved, the same holds true if you go to bed with a potential partner – having sex is a choice on both your parts.

You can also try to explain the cause of your negative feelings accurately. You may feel less well disposed towards and unnecessarily narrow your field of potential partners if you explain another's difference from you as her or him being inferior to you. Examine closely how you explain your feelings associated with specific situations in the dating and courtship process. For example, misunderstandings in starting up relationships may be due to your hypersensitivity and jealousy rather than to another's negative behaviour. You may be on the lookout for signs of unreliability and betrayal. Alternatively, your negative feelings may be due to another's behaviour and yet you find ways of blaming yourself.

Try to be honest in explaining the causes of previous relationship breakdowns with potential or actual partners. You can use this knowledge to develop a clearer concept of yourself as a partner which, in turn, should help you think more clearly about what characteristics you prefer in a future partner. You can also learn from mistakes to improve your relationship skills in areas in which you showed vulnerability in previous relationships. In addition, explain accurately what you did right in previous relationships so you can maintain your confidence and build on your skills strengths.

## Creating expectations

The process of selecting a partner involves continually assessing and reassessing the probability of a successful relationship (see Activity 6.2). During this process you gain more information both about your potential partner and your reactions to him or her. If you are not already cohabiting, try predicting what it will be like spending 24 hours a day, year in, year out with a potential partner. The following are a number of relationship myths. These myths represent unrealistic expectations that have the potential to interfere with the realism with which you select a partner. If you recognize that you possess any of these myths, seriously consider discarding or modifying them:

- People who are in love live happily ever after.
- Love overcomes all.
- Love lasts forever.
- Once we're married, I can change her/him.
- My marriage/partnership is not going to run into trouble; it can't happen to me.
- She/he will always be the same.
- The qualities in her/him, I like now I will always like.

| ACTIVITY 6.2 | Assess my mind skills weaknesses in choosing a partner |
| --- | --- |

Identify the mind skills weaknesses that you possess or might possess when choosing a partner. First assess each mind skill on your own, before discussing with another or others.

*Creating rules*

1. Identify any parental rules that might influence you in choosing a partner. Are these rules helpful or harmful?

2. Identify and assess the realism of your rules concerning how men and women should behave, how husbands and wives should behave, and how fathers and mothers should behave.
3. Identify and assess the realism of your rules about how people should behave in close relationships.

### Creating perceptions

1. When dating and courting, do you overestimate or underestimate your attractiveness? If either, what are the consequences?
2. When choosing a partner, are you at risk of inaccurately perceiving a potential partner in any of the following ways:
   - infatuation
   - idealisation
   - exaggerating similarity
   - transference
   - falling victim to impression management?

### Creating self-talk

When choosing a partner do you engage in self-statements that are:

1. Insufficiently calming
2. Insufficiently coaching
3. Insufficiently affirming.

### Creating visual images

1. Work with your potential partner to develop a visual 'history' of how they were before they met you.
2. Visualize how you see yourself and your potential partner changing as the years go by.
3. Visualize yourself and your potential partner as parents.

### Creating explanations

When choosing a partner, how accurately do you explain cause for:

1. Your positive feelings and communications with them
2. Your negative feelings and communications with them
3. What went wrong and right in your previous relationships.

### Creating expectations

Do you possess any false predictive myths about love lasting forever, perfect relationships, and both partners never changing?

### Summary

Summarize your main thinking skills strengths and weaknesses in choosing a partner.

# SOME CRITERIA FOR CHOOSING A PARTNER

What are you looking for when searching for and choosing a compatible part-ner? How realistic are your expectations and goals? Especially if marriage or its equivalent is intended, what you make is a choice for all seasons. What matters to you in the short term may be different from what matters in the long run. Sternberg considers that among the things that increase in importance as relationships grow are willingness to change in response to each other and willingness to tolerate each other's imperfections (Trotter, 1986). Additionally, the sharing of values, for instance, religious values, can become important. A common shift is that from passionate love to compassionate love.

As Aesop observed: 'There can be little liking where there is not likeness.' Couples tend to be similar in many ways. Argyle and Henderson (1985: 105) state: 'They are more similar than by chance in age, social class, religion, height, intelligence, values and beliefs and in some measures of personality.' Though complementarity may add spice and interest, most relationships require ground-ing in a high degree of similarity.

Though the initial saying 'yes' to another human being may be on first sight or meeting, it can take time to gather appropriate evidence to justify your initial choice. Hamburg writes that 'partners find out just how suited to each other they actually are only when the sexual fuel for romantic love has run out' (2000: 53). Below are a few suggestions to help you set realistic goals for selecting a partner. Trade-offs, compromises and negotiations are inevitable. Each person and each couple will weigh the importance of the following criteria differently. Also their importance for either or both partners is likely to change over time, which can either enhance closeness or draw partners apart.

## Physical attraction

Individuals tend to match themselves on physical attractiveness. People who consider themselves less likely to be accepted may trade down to a less attractive partner. Physical attractiveness is not just a matter of natural attributes. How the individual uses body language, for instance, use of gaze and eye contact, also contributes to it.

## Sexual compatibility

With premarital sex and cohabitation now so widespread, awareness of sexual compatibility is more important than previously in choosing a partner. Passion as expressed by kissing, hugging and touching and intercourse needs to be satis-factorily given and received. Furthermore, partners need to be able to talk freely about their sexual relationship, including sharing their fantasies. In the first flush of a relationship, when sexual relating is often at a high level, you may find it difficult to assess your longer term sexual compatibility. Since people vary enormously in the importance they place on sexual relating and on the activities they enjoy, a reasonable level of sexual compatibility can be critical for the stability of a relationship. As well as your experience together, further information about sexual compatibility can come from honestly sharing your previous sexual histories.

## Respect

How much respect do you and your potential partner have for each other? Respect means concern that, within our interdependence, we accept each other, see and allow each other to grow as separate human beings. Possessiveness and control are the antithesis of respect. We are secure enough in ourselves that we allow each other the psychological space to be ourselves. A good test of how well another respects you is how well they listen to you. Poor listeners tend to be too bound up with their own agendas to respect you fully.

## Trustworthiness and commitment

All relationships involve contracts of varying degrees of implicitness and explicitness. These contracts or agreements relate to such matters as not engaging in sexual activity with others, not criticizing and standing up for the other person in public, keeping confidences, keeping promises and generally acting in reliable and dependable ways. Another aspect of trust is that of trusting another not to reject or hurt you needlessly. The notion of commitment is closely allied to that of trust. A committed partner does not breach trust. Instead a committed partner keeps trust by staying with the relationship through the hard times which inevitably occur.

## Emotional responsiveness

People differ in how important they consider it for themselves and their partner to be emotionally expressive and responsive. A common pattern is that of one partner, more often the woman, wanting to ventilate feelings while the other partner, usually the man, responds by withdrawing or getting into an intellectual problem-solving mode too soon. Where differences in expressiveness exist, partners may need to work towards either changing and/or accommodating the differences. Genuineness in the expression of feelings is very important. Verbal, vocal, body, touch and taking action messages should speak in the same direction.

## Intimacy

In his book *The Art of Loving*, Fromm (1957) emphasized the importance of knowledge in loving relationships. Your knowing yourself and willingness to be known can help me relate to you as you are rather than in terms of my inaccurate personification of you. It also makes it easier for me to drop my social masks and defensive facades. Capacity for intimacy and emotional responsiveness come together in that if you can feel free to disclose not only personal information but also your feelings, you share the flow of your being with me. This encourages me to do the same. Our relationship becomes a vibrant process rather than something that is static and dull. We have an open rather than a closed communication system. People differ in how much they value emotional closeness and distance. Consequently, there are risks attached to selecting a partner whose needs for intimacy differ greatly from your own.

## Sense of humour

Does the child in the other person appeal to the child in you? Do they have a similar sense of fun and humour? Do you enjoy being silly and playing together? Enjoying each other's sense of humour can both enhance the good times and ease the bad times in your relationship. The capacity to laugh at yourself can be an invaluable asset in close relationships.

## Caring

Caring entails thoughtfulness and having regard for another's feelings. You are sensitive to each other's wishes and, where reasonable, try to meet them, which can involve being positive in finding out the other's wishes as well as reacting to them. Caring plays a very important role in people's judgements of love. Caring also involves considerateness. A potential partner can lack considerateness by hurting you unnecessarily.

## Companionship

Do you enjoy doing things together and just being together? If relationships are to remain happy, you need to engage in a reasonable number of shared pleasant activities. You can still enjoy individual activities as well. You need personal space as well as togetherness. Frequent conversations, both intimate and less intimate, are important ways of keeping in touch with one another both emotionally and practically. Couples vary in the activities they enjoy. Both your own and your potential partner's preferences for enjoyable activities are likely to change over the course of your relationship. You may then need to work to keep sharing some pleasant activities.

## Intellectual compatibility

To what degree is it important to you to have a partner of your own intellectual capability? You may find it boring to be conversing on a daily basis with someone you perceive as much less bright than you. Alternatively, you could feel inferior with someone who seems to think much more quickly than you do. Academic intelligence is no guarantee of social intelligence and sensitivity. Nevertheless, many people are likely to feel more comfortable with a partner of roughly the same intellect than where there are wide discrepancies.

## Compatibility of values

Values are the underlying principles and priorities on which people base their lives. Sample values are family life, religion, achievement, materialism, security, excitement, conformity, career and personal growth. At any time partners and potential partners have profiles of values, some of which are more important than others. Differences in values are inevitable. However, you need to feel comfortable with each other's major values to sustain a long-term relationship without great strain. Your values are likely to be heavily influenced by cultural and sex-role considerations.

Values are the basis on which you and your partner develop goals for your relationship. You may discover on closer examination that each of you wants and expects different things. This need not be an insuperable obstacle if you can resolve the value conflicts to your mutual satisfaction. However, major unresolved value conflicts are unlikely to go away. Under these circumstances, you should then consider whether it is worth the risk of committing yourself to a long-term relationship.

## Compatibility of daily activities

A host of daily living considerations may be important: what sort of television programmes, music and food each of you likes; your sleeping habits; your attitudes towards tidiness, and so on. Can you work through your differences and arrive at mutually satisfactory solutions?

## Earning and spending money

Hamburg (2000) writes that money is the number one fight topic in marriage. You need to have a reasonable degree of agreement over how you each contribute to keeping the relationship intact materially. This refers to both income and expenditure. There are no hard and fast answers to the numerous questions that money raises in relationships. Issues about earning money in a relationship include how much each person contributes, whether differences in contribution are acceptable to both, how much each partner is working for money and whether this is too much or too little for the wellness of the relationship. Issues about spending money include possible differences in what partners want to spend it on, degree of savings orientation and degree of debt tolerance.

## Balance of power

You can assess a potential relationship on the degree of power and influence you are likely to obtain in it. You need to be comfortable with how much power you are likely to have. Glasser (1995: 25) observes that 'love cannot take root in a relationship in which one or both of the partners believe that they have little or no power'. Partners can have strong needs for power and still treat each other with respect. Especially if they possess the inner strength to examine their own behaviour, powerful personalities can find ways of working around and solving their relationship problems. However, if you detect that a potential partner is very bossy, controlling and always wants her or his own way, listen to the alarm bells in your head. Such people are not strong, but weak. In fact, if you enter a long-term relationship with one you risk subjecting yourself to 'the tyranny of the weak'. Beware of potential partners who are physical and/or psychological bullies and those who attempt to control you with passive aggression.

## Relationship skills strengths and weaknesses

Though most people do not think of their relationships in skills terms, there is no reason why you should not. Throughout this book various skills for initiating, maintaining and developing relationships are described. You can assess the relationship skills of potential partners. How well you get on both now and in the future heavily depends on your own and your potential partner's relationship skills. Teamwork is important. How good are you at working together both to build your strengths and to minimize the negative effects of your weaknesses? The engagement period is a time of increased commitment when couples can assess each other's relating skills more closely. Cohabitation offers a further opportunity for this.

Getting to know another person well invariably takes time. The wisdom of not hurrying your ultimate choice of long-term partner is well summed up by Hamburg (2000: 101): 'To really get to know your partner, you need to spend enough time with your partner, in enough different situations, with enough of your partner's friends, associates, and family members, so that you know not only your partner but your partner's personal world.' When making a long-term commitment, your warmth of affection and degree of attraction to another needs to be balanced by collecting sufficient evidence and judging it reasonably coolly (see Activity 6.3).

**ACTIVITY 6.3**　　　　　　**What am I looking for in a partner?** ❘

Complete Part A on your own and, if appropriate, Part B with a potential partner.

## Part A  On your own

Write down how important each of the following criteria is for you in choosing a partner and your main reasons for its importance.

| *Criteria* | *Importance and main reasons* |
|---|---|
| Physical attraction | |
| Sexual compatibility | |
| Respect | |
| Trustworthiness and commitment | |
| Emotional responsiveness | |
| Capacity for intimacy | |
| Sense of humour | |
| Caring | |
| Companionship | |
| Intellectual compatibility | |
| Compatibility of values | |
| Compatibility of daily activities | |
| Earning and spending money | |
| Balance of power | |
| Relating skills strengths and weaknesses | |
| Other criteria not mentioned above | |

Summarize your main criteria for choosing a partner.

## Part B  Working together

You and your potential partner now share and discuss your answers to Part A of this activity. Together, answer the following questions.

1. How well do you think you are matched?
2. Are there any major areas of incompatibility in your potential partnership? If so, please specify.
3. If in question 2 you identified major areas of incompatibility between you

   (a) What impact might they have on your future relationship?
   (b) What, if anything, can you do about them?

---

## ACTIVITY 6.4       Group discussion: choosing a partner skills ▌

This is intended as a group activity, though it may be done individually or in pairs.

For each part:

1. Spend five to ten minutes answering the question in groups of three or four.
2. Each subgroup shares its findings with the whole group.
3. The whole group ranks the four most important points or skills from the most important to the least important.

## Part A  Identifying danger signals

List the four most important characteristics to avoid in a potential long-term partner.

## Part B  Identifying strengths

List the four most important strengths that you would like a potential long-term partner to possess.

## Part C  Search and find skills

List important skills people require to search for and find a suitable long-term partner.

---

# 7

# *Intimacy skills* |

**Chapter outcomes**
By studying and doing the activities in this chapter you should:

- know about what is intimacy
- understand some different dimensions of intimacy
- understand some limitations of intimacy
- know about some communication skills for intimacy
- know about some mind skills for intimacy.

Everyone craves the reward of intimacy in their close relationships. Intimacy does not always come with the territory in relationships that possess the outward form of closeness, for instance, marriage. Rather partners attain, maintain and develop differing degrees of intimacy in their relationships. Furthermore, at any time partners can withdraw and regulate the degree of intimacy they offer each other. Such holding back is more likely to be ongoing when relationships deteriorate.

## MEANINGS OF INTIMACY

### Defining intimacy

Adjectives associated with the noun intimacy include private, personal, close and familiar. Frequently, in everyday usage, intimacy means either expressing personal feelings or sexual closeness. Beck (1988: 242) observes: 'Intimacy can range from discussing everyday details of your life, to confiding the most private feeling that you would not share with anybody else, to your sexual relationship.'

The Latin word *intus*, meaning within, is the basis of the word intimacy. Nonsexual intimacy entails partners getting in touch with their internal worlds and sharing them with each other. Alberti and Emmons (2001) talk about intimacy as a quality of relationship between two people who care deeply about each other. Such a relationship quality is characterized by a complex blend of dimensions: '*attraction*, open and honest *communication*, *commitment* to continuation of the partnership, *enjoyment* of their life together, a sense of *purpose* for this relationship, and mutual *trust* which honors and respects each other' (Alberti and Emmons, 2001: 156). These six major dimensions form the acronym ACCEPT. They see acceptance of oneself, each other and of the relationship as the true heart of intimacy.

To have a truly intimate relationship with another person, it is necessary to be on the same wavelength. Prince Charles and Princess Diana were outstanding examples of people on different wavelengths. They did not grow apart as much as discover that their individual identities had been apart from the very beginning. Hamburg (2000) observes that being on the same wavelength means that a couple have the same attitudes about what makes life worth living, what kind of world they want to see around them, and about what love is and the part it plays in their lives.

## Dimensions of intimacy

The following are some important dimensions of intimacy. Simply stated, intimacy with yourself is knowing your internal world; reaching out is sharing your internal world; receiving intimacy is sharing another's internal world; and your interactive pattern of intimacy is how you and your partner coordinate the sharing of your internal worlds.

### *Intimacy with yourself*

Intimacy with yourself provides the foundation for intimacy with others. The process of intimacy is best served by partners developing a secure sense of themselves as separate persons. Rogers regards it as a paradox that in a 'process partnership', 'when each partner is making progress towards becoming his or her own self, the partnership becomes more enriching' (Rogers, 1973: 212). Intimacy with yourself involves knowing and exploring your internal world. You possess sufficient emotional literacy to experience, identify and accurately label your feelings and thoughts. Your significant feelings are either present or readily accessible to your awareness. You possess a basic acceptance of yourself as a person that allows you to be open to your contrasting emotions.

Intimacy is a process that takes place both within partners and between them. The degree of intimacy that partners can offer to each other is likely to be limited by the degree of intimacy they are able to provide for themselves. If you are out of touch with your own feelings, you are unlikely to experience other's feelings accurately. If you think defensively and rigidly, you will be restricted in how you respond to others' thoughts and feelings. However, if you possess a secure sense of your identity and a genuine acceptance of yourself as an independent, yet fallible, human being, you are more likely to experience the full of humanness of another. Intimacy with yourself is not to be confused with selfish individualism. Rather your level of inner strength and insight is such that you can reach out and experience others without needing to distort or manipulate them for your own ends.

## Reaching out

Intimacy with another involves reaching out and sharing your internal world with them. Authenticity, genuineness, honesty and realness are nouns that describe the process of reaching out intimately. If your relationship develops, you increasingly drop your social masks, facades and defences. You are willing to be known and to share vulnerable and childlike parts of yourself as well as your strengths. Eric Berne, the founder of transactional analysis, regarded intimacy as 'a candid game-free relationship, with mutual free giving and receiving and without exploitation' (1972: 25). Frequently, the notion of encounter is used to describe special moments of intimacy. Partners experience and communicate their thoughts and feelings in a way that transcends the boundaries of their existential isolation and is deeply enriching. They encounter each other in an 'I–Thou' relationship (Buber, 1970).

## Receiving intimacy

Receiving intimacy entails allowing yourself to become open to the internal world of another and to be influenced by it. Openness to your partner's internal world requires you to accept and respect them as different. You strive to create an emotional climate whereby they feel safe to risk revealing themselves to you authentically. You listen to them empathically and assist them to explore and experience their thoughts and feelings. Where appropriate, you share your own experiencing, ask questions, provide feedback or challenge them. You gently, or otherwise, allow your partner to be vulnerable, happy, sad or whatever they may feel at the time.

Receiving intimacy means that you are concerned enough about your partner to want to know them fully. Such knowledge includes their thoughts and feelings about their childhood, their subsequent background, their present lives and their relationship with you. Fromm (1957) writes of knowledge of another being not just at the periphery, but penetrating their core. You sense the underlying meanings and nuances that their surface behaviour masks: for instance, angry behaviour which masks hurt and worry. In effective relationships, partners also acquire more information about each other in terms of breadth of topics as well as depth, or revealing more risky information.

## Interactive patterns of intimacy

What are some patterns of partners influencing each other with their intimacy behaviour? One of the most consistent findings of the self-disclosure research is that people tend to reciprocate the intimacy level of each other's disclosures (for example, Berg and Derlega, 1987). If you both wish to develop your relationship, you are likely to coordinate the deepening of the intimacy level of your disclosures. However, more often than not relationships do not make a smooth progression to more intimate disclosures, but instead trace a jagged line in that direction.

The progressive matching of the intimacy level of disclosures deepens relationships for a number of reasons. One explanation is that your disclosure is a reward to another, indicating liking. The disclosure is to be matched if the relationship is to remain in balance. Another explanation emphasizes how disclosures are received. If another accepts your disclosure, this acceptance not only establishes the other as less threatening and more like you, but also gives her or him permission to make a similar disclosure. Consequently, by accepting disclosures as well as by disclosing, you develop trust in your relationships.

Dysfunctional patterns of intimacy can be too distant, too enmeshed, or in imbalance. Reciprocating a shallow level of disclosure exemplifies too distant an intimacy pattern. Possibly both partners fear intimacy and, hence, relinquish some of their capacity to reap its rewards.

The word enmeshment means entangled as in the meshes of a net. Either or both partners lose some of their individual sense of self if they become too fused. When enmeshment occurs both partners settle for a less than genuine intimacy by developing an emotionally constricting 'we–self' at the expense of their individual selves. Often in enmeshed relationships, one partner's viewpoint dominates more than the other's. This is a 'lose–lose' situation with the dominant partner deprived of some of the individuality of the less dominant partner. Relationships can also become enmeshed if partners spend all their time with each other. To be intimate with your partner does not mean all the time you need be with her or him.

An example of an unbalanced intimacy pattern is that of one partner, frequently the female, striving for greater emotional closeness, with the other partner, usually the male, preferring to keep emotionally distant (Christensen and Jacobson, 2000). Sometimes a pursuer–distancer pattern develops in which the harder the partner requiring closeness pushes, the more the other partner withdraws. The following is a vignette that illustrates this pattern:

> Ted and Debbie are a couple in their late twenties who have been married for three years. When they were courting and in the first year of marriage, Debbie used to admire Ted's calm and collected attitude to life. She saw this as a sign of quiet strength. Over the past year or so, Debbie has increasingly perceived Ted's calmness as evidence of lack of real caring for her. The more she resents his behaviour and pressures Ted to show more love, the more he withdraws. Debbie has insufficiently acknowledged that Ted was brought up in a family where his father showed little emotion, was physically absent much of the time, and his mother overwhelmed him with the amount and intensity of her feelings, including her hatred for his father. Ted grew up with no role model of a man

showing feelings. Debbie's behaviour reactivates anxieties associated with Ted's childhood feelings of powerlessness at the strength of his mother's feelings.

## Limitations on intimacy

Before examining some communication skills and mind skills for developing and maintaining intimacy, I draw your attention to some limitations on intimacy.

### Existential isolation

Humans enter and leave the world alone. As the saying goes: 'You cannot die another person's death for them.' Throughout their lives humans exist in their separate skins. Yalom (1980) states that one of the important facts which patients in existential counselling need discover is that, no matter how close they get to other people, they must still face life alone. Patients have to learn the limits of intimacy as well as its rewards. In relationships, no matter how much partners care and share, ultimately they exist separately. Partners cannot avoid the mandate to assume personal responsibility for their individual lives.

### Individual differences

People are different. The ways in which they wish to give and receive intimacy vary. Their wishes for emotional privacy vary. Imagine each partner as a large house. Independent of any good or poor intimacy skills that they possess, each partner may want the other to enter most rooms in their house, but not necessarily all the rooms all of the time. Each partner may also have more interest in entering some rooms than others. To expect a perfect situation of total openness and total interest is unrealistic. Partners can respect each other's wishes for privacy, though as relationships develop these private areas are likely to become fewer. Partners need to acknowledge that they cannot always expect to give and receive total interest.

### Sex-role learning

Frequently, women are thought to have better intimacy skills than men. Derlega and Chaikin (1975) write of the 'inexpressive male'. They note that wives are more interested in communicating personal feelings than their husbands. Males are brought up to hide their feelings more often than females. Males are more likely to deny and distort feelings and, consequently, to seem distant from them. However, as the work on sex roles of Bem (1974, 1981) indicates, men and women have been encouraged to value and express different feelings: for instance, sensitivity in women and ambition in men. Furthermore, men and women tend to have different ways of reacting to disclosures of feelings: women being more inclined to listen and empathize and men more inclined to problem solve. These are generalizations. Differences exist within the sexes and differences between the sexes may be lessening over time. Nevertheless, the learning of sex roles can present barriers to, if not limitations on, sharing intimacy.

### Realistic negative consequences

A Hungarian proverb warns 'Tell the truth and you get your head bashed in.' Should partners 'let it all hang out' in disclosing about themselves and giving feedback to their partners? Total honesty may not always be the best policy. You have to consider the consequences of what and how you disclose your inner world. An example of the limitations of total honesty is that of Marvin who criticized his wife so frequently and brutally that she divorced him (Lazarus *et al.*, 1993). Possibly, if Marvin had been more honest about his own limitations as well as his wife's, he would have been more tactful and diplomatic.

### Practical considerations

A host of practical considerations can limit intimacy. Such considerations include cramped living space, noise, shortage of money, fatigue, dependent children, caring for in-laws, work pressures, health problems, and so on. If possible, in the interests of themselves and their relationship, partners need to find ways of addressing or circumventing such practical limitations.

## SOME COMMUNICATION SKILLS FOR INTIMACY

The following are some suggestions for skills of sharing your internal world, allowing another to be open with you, and maintaining an effective interactive pattern of intimacy.

### Reaching out

#### Express feelings

Expressing your feelings involves revealing to the external world the emotions of your internal world. Thus expressing feelings entails a translation of your inner sensations into outer expressions. Sometimes the process of translation is immediate – for instance, your startled reactions to a loud noise. On most occasions, expressing feelings involves conscious choices regarding both how you label feelings and also whether and how you reveal them.

Identifying and labelling your feelings accurately requires intimacy with yourself. For instance, Oliver asks his partner Karen if she will go out to dinner with him that evening, and she politely but firmly refuses. Oliver might have a range of possible feelings including hurt, anger, anxiety, relief, resignation, cheerfulness and concern. If Oliver thinks about his feelings or wants to talk about them to Karen, he needs to put them into words. Some slippage may occur between Oliver's feelings and their verbal description. For instance, he may find it difficult to admit that he is hurt, finding it more comfortable to label his feeling as anger. Oliver's other poor skills include insufficiently acknowledging his ambivalence and the nuances in the intensity of his feelings. In addition, Oliver may lack the vocabulary to identify and express his feelings adequately. To send good feelings messages, it is useful to build up a repertoire of words to describe and to catch the nuances of your own and others' feelings.

Apart from identifying and labelling your feelings accurately, other skills for expressing feelings include: sending 'I' messages and consistent verbal, vocal and body messages. With feelings you find difficult to express, you can sometimes think through and rehearse how best to communicate them prior to taking the risk of doing so (see Activity 7.1).

## ACTIVITY 7.1        Develop my expressing feelings skills

First do each part of this activity on your own. Then, if appropriate, discuss with your partner, another or others.

### Part A   Feelings I find easy and difficult to express

1. Take a piece of paper. At the top write 'Feelings I find easy and difficult to express'. On the next line, at the top of the left column write 'easy', and at the top of the right column write 'difficult'.
2. In each column write feelings you find easy and difficult to express. You may do this with regard either to a specific relationship or to people in general.
3. Do you detect any theme(s) in the feelings you have listed as either easy or difficult to express? If so, please specify the theme(s).

### Part B   Sending feelings messages

1. For each of the following feelings write down (a) verbal messages, (b) vocal messages, (c) body messages that you could use to express the feeling appropriately either in a specific relationship or to people in general.

Love _____     Anger _____

_____     _____

_____     _____

Fear _____     Sadness _____

_____          _____

_____          _____

Happiness _____          Boredom _____

_____          _____

_____          _____

2. Look at the feelings you listed as difficult to express in Part A of this
   activity. For each of these feelings write down (a) verbal messages,
   (b) vocal messages, (c) body messages that you could use to express
   the feeling appropriately. Rehearse and practise expressing these
   feelings.

## Let yourself be known

Intimacy requires letting yourself be known. You need to reveal personal
information as well as your feelings. Following are some communication skills
for letting yourself be known:

- *Take the initiative*. Instead of waiting to be asked questions about yourself,
  you can take the initiative in talking about yourself. You can help your
  partner gain knowledge of your past, present and future.
- *Request disclosure time*. You can develop skills of letting your partner know
  that you want their attention. If you want to share a sensitive disclosure, you
  can either choose or arrange a time when you can talk the matter through.
  You can signal the importance of such a discussion to you.
- *Assert yourself*. You may need to use assertion skills to ensure that your
  partner listens to you. For instance, if they switch the focus back to themselves, you can let it be known that you wish to continue. They can have
  their turn to talk about themselves either later or another time.
- *Take calculated risks*. Revealing negative aspects of yourself can deepen relationships. You can attempt to attain greater intimacy by taking calculated
  risks. If you have never tried, you have not collected the evidence that you
  will worsen rather than improve your relationship by risking specific
  disclosures. You need not 'let it all hang out'. Some things may be better left
  unsaid (Lazarus *et al.*, 1993).
- *Reciprocate intimacy*. If your partner reveals something more intimate about
  themselves, you can choose whether or not to match their intimacy level by
  self-disclosing in the same or another area. Over time successful couples are
  likely to be close to matching the intimacy level of their disclosures.

- *Tune into your partner's reactions.* You can not only notice but also be responsive to how your partner reacts to your disclosures. If you have revealed something that changes their picture of you, they may require your help in dealing with this change. You also need to learn what interests your partner about you and how not to bore them.

- *Be worth knowing.* You need to develop as a person by keeping actively engaged in life. If you allow your internal world to become impoverished and have few external interests, you will have little of interest to disclose. For example, Becky came to spend so much time and energy on her career that she had little else to talk about with her partner Irvin.

## Receiving intimacy

This section focuses in particular on assisting your partner to share very private information. Each of us has imperfections that we fear to reveal to others. Words and phrases to describe such information include negative or risky self-disclosure, unacceptable parts of ourselves, secrets, skeletons in the cupboard, or stigmas. The following are some skills of assisting your partner to share negative aspects of her or his internal world:

- *Show unconditional acceptance.* Unconditional acceptance means accepting another unconditionally as a valuable person independent of their specific behaviours. If your partner struggles to tell you something of which they are ashamed, be careful not to be judgemental about them and it. The fact that your partner fears telling you means that they already judge the information negatively, but trust you sufficiently to not make matters worse.

- *Encourage the experiencing and exploring of feelings.* Use active listening and showing understanding skills to help your partner experience the feelings attached to the disclosure, for instance, anxiety, relief or tears. Assist them to reveal as much of the story as they are comfortable with at this stage. Give your partner space to explore their thoughts and feelings about what they are telling you. Where appropriate, ask questions that encourage them to continue and elaborate their story.

- *Show involvement.* You can show that you care for your partner not only by listening, but also by actively showing your support. If your partner appears hesitant, you can tell them of your concern and willingness to be there for them. You can also respond to specific parts of their story with comments like 'That must have been awful for you'. In addition, you can express appreciation for their trust in you as well as admiration for their courage.

- *Use effective vocal messages.* You can show that you understand the intensity of their feelings by varying the emphasis of your voice. You can also show compassion by speaking gently.

- *Use effective body and touch messages.* Use body messages such as interested and responsive facial expressions and good use of gaze and eye contact. Consider also using touch messages: for instance, either placing your hand on theirs or your arm round their shoulders.

- *Choose whether or not to reciprocate.* What your partner says may trigger something that you would like to reveal about yourself. Be sensitive that this may not be the best time to switch the agenda from your partner's concerns. Nevertheless, on some occasions, sharing something shameful about yourself may ease your partner's burden of self-devaluation as well as yours.

Above, I have focused on skills of helping another to reveal negative information. However, intimacy also entails sharing and receiving positive information. You may help your partner to feel more positively by accepting aspects of them that they find unacceptable. In addition, you may need to use good receiving intimacy skills to assist your partner to reveal what they like about themselves. Many people require loving assistance in owning and revealing their strengths (see Activity 7.2).

---

**ACTIVITY 7.2        Develop my disclosing and receiving personal information skills** |

---

Complete each part of the activity on your own. Then, if appropriate, discuss with your partner, another or others.

## Part A  Disclosing personal information

1. Assess your strengths and weaknesses in each of the following skills of revealing personal information:

   (a) Taking the initiative
   (b) Requesting disclosure time
   (c) Asserting myself
   (d) Taking calculated risks
   (e) Reciprocating intimacy
   (f)  Tuning into my partner's reactions
   (g) Being worth knowing.

2. If appropriate, identify one or more of your poor skills at disclosing personal information and develop a plan to change how you communicate. In your plan, specify:

   (a) Your goals, including a time frame
   (b) The steps you intend taking to attain each of your goals
   (c) How you will monitor your progress.

## Part B  Receiving personal information

1. Assess your strengths and weaknesses in each of the following skills of receiving personal information.

(a) Showing unconditional acceptance
(b) Encouraging the experiencing and exploring of feelings
(c) Showing involvement
(d) Using effective vocal messages
(e) Using effective body and touch messages
(f) Choosing whether or not to reciprocate.

2. If appropriate, identify one or more of your poor skills at receiving personal information and develop a plan to change how you communicate. In your plan, specify:

(a) Your goals, including a time frame
(b) The steps you intend taking to attain each of your goals
(c) How you will monitor your progress.

---

## MAINTAINING YOUR INTERACTIVE PATTERN OF INTIMACY

The following is a vignette of a couple who allowed their pattern of intimacy to run down and then took steps to repair it:

Andy and Stephanie, a couple in their late thirties, had been married for 13 years and had two boys, aged 9 and 10. Until recently Andy had been a company lawyer who worked long hours, including taking work home on evenings and weekends. Stephanie was a social worker. Not seeing much of Andy, she adjusted her schedule to include numerous committees and outside activities. When Andy's company was unexpectedly taken over, he lost his job. As part of his soul-searching on being made redundant, Andy decided to seek a less demanding job so he could spend more time with his wife and family. This prompted a series of discussions with Stephanie about how they wished to relate in future. Stephanie was sceptical that Andy would change his ways. Nevertheless, they agreed to set aside an evening a week to have a social evening together, to do the shopping together on Saturday mornings and have coffee out afterwards. They also agreed to go bowling more. To Stephanie's delight, Andy turned down some job offers that would have left them little time to have a relaxed intimate relationship. Eventually he took a job where he could restrict his work. Stephanie relinquished some of her outside activities to spend more time at home. Andy and Stephanie discussed early warning signals for their relationship becoming distant again, for instance, Andy's irritability, Stephanie experiencing difficulty getting through to him, and Stephanie looking for satisfaction outside the home. They agreed in future to confront the problem of distance in their relationship early on.

### Talk about how you relate

An important skill in maintaining an effective relationship is to talk to each other about how you relate. Egan calls this skills immediacy, or 'you–me' talk. He distinguishes between relationship immediacy, 'Let's talk about how we've been relating to each other recently', and here-and-now immediacy, 'Let's talk about what's going on between you and me right now as we're talking to each other' (Egan, 1977: 235). Thus Egan's 'you–me' talk can either have a recent past or a present focus. Another focus for 'you–me' talk sessions is how partners want their relationship to develop in future. For instance, in the above vignette Andy became dissatisfied that he was a status-seeking and money-making machine rather than a person. Then he and Stephanie engaged in some 'you–me' talk to establish different goals for their relationship. Andy would have found it harder to maintain his change if Stephanie had maintained her high level of outside activity.

When talking about how you relate, partners require skills of giving and receiving feedback. Partners can share positive and negative feelings about how each other relates. Other areas for feedback include how committed we are to the relationship, what issues we have avoided in the past, what issues we are not bringing up at this moment, what we want from our relationship, what are the strengths in our relationship, what is missing in our relationship, the influence of one another on how we give and receive intimacy, how we might improve our relationship, and the impact of other relationships on our relationship. Skills for 'you–me' talk sessions include getting in touch with what you think and feel, sending 'I' messages, being specific, and inviting rather than cutting off discussion of the points made. In addition, tact and diplomacy can help soften painful communication (see Activity 7.3).

## ACTIVITY 7.3                         Develop our 'you–me' talk skills

If you are in a relationship, complete the first part of this activity on your own and ask your partner to so the same. Then, if appropriate, do the second part of the activity together.

## Part A  Assessment

1. What positive feelings and thoughts about how your partner to you relates have you left unsaid?
2. What negative feelings and thoughts about how your partner relates to you have you left unsaid?

3. To what extent do you and your partner avoid talking about what is going on in your relationship in the 'here-and-now'?
4. How might you and your partner work together to improve your relationship?

### Part B  Hold a 'you–me' talk session

1. Set aside a time to hold a 'you–me' talk session with your partner about your relationship.
2. Conduct a 'you–me' talk session. Remember to send 'I' messages, be specific, invite rather than cut off discussion, and use tact and diplomacy.
3. Evaluate with your partner the benefits, if any, of holding 'you–me' talk sessions about your relationship.
4. Hold further 'you–me' talk sessions as you both see fit.

---

*Allocate time to maintain your relationship*

As the statistics for divorce and separation show, relationships can easily deteriorate into serious conflict. Stresses of work, family and outside activities interfere with couples spending quality time together. There is no magic wand to wave for maintaining intimacy in your relationship. Like Andy and Stephanie, you and your partner can deliberately allocate time for enjoying each other's company and conversing. Then at least, you give maintaining intimacy a chance. You can become aware when you start spending less time together and repair your intimacy pattern before it is too late.

## SOME MIND SKILLS FOR INTIMACY

This section explores some mind skills you can use to increase your chances of achieving intimacy.

### Creating rules

You may possess unrealistic rules concerning intimacy. You may turn your preferences into demands that restrict your freedom to think and act rationally in relation to yourself, others and your relationships. The following are examples of intimacy rules that may be unrealistically rigid.

*Intimacy with yourself*

- Males must not focus on their feelings.
- I must not have negative feelings about others.
- I must not have positive feelings about myself.

*Reaching out*

- I must always keep my distance.
- I must always be in an intimate relationship.
- I must have immediate and total affection.

*Receiving intimacy*

- I must always be polite.
- I must always actively help her/him solve her/his problem.
- Others must always treat my feelings with great respect.

*Interactive patterns of intimacy*

- We must have the same needs for emotional closeness.
- We must not share intimacies outside our relationship.
- We must put career and other daily activities ahead of creating time to talk to each other about our relationship.

To reiterate, dealing with unrealistic rules requires three steps. First, identify any unrealistic rules and their negative consequences. You can use the STC framework to help you analyse specific situations in which you possess one or more unrealistic rules. Second, dispute or challenge the logic of unrealistic rules by asking questions like: 'Where is the evidence that I must have immediate and total affection?' 'Could I stand it if I did not receive immediate and total affection?' 'Does not having immediate and total affection make me a rotten person?' 'Do I expect to give immediate and total affection to others?' Third, restate the unrealistic rule into something less rigid: for example, 'In the context of a supportive relationship, I prefer my partner and me to be honest about our feelings for each other.'

## Creating perceptions

*Perceive yourself accurately*

You may fail to perceive yourself accurately. To maintain your self-picture you may edit out significant personal information, both positive and negative. For instance, you can exaggerate either your strengths or weaknesses or a mixture of the two. You may consider yourself so unlovable that you cannot accept another's affectionate interest. You may engage in various defensive processes to contain your anxiety and maintain your current way of viewing yourself. The following are some defensive processes that can block intimacy – frequently people remain unaware that they use them (Freud, 1949; McKay *et al.*, 1994; Yalom, 1980):

- *Avoiding.* You may avoid people and situations that you find threatening: for example, situations where you may be asked to share your internal world or allow another to open up deeply to you.
- *Withdrawing.* When situations become emotionally charged, you may lower the temperature by either psychologically or physically withdrawing or both. You may play various roles and psychological games that create distance in your relationships (Berne, 1964; Powell, 1969).
- *Compulsive activity.* You may always be too busy to engage emotionally with another person. You may take refuge in your work, hobbies, or outside friendships.
- *Compulsive relating.* You may enter relationships not because you genuinely find another person attractive, but because you cannot stand the pain of loneliness or the social stigma of not being in a relationship. Because you have entered a relationship under false pretences, it may be difficult for you to attain intimacy.
- *Serial relating.* You do not allow yourself to develop a deep relationship with anyone. When genuine intimacy threatens, you end the relationship and move on to the next.
- *Compulsive sexuality.* You may avoid intimacy with anyone by focusing on them as bodies to be used for sexual pleasure rather than as persons with whom to develop relationships.
- *Dependency.* You may allow yourself to become dependent on another person rather than acknowledge and develop your own strengths.
- *Denial.* You may repress significant aspects of yourself: for instance, anger, concerns about death, or altruistic feelings. You may also deny certain aspects of the feedback you receive from others: for instance, their love for you.
- *Distortion.* You may filter incoming information by magnifying or minimizing it: for example, not acknowledging the full extent of a compliment or criticism. You may also fail to acknowledge sufficiently the effect of your upbringing on how you think and feel.
- *Projection.* Rather than acknowledge aspects of yourself that you do not like, you may become very conscious of these qualities in others: for instance, *their* need to control and *their* manipulation.
- *Rationalization.* Excuses, excuses, excuses. You may be adept at finding reasons for your less acceptable thoughts, feelings and behaviours.
- *Competing.* You may need to see yourself as superior to your partner and to others with whom you relate. You exaggerate your virtues and their faults.
- *Attacking.* You avoid acknowledging your own hurt and inadequacies by

inwardly attacking your partner. Outwardly, you may criticize, ridicule, nag and blame them. Verbal abuse may be accompanied by physical abuse.

- *Identification with the aggressor.* You may start making excuses for another's aggressive behaviour and secretly admire their strength at the same time as denying how furious you are with them.
- *Sex-role stereotyping.* You may resist seeing qualities in yourself that do not accord with the traditional stereotype of your sex. You think in rigid terms: 'Women are . . .' and 'Men are . . .'

Since you may not be aware of it in the first place, letting go of defensive thinking can be difficult. Anything you do that increases your self-esteem is likely to lower your need to defend yourself. In addition, if you become aware that you are using a defence, review the negative consequences to yourself and your relationships of maintaining it. Review also the possible gains of relinquishing it. Then, either on your own or with the help of your partner, you can strive to see yourself more accurately.

### *Perceive another accurately*

The corrosive effects on intimacy of each partner's defensive thinking can scarcely be overemphasized. Partners expand their defensive thinking because, in order to protect their own distorted self-pictures, they need to distort their pictures of one another. Thus intimacy becomes doubly difficult. However, by striving to overcome your own defensive thinking, you can perceive others more accurately.

Partners can also perceive each other inaccurately through insufficient information. Here they may attain greater intimacy by continuing to collect information about each other – their pasts, presents and hopes for the future. Taking the trouble to know your partner well can also protect you against insufficiently acknowledging how they differ from you. In addition, partners can perceive each other inaccurately through jumping to conclusions about each other's thoughts, feelings, motivations and actions. People tend to perceive in others only the thoughts and emotions they are capable of in themselves. You can protect yourself against misinterpreting your partner if you listen to them carefully and, if necessary, ask them to explain themselves.

### Creating self-talk

You may perceive that there are risks attached to disclosing specific aspects of your internal world, be they positively or negatively evaluated by you. Assuming that you decide to make a specific disclosure, you can use self-talk to help yourself do it in an appropriate way. Correctly using self-talk can assist you to feel better and act more effectively. Remember, self-talk consists of calming, coaching and affirming self-statements.

Let's take the example of Christine who decides to reveal to her partner Tony that, as a child, she was sexually abused by an uncle. Christine has never told anyone this before. Christine's calming self-statements include: 'Calm down' and 'Breathe slowly and regularly.' Christine's coaching self-statements include: 'Tell Tony that I have something important about my past that I want to share with him' and 'Be honest about the details of what happened and how I now feel.' Christine's affirming self-statements include: 'I'm a valuable person in my own right' and 'I have some good skills at sharing sensitive information and handling other people's reactions to it.'

Often partners require good self-talk when receiving disclosures. For example, if Tony starts feeling anxious when hearing Christine's disclosures, he can tell himself to calm down and use his listening skills.

## Creating visual images

You can use creating visual images skills to increase intimacy. For example, by using your imagination, you can develop a better understanding of another's life experiences, both past and present. In addition, you can visually rehearse how best to reach out to another. Such imaginary rehearsal can have the twin goals of calming your anxiety and increasing your chances of behaving competently.

You can use visual images to remember your partner when you are parted, be it for a working day or for longer periods. Such visual remembrance may stimulate you to contact them and ask how they are going. You can also use visualizing skills to strengthen your motivation for positive displays of intimacy by imagining another's pleasure in receiving what you say and do. In addition, you can inhibit actions that impede intimacy by imagining their negative consequences: for example, criticizing your partner in public.

Together you and your partner can develop intimacy by sharing your dreams and fantasies. You can also develop visual pictures of life you want to lead, both now and in future.

## Creating explanations

You can offer all sorts of reasons why you are less than successful in developing and maintaining intimacy in your relationships. Illustrative explanations for insufficiently reaching out to another person include: 'It's my nature', 'It's my upbringing', 'It's my culture', 'It's my sex-role conditioning', and 'I've tried to get through in the past, so it's no use trying again.' Illustrative explanations for not receiving another's intimacy include: 'She/he is manipulating me', 'She/he is trying to gain power over me', 'She/he never listens to me', 'I don't really care about her/him (when underneath I really do care)' and 'It's up to her/him to make the first move to improve communication in our relationship.'

If any of the above explanations are ways in which you block intimacy, challenge their accuracy. Often what happens is that people convert partial truths into whole truths. For instance, you may have been brought up in a family of under-disclosers. However, that is no reason why you cannot now assume responsibility for developing your intimacy skills.

In addition, you can challenge the accuracy of your explanations for not receiving another's disclosures. For instance, you can challenge the explanation 'She/he never listens to me?' by asking yourself questions like: 'How well do I disclose and listen to her/him?' and 'Can I think of any occasions where she/he has listened to me?' and 'Why should I let how I think and behave be controlled by how she/he thinks and behaves?'

## Creating expectations

You can be poor at predicting the risks and gains of intimacy with yourself, reaching out, receiving another's intimacy, and developing and maintaining yours and your partner's pattern of intimacy. Fears attached to knowing yourself better include acknowledging existential anxiety, guilt, vulnerability, your shadow side and ways in which you have fallen short both of parental teaching and of your potential. Fears attached to intimacy with others include losing yourself in the relationship, having your disclosures used against you, breaches of confidentiality, getting badly hurt and losing your partner when the relationship ends. Fears attached to changing interactive intimacy patterns include being taken advantage of and facing the unwillingness or inability of your partner to change.

You require the ability to be realistic about assessing the gains of seeking greater intimacy as well as the risks. You can ask yourself questions such as: 'What is the upside as well as the downside of risking greater intimacy?' 'Where is the evidence to support or negate my predictions?' 'What is the level of trust in the relationship?' 'What are my strengths and where are my support factors if my efforts at increasing intimacy get rejected?' 'If my initial efforts at greater intimacy get rejected, what are the pros and cons of trying again?' 'What communication skills do I need to deepen or repair the intimacy level of the relationship?' (see Activity 7.4).

## ACTIVITY 7.4      Develop my mind skills for expressing intimacy |

First do each part of this activity on your own. Then, if appropriate, discuss with your partner, another or others.

*Mind skills*

The following are six mind skills:

1. Creating rules
2. Creating perceptions
3. Creating self-talk

4. Creating visual images
5. Creating explanations
6. Creating expectations.

## Part A  Intimacy with myself

1. Assess your mind skills strengths and weaknesses.
2. Identify your main weakness or weaknesses and specify the steps you intend taking to change it/them.

## Part B  Reaching out

1. Assess your mind skills strengths and weaknesses.
2. Identify your main weakness or weaknesses and specify the steps you intend taking to change it/them.

## Part C  Receiving intimacy

1. Assess your mind skills strengths and weaknesses.
2. Identify your main weakness or weaknesses and specify the steps you intend taking to change it/them.

## Part D  Interactive pattern of intimacy

Focus on a specific relationship.

1. Assess your own and your partner's mind skills strengths and weaknesses.
2. Identify your main weakness or weaknesses and specify the steps you intend taking to change it/them.

---

**ACTIVITY 7.5**                    **Group discussion: intimacy skills**

This is intended as a group activity, though it may be done individually or in pairs.

For each part:

1. Spend five to ten minutes answering the question in groups of three or four.

2. Each subgroup shares its findings with the whole group.
3. The whole group ranks the four most important skills from the most important to the least important.

## Part A  Reaching out

List the four most important skills partners can use to reach out to one another.

## Part B  Receiving intimacy

List the four most important skills partners can use to receive intimacy from one another.

## Part C  Maintaining intimacy

List the four most important skills partners can use to maintain intimacy in their relationship with each other.

# Companionship skills

**Chapter outcomes**
By studying and doing the activities in this chapter you should:

- understand what is companionship
- understand what is personal space
- know why both companionship and personal space are important
- know about some activities for companionship
- know some communication skills for companionship
- understand how to use some mind skills to enhance companionship.

Romantic love, where doing just about everything is fun, can make it seem that partners have more in common with one another than is the case. Once romantic love runs out, those 'fun' things, for instance, going out to dinner, do not necessarily produce the sense of closeness that they did at the beginning. Partners need to ask how similar they are in how much free time they like to have and how they spend it. Hamburg (2000) thinks it particularly important that partners have at least one shared serious interest. Other issues relevant to companionship are the amount of time each partner wants to spend free time alone, and the amount of time each partner wants to spend time alone as a couple rather than together with other couples. Partners can also vary in whether they want to do expensive versus inexpensive things and exciting versus quiet things. Partners need to feel reasonably comfortable with how they decide such issues.

The amount of free time and what you do in it is also about revitalizing yourself and your relationship. However, there is a pervasive trend for people to work more that reduces time and energy for other activities (Haworth and Lewis, 2005). If you and/or your partner 'work around the clock', you either may or may not gain the tangible rewards of high productivity. What is more certain is that your relationship is likely to suffer. Glasser (1995: 34) observes: 'The key to friendship is sharing and expanding common interests and, at the risk of being repetitious, friendship is the key to a good marriage.' Your relationship is more likely to stay fresh and be fun if you are creative about how you spend time together. However, you also need the freedom to engage in some separate activities. Though couples differ in the mix between doing things together and separately, those that are successful tend to arrive at solutions which are acceptable to both parties.

Tania and Vince have been married for over ten years. They are committed Christians and spend time working for the local church. They also have separate activities too: for instance, Vince plays golf and Tania does embroidery. Every evening when they come home from work they spend at least an hour having a drink and talking over the main events, thoughts and feelings of their days. On fine days they sit in their garden to do this. They are each other's best friends.

Jon and Lucie have been happily married for nearly 20 years and have three children. Each family member plays a musical instrument. Often the family makes music and sings together. Jon also plays the guitar in a rock band that does gigs in the local area. Lucie is not threatened when Jon does this. She sees it as a chance for him to have space away from the family and a complete break from his factory work.

Partners often spend a large proportion of their lives in leisure activities. Argyle (1992) provided the following breakdown of average daily time spent on non-work activities. These figures come from the British General Household Survey, which interviews about 20,000 households each year.

| | |
|---|---|
| Domestic work (including child care) | 3 hours 42 minutes |
| Personal care (including sleeping, eating) | 10 hours 38 minutes |
| Leisure outside home | 1 hour 39 minutes |
| Leisure at home | 4 hours 3 minutes. |

Survey findings indicate that British men and women enjoy different quantities of leisure time: men 380 minutes and women 307 minutes. Of their total leisure time, men spent 110 minutes outside the home and 270 minutes inside. The corresponding figures for women were 89 and 218 minutes inside (Argyle, 1992). Haworth and Lewis (2005: 71) reinforce this finding: 'Many studies have shown that, even when both partners are working, women still make a significantly greater contribution to domestic tasks, and there are key differences between men's ability to preserve personal leisure time, and the much more limited capacity of women to do so.'

# PATTERNS OF COMPANIONSHIP

## Togetherness

How can doing things together strengthen and deepen your relationship? First, you find out more about one another's likes and dislikes and whether you are still compatible. You discover whether you each enjoy spending time with the other. Second, your companionship helps both you and your partner avoid loneliness. Third, many domestic activities become less wearisome if jointly performed. Fourth, leisure activities enable you to play, have fun and enjoy each other's company. Arguably, partners who play together, stay together. When dating, couples engage in many rewarding leisure activities, for instance, going out to dinner and to movies. In long-term relationships you still require amusement and diversion from the daily grind. You continue needing opportunities to smile, laugh and be humorous. Fifth, doing things together provides a vehicle for your ongoing relationship conversation. Shared activities have an emotional as well as a functional purpose. Sixth, you can avoid boredom and find meaning in leisure. Seventh, sharing activities can be a source of strength during rough times in your relationship. Such activities may help you keep in contact despite feelings of hurt, pain and anger.

## Personal space

In the context of this chapter, personal space means the freedom to pursue your own activities, interests and friendships independent of your partner. Each of you comes to a relationship with a history of previously developed activities. Many of these activities you can share with your partner, but there may be others where your interests differ. In addition, as time goes by each of you may develop new and different pursuits.

In good relationships, the distinction between personal and shared activities becomes blurred. For example, partners can be sitting in the same room, one reading the paper and the other knitting and both enjoying each other's company. Furthermore, partners can be doing different things in different parts of the house or flat and still provide each other with a sense of companionship.

Partners can take pleasure in the stimulation the other derives from their separate interests. The relationship is strengthened by the fact that it is not based on the 'joined-at-the hip' or 'ball-and-chain' principles. Each partner feels free to develop separately as well as together. Furthermore, separate interests can add spice and stimulation to relationships. In addition, sometimes it is a good idea if you can witness your partner being valued by other people for part of themselves not shown in your relationship.

Talking to a carbon copy of yourself is intensely dull. People living in close contact sometimes can see too much of each other. Separate leisure pursuits can prevent relationships from becoming unhealthily intense and suffocating. Allowing one another personal space can foster rather than militate against enjoying shared activities.

## Interactive patterns of companionship

The following are three main interactive patterns of companionship.

1. *Total togetherness.* Lazarus (1985: 31) remarks about total togetherness: 'This represents the romantic ideal where two people merge so completely that they become as one. In practice, where this is possible, it would probably result in emotional suffocation.' Enmeshment is another term for total togetherness. Lazarus advocates due consideration for your partner, especially on major decisions, at the same time as some latitude to make unilateral decisions. Total togetherness is more likely to be a problem in English-speaking western cultures, with their emphasis on the nuclear family and possessive individualism – 'my spouse is my property' – than in eastern cultures, where more value is placed on group harmony and the extended family.

2. *Much distance.* Partners mainly go their separate ways. For instance, Angie's main recreational interest is gardening and Colin's is boating. This might be fine, but they also differ so much in their pattern of other recreational activities that overall there is much distance and very little common ground in how they spend their leisure time. Furthermore, Angie and Colin take little interest in hearing about each other's recreational interests.

3. *Mainly togetherness, but some personal space.* Partners engage in some recreational activities together, but respect each other's difference and wish to develop as separate persons. Enjoying personal leisure activities strengthens them individually and as a couple. Lazarus (1985) suggests 75–80 per cent togetherness represents an excellent marriage. Many couples settle for less than this, for instance, 60–70 per cent, yet still enjoy strong relationships. Some emotionally close couples may spend still fewer hours together, but enjoy their quality. Shared activities in themselves do not guarantee satisfaction. Habituation can lead to boredom. Togetherness is sometimes enhanced by partners sharing stimulating or exciting activities.

These are balanced or symmetrical companionship patterns where each partner either wants the same as the other or, willingly or unwillingly, has adjusted to the other's wishes. Companionship patterns may also be unbalanced, with one partner seeking more recreational investment than the other is prepared to give. The total togetherness and much distance companionship patterns are especially vulnerable if either or both partners change in incompatible ways. Sometimes outside factors cause one partner to have more leisure time than the other, for example, either differences in job demands or if one partner becomes unemployed.

## COMPANIONSHIP ACTIVITIES

What activities can partners jointly engage in to bring them the rewards of companionship? Much of your relationship will centre around routine activities. A portion of these activities is domestic chores, some of which you do together. Other activities may be more enjoyable parts of your daily routine, like having meals together, being in bed, watching television or listening to music. Still others may be special events – for instance, eating out or going to a concert.

MacPhillamy and Lewinsohn developed a Pleasant Events Schedule of 320 items (Lewinsohn *et al.*, 1986). They ask respondents to rate each item according to how often each event happened in the past month and how enjoyable or rewarding it was in this period. As in the Pleasant Events Schedule, frequency and the degree of pleasure each of you derives from different joint activities are two major considerations when assessing the amount and quality of companionship in your relationship. For instance, frequently watching large amounts of television may provide only moderate pleasure and a limited quality of companionship.

## Companionship at home

The home-based activities discussed here relate more to leisure than to domestic work. Watching television is the main leisure activity at home. In Britain, women spend on average four and a quarter hours and men three and three-quarter hours a day watching it (Argyle, 1992). Television watching can both promote and impede companionship. Couples can share their interest and enjoyment in the same programmes. On the other hand, too much television watching may interfere with couples conversing and engaging in more active rewarding activities. What can you do together at home to enjoy each other's company. Box 8.1 provides some suggestions. Some of these activities may be done individually as well as together.

---

### Box 8.1   Home-based companionship activities

| | | |
|---|---|---|
| Art activities | Having coffee/tea | Playing with pets |
| Conversing in bed | Having sex | Praying together |
| Cooking | Listening to CDs/cassettes | Reading |
| Craft work | Listening to the radio | Singing |
| DIY | Massaging/back rubbing | Sitting outdoors |
| Eating snacks | Meditating/doing yoga | Sleeping |
| Entertaining friends | Petting/necking | Sunbathing |
| Entertaining relatives | Planning holidays | Talking about people |
| Gardening | Playing indoor games | Telling jokes |
| Having a bath/shower | Playing music | Telling funny stories |
| Having a drink | Playing with computers | Watching television |

# Companionship outside the home

Couples spend much less leisure time outside than inside the home. Activities that get couples out of the house are important. They provide variety and stimulus to the relationship. They can also prevent otherwise enjoyable home-based activities from becoming monotonous. Many outside activities are extensions of home-based activities: for example, giving and receiving entertainment with friends and relatives. There are limits to which you can pursue many activities in the home, for instance, fitness activities and playing music. Other activities are impossible to do at home, for instance, horse-riding. Box 8.2 provides suggestions for outside the home companionship activities (see Activity 8.1).

---

**Box 8.2   Outside the home companionship activities**

| | | |
|---|---|---|
| Amateur drama | Driving | Picnicking |
| Amateur music | Enjoying nature | Pop concerts |
| Art activities | Evening classes | Rock-climbing |
| Athletics | Field trips/nature walks | Shopping |
| Attending concert/opera/ | Fishing | Skiing |
| ballet | Folk dancing | Snooker/billiards/ |
| Badminton | Gambling | pool |
| Barbecuing | Golf | Squash |
| Basketball | Health clubs/saunas | Surfing |
| Birdwatching | Helping someone | Swimming |
| Bingo | Hiking/rambling | Table tennis |
| Boating | Holidaying | Tennis |
| Bowling | Horseriding | Visiting the countryside |
| Camping | Going to parties | Visiting downtown |
| Card playing | Going to pubs | Visiting museums |
| Choral societies/choirs | Going to restaurants | Visiting friends |
| Church activities | Going to talks/lectures | Visiting historic sites |
| Computer games | Going to the theatre | Visiting libraries |
| Craft activities | Jogging | Visiting parks |
| Cinema | Leisure classes | Visiting relatives |
| Community service | Looking at stars/ | Visiting the seaside |
| Cricket | moon | Voluntary work |
| Cycling | Motorcycling | Walking |
| Dancing | Nightclubbing | Walking the dog |
| Darts | Overseas travel | Watching sports events |
| Discos | Photography | Yoga/meditation classes |

**ACTIVITY 8.1**              **Identify and choose companionship and personal activities**

This activity assumes you are in a relationship. Complete Part A on your own and Part B with your partner.

## Part A  Identify activities

*Companionship activities*

1. Using the following rating scale:

   0  no good as a companionship activity
   1  I do or would enjoy this as a companionship activity
   2  I do or would very much enjoy this as a companionship activity

   (a) Rate each item in Table 8.1 Illustrative home-based companionship activities.
   (b) Rate each item in Table 8.2 Illustrative outside the home companionship activities.

2. For each activity you rated 1 or 2, estimate how many times you engaged in it in the past week?
3. How satisfied are you with your current pattern and frequency of companionship activities?

*Personal activities*

1. Using the following rating scale:

   0  no good as a personal activity
   1  I do or would enjoy this as a personal activity
   2  I do or would very much enjoy this as a personal activity

   (a) Rate each home-based item in Table 8.1 that you would prefer to do on your own, at least sometimes.
   (b) Rate each outside the home item in Table 8.2 that you would prefer to do on your own, at least sometimes.

2. For each activity in Tables 8.1 and 8.2 you rated 1 or 2, estimate how many times you engaged in it in the past week?
3. How satisfied are you with your current pattern and frequency of personal activities?

## Part B  Choose activities

1. Share and discuss your answers to both sections of Part A of this activity.
2. Share and discuss your views on the balance of togetherness and personal space in your relationship.

3. Share and discuss your views on the balance of home-based and outside the home companionship and personal activities in your relationship.
4. Discuss how, if at all, you might increase the satisfaction each of you can obtain from existing or new companionship activities. If appropriate, choose new companionship activities and drop or lessen some current activities.
5. Discuss how, if at all, you might increase the satisfaction each of you can obtain from existing or new personal activities. If appropriate, choose new personal activities and drop or lessen some current activities.
6. Together develop a step-by-step plan to initiate and/or develop, during the next week or month, one companionship activity.
7. Either individually or together, develop a plan to initiate and/or develop during the next week or month one personal activity each.

---

## SOME COMMUNICATION SKILLS
## FOR COMPANIONSHIP

The following are some communication skills that you can use to increase the quantity and quality of companionship in your relationship. Many of the mind skills discussed in the next section influence how effectively you can act.

### Manage time effectively

Both individually and as a couple you may be poor at managing time. The following are two examples of people with poor skills at doing so:

Diane, age 19, is disorganized in her work as a student. She never feels on top of her studying and complains about lack of time to spend with her boyfriend Rick, 20.

Paula, 33, is a computer programmer and her husband Andre, 30, is a car salesperson. Both have busy schedules that allow for some spare time. However, Paula and Andre are poor at letting each other know their schedules and coordinating them so that they can spend recreation time together.

You may, like Diane, think that being insufficiently organized about your work interferes with your personal life. If so, you can try and gain more control over your work by listing what you have to do, setting priorities and timetabling when you will do them. In addition to your timetabling skills, you may require other skills like getting started on assignments skills and saying no to requests that help you to avoid work. Some individuals are very organized in their work. However, they place such high value on work that they need to timetable more recreation and organize their work accordingly.

Couples like Paula and Andre need to coordinate how they manage time. A starting point might be for both partners to monitor how they currently spend time by filling out for the next seven days a timetable broken down by hours. Then partners can compare timetables and discuss how best to spend more time together.

## Schedule activities and abide by contracts

Apart from scheduling work time, partners require skills at scheduling domestic chores, time together and personal space. Much of this scheduling can be achieved by informal discussion. However, some couples require a more systematic approach to scheduling joint activities. For instance, couples trying to repair a relationship by increasing the amount of shared pleasant activities should agree not only on which activities to share, but also on when and how frequently to do them. Then they can consider timetabling agreed companionship activities for the next week, few weeks or a month.

Each partner's agreement to participating in the activity at a given time constitutes a form of contract with the other. Especially when relationships are fragile, realize that keeping or breaking such contracts increases or decreases trust. Consequently, renegotiate agreements rather than break them unilaterally. Misunderstandings may be avoided if you write down agreements. This may just be a simple matter of writing agreed activities in your diaries. A more formal approach is writing out agreements in contract form, with or without signing them. Then you can post such contracts prominently.

## Gather information

Often partners can gain enrichment in life by gathering more information about available activities. People vary greatly in how good they are at this. Possibly more attention is paid to teaching people job search information skills than leisure search information skills. Once you have identified activities you may be interested in, you can then require information as to what they involve, how difficult or easy it is to learn them, and what facilities there are in your locality for participating in them.

Doug and Carol, a couple in their late twenties, think they might enjoy playing tennis. Neither has played much tennis in the past. They decide to gather information systematically about the following: where are the private and public courts in the area and how good they are, the charges and reputations of the tennis clubs that have good courts, and who are the good coaches in the area and how much they charge. Sources of information about where and how good the local tennis courts are include the classified section of the telephone directory, phoning the council, getting in touch with national or local tennis associations, looking at maps of the area, asking friends and acquaintances, and going along and seeing the different facilities. Doug and Carol apply the same systematic information-gathering skills to finding out about tennis coaches.

## Develop skills for specific activities

Some joint activities, like walking, you can do without assistance. However, there are many other activities that are more enjoyable both functionally and socially if you possess a certain level of skill. Examples abound of shared activities that require a commitment to attaining a certain level of performance to gain full enjoyment from them: for instance, bridge, craft activities and most outdoor sports. Continuing the above example, Doug and Carol decided that they would find tennis more enjoyable if they took some tennis lessons together. To do this, they joined a tennis club that had a combination of reasonable fees, good courts and a strongly recommended coach. They were confident that once their tennis improved they possessed the socializing skills to integrate into the club. Like Carol and Doug, you and your partner may need to put in the time and effort to develop the skills of specific activities. In addition, each of you needs to maintain a minimum level of skills for your mutual enjoyment.

Partners can help each other develop skills for shared activities. When learning a new skill you can offer support to and practise with each other. Sometimes, one of you already has an existing interest, for example, folk dancing, in which you can help your partner. Where there are obvious imbalances in domestic duties, by pulling more of his or her weight the less domestically active partner can free up the other partner's time and energy to develop specific skills.

## Develop socializing as a couple skill

Some couples find that, for various reasons, their social life becomes increasingly restricted. Sometimes this restriction reflects either or both partners possessing poor time management and activity scheduling skills. Partners may also restrict their social life when there are serious difficulties in their relationship. On other occasions, a restricted social life may be due to factors such as moving house or country, language difficulties, parenting responsibilities and shortage of money.

Partners enter relationships with previous friendships and commitments. You may decide to socialize together with some of these people, socialize separately with others and see much less of the remainder. In addition, partners require skills of networking and making new friends. While retaining your individuality, partners need to socialize as a couple. For example, you may require the skills of preparing and serving food and drink. Partners also require conversational skills that support and enhance one another, for example, bringing the other into the conversation, knowing when to keep quiet and retrieving mistakes. In most social relationships, be careful about seeming to criticize one another and making intimate disclosures. However, partners who develop genuinely close relationships with other individuals or couples may feel safe in talking more openly about their relationship.

## Be rewarding to one another

Partners are more likely to continue being companions if each finds what you do together to be rewarding. You can reward each other by making many shared activities fun. For instance, you can use humour to see the funny side of situations, tell jokes and stories and clown about. You can show enjoyment at each other's pleasure and achievements. You can express appreciation for each other's companionship. In addition, you can be a receptive audience as you share thoughts and feelings about what you do.

Some partners may need to develop some of the above skills. All partners need to maintain them. When relationships run into trouble, partners can go some way to repairing the relationship by relearning how to have fun together again. One approach is to try to recapture some of the magic from fun things you did when courting.

## Assertively request and decline companionship

Do not expect your partner to be an expert mind reader of how much and what sort of companionship you want. Ineffective ways of requesting companionship include silence, complaining, nagging and become aggressive. It is preferable to specifically, tactfully and, if appropriate, firmly and persistently request what you want. In addition, you can provide your partner with feedback that improves the kind of companionship she or he already offers: for instance, what kind of affection you like receiving in public.

Partners can also assertively set limits on the amount of companionship they are willing to provide. When Iris's husband Steve retired, she became frustrated with his always wanting her to be available to do things with and for him. She saw herself as being placed in an unwanted mothering role to a dependent child. Accordingly, she set limits on what she was prepared to do. In addition, Iris encouraged Steve to develop some interests of his own and share more of the domestic chores.

Sometimes, you may need to decline requests to attend events or participate in specific activities that you do not enjoy. Lazarus (1985) gives the example of Fred and Kay, whom he was seeing for marital therapy. A problem in their relationship centred around attendance at cocktail parties, which Kay loved and Fred hated. Fred had no objection to Kay going to cocktail parties on her own. Once Kay addressed her anxiety about how she could explain Fred's absence by her side, both she and Fred found a new freedom that spread to other areas of their relationship. Compromise, whereby you limit the number of football matches or cocktail parties you go to, is another way of assertively setting limits on companionship. Alternatively, you may trade presence or absence of companionship at football matches for presence or absence of companionship at cocktail parties (McKay *et al.*, 1994).

## Develop your own and support your partner's personal activities

Many of the skills already discussed, for instance, managing time and gathering information, are relevant to developing your own personal activities. Partners can also support each other in gaining and maintaining enrichment from personal activities. For instance, you can be a sounding board for your partner's ideas about engaging in new activities; support them in taking the first steps to learn new activities, either on their own or with others; do domestic chores to free up their time for personal interests, for instance, preparing a meal when your partner has an evening class; be an audience for their achievements, such as attending their amateur dramatics presentations; and share their enjoyment and frustrations. You can also respect your partner's wishes to set some limits on talking about what they are doing. Showing support and interest differs from being nosy. Your partner may request some emotional privacy along with space for personal activities (see Activity 8.2).

---

**ACTIVITY 8.2**     **Develop my communication skills for companionship**

---

This activity assumes you are in a relationship. Do Part A on your own and Part B with your partner.

## Part A  My communication skills for companionship

1. Assess your strengths and weaknesses in each of the following communication skills for companionship:

   (a) Managing time effectively
   (b) Scheduling activities and abiding by contracts
   (c) Gathering information
   (d) Developing skills for specific activities
   (e) Socializing as a couple skills
   (f) Being rewarding to each other
   (g) Assertively requesting and declining companionship
   (h) Developing your own and supporting your partner's personal activities.

2. If appropriate, identify one or more of your poor companionship skills and develop a plan to change how you communicate. In your plan specify:

   (a) Your goals, including a time frame
   (b) The steps you intend taking to attain each of your goals
   (c) How you will monitor your progress.

## Part B  Working together

1. Share and discuss your answers to Part A of this exercise.
2. If appropriate, identify one or more of your poor companionship skills and develop a plan to work together to change how you communicate. In your plan, specify:

   (a) your joint goals, including a time frame
   (b) the steps you as a couple intend taking to attain each of your joint goals
   (c) how you will jointly monitor your progress.

---

# SOME MIND SKILLS FOR COMPANIONSHIP

The following are some mind skills that can influence how well people offer and receive companionship.

## Creating rules

You and your partner, both individually and as a couple, may possess unrealistic rules concerning companionship and personal space. Often you may have an unrealistic rule for yourself that you expect to hold good for your partner as well. Following are examples of companionship rules that may be unnecessarily rigid.

*Personal rules*

- I must never do anything without my partner.
- I must always be approved for my companionship.
- I must never be lazy.
- I must always do everything very well indeed.
- She/he must like what I like.
- Work must come before leisure (or vice versa).
- I must never be bored.
- I must never be alone.

*Relationship rules*

- We must do everything together.
- We must mean everything to each other.
- We must not differ in what we want to do.
- All leisure decisions must be jointly made.
- We must never intrude on each other's personal space.
- Good husbands do household repairs/good wives do the laundry.
- We must never be bored.
- We must be the life and soul of the party.

As with any other unrealistic rules, dealing with unrealistic companionship rules requires identifying them, challenging their logic, and restating them in a more realistic format. For instance, Helen and Kenny, both aged 18, have been in a relationship for three months and are starting to feel suffocated by thinking they must do everything together. Rather than blame each other and then break up, they decide to question how rational is their rule: 'We must do everything together.' Following are some questions that they can ask themselves:

- Where is the evidence that we must do everything together?
- What will be the consequences if we continue doing everything together?
- Do we expect other couples to do everything together?
- Is there room for any acknowledgement of difference in our relationship?
- What is the role of personal space in our relationship?

By challenging their relationship rule 'We must do everything together' Helen and Kenny decide that they want to replace it with something more realistic. They agree on the following restatement: 'We care for each other very much and are committed to our relationship. We want to spend most of our free time together. However, we support each other in pursuing individual interests as well. We can jointly decide the balance we want between togetherness and personal space.'

## Creating perceptions

*Perceive yourself accurately*

How accurately do you perceive your attitude towards recreation? For instance, you may talk about having fun, but underneath consider that recreation is a waste of time (Lazarus *et al.*, 1993). As a result, you and your partner may fail to enjoy the amount and range of shared activities that could make your relationship more mutually satisfying. You may notice the signs of stress in others, but fail to notice them in yourself. Instead of being fun to be with, you are tense and irritable. Alternatively, you may be so focused on your own recreation that you fail to perceive the effect this has on others: for instance, drinking or gambling away the family finances and/or expecting your partner to act as your domestic help.

How good a companion are you and how do you know? As relationships move out of their 'honeymoon' period, you may become a less good companion (Beck, 1988). You can become wrapped up in your career and interests and take your partner's companionship for granted. Together you may progressively invest less of yourselves in your relationship. Watch out for signs that personal space is turning into interpersonal distance before this process becomes irrevocable.

Anxiety can cause you to be a less good companion than you otherwise might be. For example, at two extremes you may either avoid social activities or compulsively engage in them. You may also have tendencies towards controlling what your partner does and says rather than supporting her or him. In addition, you may inappropriately compete with your partner in activities that are intended to be relaxing.

### *Perceive your partner accurately*

How accurately do you perceive your partner in the area of companionship? You may inaccurately perceive your partner's wishes for companionship and personal space and also your partner's perception of what kind of companionship and personal space you want. Asking them what companionship they want is one way of collecting evidence and reality testing your perceptions. You can also tactfully tell them what sort of companionship you like. In addition, you require sensitivity to their reactions to the quantity and quality of companionship you provide. For instance, you may be quick to sense their pleasure and poor at sensing their displeasure and resentment. Alternatively, you may be hypersensitive to signs that what you do is never good enough.

Especially during periods of strain in your relationship, you need to beware of negatively labelling your partner as 'selfish', 'insensitive' and 'always wanting his or her way' and 'never taking your feelings into account'. If anything, there may be a bias towards perceiving a partner's companionship too positively at the start of a relationship and too negatively as the relationship develops (Beck, 1988). At times you may need to search for positive evidence and give each other the benefit of the doubt in ambiguous situations.

### Creating self-talk

Often people feel anxious about changing their pattern of activities. Take the example of Ellie and Dave who want to become more socially active and decide to give a dinner party. As the event comes nearer, both become increasingly anxious about its success. Ellie worries about her culinary skills and Dave about his conversational skills. However, using creating self-talk skills should help them contain their anxiety and stay task oriented. As mentioned earlier, creating self-talk skills consist of making calming, coaching and affirming self-statements.

Both Ellie and Dave can tell themselves the following calming self-statements: 'Stay calm' and 'Breathe slowly and regularly.' Sample coaching self-statements for Ellie include: 'Prepare as much as possible in advance' and 'Make a list of things I need to do when the guests arrive, so I don't forget.' Sample coaching self-statements for Dave include: 'Prepare in advance a number of topics that I can talk about' and 'Make sure to use active listening skills.' In addition, Ellie and Dave can each affirm themselves with self-statements reminding them about their strengths and about occasions in the past where they have used good culinary or conversational skills.

## Creating visual images

Creating visual images skills can help increase your participation in and enjoyment of companionship activities. For example, visualizing can help you choose what you want to do by imagining what it would be like doing it. You can increase motivation for specific shared activities by picturing the rewards of doing them. Alternatively, you can lessen your motivation with negative images.

Sometimes due to anxiety people get negative images about activities they might otherwise enjoy. Mental relaxation and mental rehearsal are two visualizing skills you can use, either singly or sequentially, to manage your anxiety when thinking about or shortly before engaging in an activity. One mental relaxation technique is to close your eyes and visualize a restful scene like lying on a beach on a warm sunny day without a care in the world. You hold this image until you feel more relaxed. With mental rehearsal, you visually rehearse performing the anxiety-generating activity competently. Often mental rehearsal is best performed in conjunction with self-talk, consisting of calming, coping and affirming self-statements.

## Creating explanations

Partners differ in the explanations they offer for the quantity and quality of companionship in their relationship. Following are some explanations for offering little companionship in the relationship:

- 'It's my nature.' One or both partners consider themselves loners or unsociable by nature.
- 'It's my upbringing.' Life has taught me to place a high value on personal space relative to togetherness.
- 'Its my sex.' Either or both partners are only prepared to engage in activities characteristic of their sexes: for instance, she will not go to football matches and he refuses to take tea with her female friends.
- 'It's my career.' My career is so important and demanding that I have neither the time, interest nor energy to offer and receive much companionship.
- 'It's my health.' I am under so much stress/ill health that I wish to avoid further demands on my energy.

- *'It's my parents/children.'* The perceived demands of looking after parents and children take precedence over maintaining companionship with a partner.

Below are some explanations for not trying to change an unsatisfactory level of companionship:

- *'My partner is too possessive.'* Either or both partners perceive it is safer to keep their distance from the controlling tendencies in the other than to engage in much companionship.
- *'We've nothing in common.'* Partners perceive their differences to be so wide that either or both does not wish to surmount them.
- *'We've tried before.'* Partners may have made previous unsuccessful half-hearted and whole-hearted attempts to rekindle the companionship in their relationship.
- *'My partner is not prepared to change her/his ways.'* Here one partner casts herself or himself as the victim of a rigid partner, hence conveniently avoiding all responsibility for the couple's companionship problems.
- *'She/he is having an affair.'* One partner, rightly or wrongly, perceives the other partner's withdrawal of companionship as due to an affair.

Partners can challenge the adequacy of their explanations to assess how much truth they contain. For instance, the explanation 'We have nothing in common' can be challenged by looking for things the couple have had in common from the start of their relationship up until now. Even the explanation 'She/he is having an affair' can be challenged. First, the affair may not exist. Second, even if it does exist it may result from and not be the cause of lack of companionship. Third, if the couple addresses their relationship problems they may still achieve a tolerable level of companionship.

## Creating expectations

For various reasons, partners can have inaccurate expectations about the risks of maintaining their companionship behaviour. For example, Jock, 28, inaccurately predicts that his partner, Tony, 27, will stay in their relationship if he continues his workaholic behaviour. Brian, 42, inaccurately predicts that his wife Sally, 35, will happily continue supplying the food and playing second fiddle to him on social occasions. Sally is going to a feminist assertiveness group and Brian's days of ruling the roost are numbered. Both Jock and Brian require greater sensitivity to their partners as persons so that they can create expectations about risk accurately.

Partners can also create inaccurate expectations of the gains from changing their companionship behaviour. In the above examples, Jock may have been afraid of jeopardizing his career by spending more time with Tony. However, had he and Tony worked out a mutually acceptable compromise, Jock might have been happier at home and at work. Similarly, Brian and Sally could possibly find a mutually acceptable formula whereby each feels valued. In short, Jock and Brian require better skills of assessing both risk and gain. They also require good skills of negotiating differences.

Frequently partners are anxious about trying new companionship activities inside or outside the home. Earlier I gave the example of Ellie and Dave who, for different reasons, worried about holding a successful dinner party at their home. Many partners fear taking up activities outside the home such as swimming, dancing, golf or going to evening classes. Again, focusing on the gains of trying something different and not just on the risks can help you feel more confident. Possessing some of the other mind skills mentioned above, for instance, creating rules and creating self-talk, can contribute to optimism about your level of performance and about attaining desired outcomes (Bandura, 1986; Seligman, 2002) (see Activity 8.3).

---

**ACTIVITY 8.3**           **Develop my mind skills for companionship**

---

This activity assumes you are in a relationship. Complete Part A on your own and Part B with your partner.

## Part A My mind skills

*Mind skills*

The following are six mind skills

1. Creating rules
2. Creating perceptions
3. Creating self-talk
4. Creating visual images
5. Creating explanations
6. Creating expectations.

*Offering companionship*

1. Assess your mind skills.
2. Identify your main poor skill or skills and specify the steps you intend taking to change it/them.

*Receiving companionship*

1. Assess your mind skills.
2. Identify your main poor skill or skills and specify the steps you intend taking to change it/them.

*Developing personal activities*

1. Assess your mind skills.
2. Identify your main poor skill or skills and specify the steps you intend taking to change it/them.

## Part B  Working together

1. Share and discuss your answers to Part A.
2. Focus on your interactive pattern of companionship and examine how you influence one another through your feelings, thoughts and actions.
3. Identify your main poor mind skills, if any, in developing and maintaining an effective companionship pattern and specify the steps you intend taking to change it/them.

---

**ACTIVITY 8.4**         **Group discussion: companionship skills** |

This is intended as a group exercise, though it may be done individually or in pairs.

For each part:

1. Spend five to ten minutes answering the question in groups of three or four.
2. Each subgroup shares its findings with the whole group.
3. The whole group ranks the four most important skills from the most important to the least important.

## Part A  Offering companionship

List the four most important skills people can use in offering companionship to a partner.

## Part B  Receiving companionship

List the four most important skills people can use in receiving companionship from a partner.

## Part C  Personal activities

List the four most important skills that partners can use in developing personal activities in their relationship.

---

# 9

# Sexual relationship skills

**Chapter outcomes**
By studying and doing the activities in this chapter you should:

- know about defining sexual relating
- have some idea about frequency of sex
- know about sexual equality
- understand the sexual response cycle
- know about different sexual activities
- know about some communication skills for sexual relationships
- know about some mind skills.

## INTRODUCTION

Sexual relationships are fraught with pleasures and difficulties: for instance, each of you may have different sexual appetites and tastes. In addition, sexual relating takes place in the context of your overall relationship in which numerous other skills are important: for instance, intimacy and companionship skills.

## Defining sexual relating

In its most basic form sexual relating is a physical activity involving mutual genital contact for the purpose of procreating the species. Other terms for this activity are sexual intercourse, copulation, having sex and a four-letter word for intercourse ending in the letter k (if you think it is 'talk', then you are wrong!). However, sexual intercourse is far from the only kind of sex act: others include, oral sex and masturbating. Numerous behaviours are sexual, but do not constitute specific sex acts: for instance, flirting, dating and having romantic dinners. Furthermore, the whole of your body can be viewed as an erogenous zone, not just your genitals.

Hamburg (2000) states that the sexual dimension in relationships has three components: comfort with sexuality, interest in sex and sexual style. Comfort with sexuality means how relaxed you and your partner are about doing all the various things that are connected with sex. In addition to physical sex, this includes thinking, reading, watching movies, telling jokes and talking about it. Interest in sex means how preoccupied each partner is with sex and how often you want to do it. Sex drive is another expression for interest in sex, which is partly influenced by heredity. Sexual style relates to who partners uniquely are during sex. Sexual style derives from a sense of what sex is primarily about – connection or pleasure, conception or relaxation – and how sex is – serious or comic, elevated or dirty. Sexual style can change with the same partner as well as with different partners. Sexual style also refers to the kind of identities that partners want to take on during sex, for instance, how active or passive. Partners can differ on each of the three dimensions and, if so, can negotiate with one another.

## Frequency of sex

The frequency with which partners have sex can guarantee neither sexual satisfaction nor relationship satisfaction. The following are some findings on frequency of sex that take age into account. Masters *et al.* (1986) observed that, in their twenties and thirties, the average American married couple had intercourse two or three times a week, after which frequency slowly declined until, past age 50, frequency of intercourse was once a week or less.

In a British national survey of nearly 20,000 respondents aged 16 to 59, sex was defined as vaginal intercourse, oral sex or anal sex (Wellings *et al.*, 1994). For both males and females, the median of the distribution never exceeded five acts of heterosexual sex in the last four weeks. (The median divides a set of values, in this case heterosexual sex acts, into two groups of equal size – half of the values are larger and half are smaller than the median.) An indication of how frequency of sex acts varied is shown in the ninety-fifth centile (95 per cent reporting less frequency) being 20 for males and 25 for females. Frequency of sex varied substantially with age for both males and females, ranging from a median of five acts per month for women aged 20 to 29 and for men aged 30 to 34, thereafter declining to a median of two for men aged 55 to 59, with more than 50 per cent of women in this age group reporting no sex acts in the last four weeks.

Regarding affairs, Wellings and her colleagues found that only one in 50 respondents believed extramarital sex 'to be not at all wrong, and some four out of five people (78.7 per cent men and 84.3 per cent women) are of the opinion that it is always or mostly wrong' (1994: 249). However, what people say and do can differ. In a Dutch study of 125 couples, 79 per cent married and 21 per cent cohabiting, 26 per cent of the men and 18 per cent of the women reported having had sex outside their primary relationship in the past year (Buunk, 1995). Also, 22 per cent of the women and 19 per cent of the men indicated that they had a partner who had been involved in such behaviour during that period.

Though caution is required in generalizing from Dutch findings, the incidence of sexual affairs in Australasia and Britain may be much higher than that indicated by the British attitudes to extramarital sex reported by Wellings and her colleagues. In the USA, sexual infidelity has been found to be both a cause and a consequence of relationship deterioration (Previti and Amato, 2004).

## Sexual equality

Though with obvious differences, anatomically males and female bodies are very alike. In terms of their sexual functioning, men and women are also 'incredibly and consistently similar' (Masters and Johnson, 1970: 38). However, women's capacity to respond to sexual stimulation is far greater than that of men and men are far more fertile than women. Emotionally females and males are also very similar. Both are highly sexual.

In all cultures, males and females are subject to sex-role conditioning. Sexual knowledge (or lack of it) and attitudes towards sensual and sexual pleasure are two key areas where males and females can receive different sexual socialization. For example, males may be more socialized than females to be sexual rather than sensual. In Australia, Britain and North America sex-role conditioning has led to many women feeling that they are second-class citizens. Often in the past, women's potential for sexual arousal and pleasure was viewed by both sexes as less than that of males. Women's wishes in regard to sex were sometimes viewed as less important. Alberti and Emmons (2001) list the following among characteristics of sexually non-assertive females: passivity, misguided compassion, silence and suffering, giving in, doing your duty and manipulation.

However, males too have not escaped unscathed from their sex-role conditioning. Jokingly, young males have been observed to need four items to measure their sexual prowess: a ruler for the length of their penis; a piece of string for its thickness; a clock for how long they can delay ejaculating; and a counter for how many times they get 'it'. Many males accept too much responsibility for the success of sexual encounters. Frequently male socialization generates counterproductive expectations and anxieties about sexual performance. Furthermore, many males have experienced difficulty in expressing vulnerability, affection and tenderness. Alberti and Emmons (2001) list the following among characteristics of sexually non-assertive and/or aggressive males: silence, lack of emotion, insulation, control, machismo, inflexibility, exploitation and score keeping.

Increasingly, there is a trend towards sexual equality. Sex is recognized as something that partners do with each other for their mutual gratification rather than something that is done to or for the other partner. Both males and females need to develop as sexual persons and to accept responsibility for the success of their sexual encounters.

## The sexual response cycle

The following reviews of the sexual response cycle assume a basic knowledge of sexual anatomy. In understanding this section, it should be noted that many if not most women require extra or different stimulation than intercourse to achieve orgasm (Clarkson, 2003).

## Masters and Johnson's version

Masters and Johnson studied by means of direct laboratory observation over 10,000 episodes of sexual activity in 382 women and 312 men. They found that human sexual response was a cycle with four phases: excitement, plateau, orgasm and resolution (Masters *et al.*, 1986). The phases are not always discrete and can vary considerably between people and with one person at different times. The physiology of sexual response is the same for males and females, be they heterosexual or homosexual. Two basic physiological reactions occur during the sexual response cycle. The first is vasocongestion, in which the amount of blood concentrated in the body tissues of both sexes' genitals and the female breasts increases. The second is increased neuromuscular tension or myotonia, in which there is a build-up of energy in the nerves and muscles throughout the body.

### Excitement phase

Humans get aroused through touching and feeling, sexy thoughts and fantasies, hearing romantic music and smelling body odours. Vaginal lubrication is the main sign of sexual excitation in the female. The walls of her vagina secrete moisture. As lubrication increases the fluid sometimes flows out of her vagina moistening her vaginal opening. Women vary in the quantity, consistency and odour of their vaginal lubrication. The amount of vaginal lubrication does not necessarily indicate level of sexual arousal and readiness for intercourse. Other female excitement responses include enlargement of the diameter of the vagina's inner lips, increased size of the clitoris and, for most women, erect nipples.

Erection of the penis is the main sign of physical erection in the male. The penis becomes harder, thicker and points outwards or upwards. Other male excitement responses include the smoothing out of the scrotum, the testes being partly drawn towards the body, and, for some men, erect nipples.

For both males and females, the build-up of excitement can vary in time and intensity with the occasion. Excitement can be dampened or reversed through distractions, for instance, a door knock or a tactless remark. Alternatively, either or both partners may choose to reverse the excitement phase with or without them choosing to return to it.

*Plateau phase*

In the plateau phase high levels of sexual excitement are maintained and set the stage for orgasm. The word plateau is somewhat inaccurate since for both sexes neuromuscular tension generally increases, particularly in the buttocks and thighs. In addition, hearts beat more rapidly, blood pressure heightens and breathing quickens.

During the plateau phase in women, vasocongestion causes the opening or the vagina to narrow by 30 per cent or more. This narrowing of the outer vagina or orgasmic platform provides for a tighter grip of the penis. The clitoris pulls back against the pubic bone and this change, combined with the vasocongestion occurring in the vaginal lips, causes the clitoris to retreat under its hood. The vagina's inner lips enlarge greatly, doubling or even tripling in thickness. The breast size of women who have not nursed a child increases markedly. However, for women who have breastfed a child increase in breast size is either less pronounced or non-existent. In about half to three-quarters of women and about a quarter of men, a sex flush starts late in the excitement stage or early in the plateau stage. This spotty skin colour change generally begins just below the breastbone and then spreads rapidly over the breasts and front of the chest.

For males, during the plateau phase, their testes continue to elevate, though for men over 50 full elevation may not be attained. With some males, small amounts of clear fluid or 'pre-cum' come from the tip of the penis.

Unwanted distractions may deter both males and females from maintaining the plateau phase. Alternatively, as part of relaxed and gourmet lovemaking, partners may choose to reverse and then rekindle this phase.

*Orgasm phase*

Climax and coming are other words for orgasm. Orgasms last for a few seconds and consist of rhythmic muscular contractions followed by rapid relaxation. Psychologically orgasm is usually a time of intense pleasure. However, the intensity of and degree of satisfaction derived from orgasms varies between people and across different occasions for the same person.

For females, orgasm is characterized by simultaneous rhythmic contractions of the uterus, the outer vagina (orgasmic platform) and anal sphincter. Mild orgasms may have three to five contractions and intense orgasms ten to fifteen. As orgasm continues the contractions diminish in force and frequency. Most women do not ejaculate during orgasm. Unlike males, if restimulated, females are capable of further orgasms within seconds or minutes of each other. Kassorla (1980: 215) observes that 'a healthy woman can enjoy repeated orgasms for as long as she wants to'. However, it is the exceptional woman who is multi-orgasmic during most of her sexual activity. Some women never experience multiple orgasms and others experience them rarely.

Unlike with females, male orgasm consists of two stages. In the first stage, a series of contractions force semen into the bulb of the urethra and the man experiences a sense of ejaculatory inevitability. At this point he cannot voluntarily stop ejaculation. In the second stage, the male experiences contractions throughout his penis that cause ejaculation involving the spurting of semen or 'cum' from the tip of his penis. Initially rhythmic contractions occur at four-fifths of a second. However, after the first three or four contractions, intensity and frequency taper off. In general, men's orgasms are more uniform than women's. Usually, men take much longer than women to become orgasmic again. However, the refractory period for potent young males may be minutes rather than hours.

### Resolution phase

In the resolution phase females and males return to the unaroused state. Heavy breathing and fast heart rate may continue just after orgasm, but gradually go back to normal. In addition, the sex flush disappears. In females, during the resolution phase, the narrowing of the vaginal lips reverses, the vagina contracts in both length and diameter, the clitoris returns to its normal size and position, breasts cease being enlarged and nipples lose their tautness. During this phase, women may experience discomfort if their clitoris, vagina or nipples are stimulated.

In the resolution phase, the male erection diminishes in two stages. First, there is partial loss of erection as the orgasmic contractions cause blood to be pumped out of the penis. Second, there is a slower stage in which the penis returns to its smaller and softer normal state. During this stage, the testes decrease in size and move back into the scrotum.

## American Psychiatric Association's version

The American Psychiatric Association (APA) provides a different version of the sexual response cycle. Here the four phases of the sexual response cycle are desire, excitement, orgasm and resolution. The desire phase consists of fantasies about sexual activity and the desire to have sexual activity (APA, 2000). The APA excitement phase combines the excitement and plateau stages of the Masters and Johnson version. In both sexual response cycle versions, the orgasm and resolution phases are essentially the same.

## SEXUAL ACTIVITIES

In close relationships, partners' sexual activity forms part of their broader emotional and sensual relationship. When relating sexually, partners are ideally responsive to the flow of their own and one another's feelings. They think about how best to give pleasure as well as how to receive it. In addition, their actions enhance and affirm their own and their partner's pleasure and well-being.

## Sexual intercourse

Heterosexual intercourse involves the male penetrating the female's vagina with his erect penis and thrusting back and forth. There are numerous positions for the 'making love' – lying down, sitting, standing up, and so on. I now mention five of the more usual positions. Partners can use more than one position during a single lovemaking session.

- *Man lying on top, face to face*. This 'missionary position' is probably the most commonly used position in Australasia and Britain. The woman lies on her back with her legs spread somewhat apart. She can also bend her knees or wrap her legs around her partner. Also, she can caress him. An advantage of this position is that partners can look at each other and kiss. For couples wanting children, another advantage is that this position gives the best chance of conception. Disadvantages include the difficulty of manually stimulating the clitoris and the man's weight sometimes being too heavy.
- *Woman lying on top, face to face*. Here the woman possesses more control over the timing and depth of her partner's thrusting. However, the man may find it less easy to thrust. Partners can look into each other's eyes and kiss. Since the man does not need to support himself, his hands are free for stroking the woman's breasts, genitals or other parts of her body.
- *Woman sitting on top, face to face*. Here the woman has even more control of the tempo and penetration of the man's thrusting than when lying on top. Partners can see more of each other and play with one another's chests or breasts. In addition, either partner can manually stimulate the clitoris. Mouth to mouth kissing is still possible, if wanted. This position can be used in the later stages of pregnancy.
- *Lying side by side, face to face*. The side-by-side position gives partners much opportunity to caress and hug one another. Neither partner carries the other's weight. Disadvantages include insufficient leverage for active penile thrusting and the greater likelihood of the penis coming out of the vagina than in other positions.
- *Rear entry, woman kneeling or lying down*. With rear entry 'doggy style', the man inserts his penis from behind into the woman's vagina as she kneels. The woman may have her back horizontal or sloping downwards. Some people object to the sheer animal nature of this position, but others find it exciting. Alternatively, rear entry may take place with the partners lying on their sides, the so-called 'spoon position'. During pregnancy some women find the spoon position especially satisfactory. In rear entry positions, eye contact and mouth-to-mouth kissing are difficult. However, usually the man can manually stimulate his partner's clitoris or breasts.

In addition to penile-vaginal intercourse, partners may engage in anal sex. Stimulation of the either sex's anus can be done manually, by using one or more fingers, or orally. Penile-anal intercourse is far from being restricted to male homosexuals. However, some heterosexuals look upon this activity negatively. In addition, penile-anal intercourse can be physically painful for the receiving partner. If vaginal penetration is to follow anal penetration, always wash the penis thoroughly to avoid transmitting germs into the vagina.

## Touching

Touching has many functions before, during and after sexual activity. Before sexual activity, touch can be a 'turn-on' message about your willingness to engage in sex. During sexual activity, touch can affirm your love and tenderness for one another as well as stimulate and excite. In addition, partners can use touch to communicate how they like to receive pleasure. After sexual activity, you can enjoy the warmth and closeness of one another's bodies.

There are many dimensions of touch. The intention of touch can be passionate or companionate. You and your partner may actively touch each other simultaneously or in turns. Your touches can be exploratory, focused or somewhere in between. Touch can be gentle or strong. Here it is important to take your partners wishes into consideration. The target of touch can be different parts of the body and not just the genitals: for example, nipples, hair and ear lobes. You can regard all of the body as an erogenous zone. Apart from lying together, cuddling or hugging your partner with your arms, legs or both, the main ways of touching one another are with your mouth and hands (Litvinoff, 1992).

- *Touching with your mouth.* Methods of touching that involve the mouth include kissing one another's lips, kissing with open mouth, kissing and exploring one another's mouth with your tongues, licking, sucking, nibbling, biting and blowing.
- *Touching with your hands.* Methods of touching that involve the hands include caressing with your finger tips, stroking, rubbing, scratching, holding, squeezing, patting, smacking, kneading, massaging and tickling.

Partners can touch each other in oral-genital sex. The term 'cunnilingus' is used for oral stimulation of the female genitals. The term 'fellatio' is used for oral stimulation of the man's genitals. The term 'soixante-neuf', French for sixty-nine, is used for partners simultaneously engaging in oral-genital stimulation.

## Masturbation

Masturbation is variously described as genital self-stimulation, producing an orgasm by genital self-stimulation, and any act of sexual self-stimulation regardless of whether it involves the genitals and orgasm. Other parts of the body used for self-pleasuring include the nipples, breasts, inner thighs and anus.

The most common form of female masturbation is lying on her back and manually stroking her clitoris, mons or vaginal lips. However, other women prefer to masturbate when lying on their stomachs. Some women rub their genitals against objects such as pillows. Few women masturbate by inserting something into their vaginas. An increasing number of women use hand-held vibrators to enhance their pleasure. The most common form of male masturbation is rubbing one hand up and down the shaft of his penis with increasingly rapid movements until ejaculation.

In close relationships, sometimes partners masturbate, either solo or simultaneously, as part of their lovemaking. Such masturbation may turn one another on. Alternatively, though not a strict use of the term, partners can masturbate one another. In addition, there may be occasions when partners masturbate alone without harming their relationship. Examples are when one of the partners is absent or ill or where great differences exist in partners' sexual appetites. In one American survey, 72 per cent of young married husbands masturbated with an average frequency of about 24 times a year, and 68 per cent of young wives masturbated averaging 10 times per year (Masters *et al.*, 1986).

Masturbation has dangers as well as advantages. Some people use masturbation as a way of avoiding the risks of entering genuine relationships. Partners in close relationships may masturbate instead of trying to improve their sex lives together (see Activity 9.1). In addition, sometimes people accompany masturbation with depraved and degrading fantasies that they later enact in real life.

---

**ACTIVITY 9.1**                **Degree of comfort with sexual activities**  |

This activity assumes you are in a relationship. Complete Part A on your own and Part B with your partner.

## Part A  My comfort zones

Assess how psychologically comfortable you feel about engaging in each of the following sexual activities.

*Sexual intercourse*

- Man lying on top, face to face
- Woman lying on top, face to face
- Woman sitting on top, face to face
- Lying side to side, face to face
- Rear entry, woman kneeling or lying down
- Other positions (specify).

*Anal sex*

- Penile-vaginal intercourse
- Other methods (specify).

*Oral-genital sex*

- Fellatio (mouth-genital contact on man)
- Cunnilingus (mouth-genital contact on woman).

*Manually stimulating my partner's genitals*
*Masturbation*

- Partner present
- On your own.

## Part B  Discuss with partner

1. Each partner shares their comfort zones and discusses the reasons for them.
2. If necessary, identify ways in which you can introduce more variety into your lovemaking.

---

## CONDITIONS FOR SEXUAL ACTIVITY

Numerous variations exist in the conditions for sexual activity. Partners' preferences may be similar or different. Variety is also important. Sometimes an analogy is made with eating: sexual appetite can be satisfied in various ways and eating the same food all the time becomes monotonous.

### In the mood

For sex to occur, at least one partner must start somewhat in the mood. If the other partner is not initially in the mood, they may like the process of being aroused. However, this may not always be the case. Partners require sensitivity concerning one another's feelings and moods about both having and not having sex. Some partners feel more randy after being out in the fresh air or exercising physically. Getting in the mood is best achieved in the context of a tender and sensual relationship outside the bedroom.

### Turn-ons and turn-offs

Partners build up a repertoire of signals that give and receive messages about when they are in the mood for sex. Good lovers become keenly attuned to what turns one another on: for instance, certain forms of eye contact, touching, breathing, clothing, conversation, and so on. Partners can also turn each other off sex: for instance, by bad breath, poor hygiene, dirty knickers or underpants, coarse language, and being too pushy. Also, beware of tactless criticism. Glasser (1995: 47) writes: 'Criticism directed at a partner's sexual performance is the ultimate sexual turnoff.'

## Surroundings

Sex need not always take place in the bedroom at home. Some partners may enjoy making love in front of a blazing fireplace, in the bath, on the stairs, in hotels and motels, or outdoors – for instance, in a field or on a beach. However, to protect your own and other people's sensitivities, privacy is important. If there is a possibility of being interrupted at home, lock the door and take the phone off the hook. The lighting of the surroundings for sex may be bright, dim or non-existent. There may be music in the background or silence.

## Timing and duration

Partners can choose to have sex at any time – not just between 11pm and midnight on Saturday evenings! For instance, you may enjoy a lunchtime 'nooner' or a leisurely afternoon of lovemaking. The duration of your lovemaking may range from a 'quickie' to as long as you can maintain your interest and energy.

## Preventing conception and sexually transmitted diseases

Both partners engaging in sexual activity need to assume responsibility for contraception and for preventing sexually transmitted diseases (STDs). Approaches to these two main preventive concerns have commonalities as well as differences. In both instances, a distinction exists between the theoretical effectiveness and actual effectiveness of the method. For instance, if a woman forgets to take the pill and then becomes pregnant, this most likely represents user rather than method failure. Using condoms that are poor quality or past their use-by date increases the risk of conception and of transmitting STDs – here, user failure and method failure can interact.

Partners seeking to control birth are well advised to consult with doctors and family planning clinic advisers to select the method or methods that best combine prevention, health and comfort. Sexual honesty is desirable so that your partner can protect himself or herself. If necessary, assertively ask direct questions about your partner's sexual health and ensure that a condom is used. If you think you have an STD, the more promptly you are tested and treated, the greater the chances of your preventing or managing well any serious complications arising from the disease.

# COMMUNICATION SKILLS FOR SEXUAL RELATIONSHIPS

Partners can communicate about sex both in and out of bed. Often partners can best talk in detail about sexual problems and difficulties out of bed, thus keeping the bed associated with pleasure and warmth. Each of you may find it difficult to communicate clearly at the best of times. When it comes to talking about sex you may be embarrassed inhibited, beat around the bush, or do your best to avoid the subject altogether. In addition, other unfinished business in your relationship may become intrusive. Following are some skills for communicating about sex.

## Express tenderness and affection

In close relationships the emotional side of sex is very important. Some partners may never have developed good skills of expressing tenderness and affection in or out of bed. Others may possess good skills, but fail to demonstrate them after courtship and the early stages of marriage or cohabitation. Partners like to feel valued not just for their bodies, but for themselves. There are many ways in which you can show affection and appreciation for your partner. Sometimes, people really love their partners but fail to say so. If you fall into that category, try finding a time to say 'I love you' to your partner in a way that reflects your true feelings for her or him. Be prepared, if necessary, to develop your skills of affectionate hugging and tender caressing.

## Develop a comfortable language for sex talk

People vary in what language they find acceptable when talking about sex. In addition to the four letter word f – k, there are many other terms that describe intercourse among them, 'bonking', 'banging', 'rooting', 'shagging', 'screwing', 'getting laid', 'having sex', 'having nookie', 'having a poke' and 'having it off'. Many different words can be used to describe other sexual acts, for example, fellatio can become 'blow job' and masturbation 'wanking'. Furthermore, slang terms exist for erogenous parts of both the female and male bodies: for instance, breasts can become 'boobs', 'tits', 'mammaries', 'headlights' and 'fun bags' and a penis can be called a 'cock', 'dick', 'prick', 'tool' or 'bed flute'. No law of nature decrees that some of these terms are right or wrong. Each couple has to develop a language in which they can comfortably discuss sex without the constant fear of giving or receiving offence.

## Tune into your partner's sexuality

Being sexually skilled in bed requires you to be responsive to the flow of feelings and sexual sensations in your partner. You and your partner can create a safe emotional climate for talking about and experiencing your sexuality by using the listening skills described earlier in this book. Be sensitive to her or his feelings of vulnerability in talking about sex either in general or in relation to specific aspects. However, much of the information you receive is not verbal, but comes from other sounds and from seeing and touching your partner. For instance your partner's vocal messages, such as their sighs and heavy breathing, can indicate the location and degree of their pleasure. In addition, by observing and physically feeling your partner's reactions, you get numerous messages about how she or he experiences various aspects of your lovemaking. Furthermore, if you allow it, your partner may guide you in how to provide more pleasure. Much of this communication may be non-verbal – for instance, placing your hand in a certain part of her or his body and applying the right amount of pressure or friction.

## Disclose your sexuality

You can talk about yourself as a sexual person. Your disclosures may make it easier for your partner to reciprocate. For instance, you can share various aspects of your sexual history so that both you and your partner understand more about the origins of your current attitudes and behaviour. You can let your partner know what you like in bed. Sometimes, you can do this by positive feedback: 'That feels great' or 'Keep doing that, I love it.' On other occasions you may wish to improve or modify an otherwise enjoyable behaviour: for instance, 'I like it when you play with my testicles, but please do it lower down and more gently.' On still other occasions, you may wish to stop a behaviour: for instance, 'Please stop biting my neck. It hurts.' In addition, you can request sex acts, for instance: 'Please lick my cunt', though be sensitive to language and to your partner's reactions. You can share your sexual fantasies, though again carefully monitor how your partner responds.

You can disclose yourself with appropriate vocal messages that frame the verbal messages you send. However, on other occasions your vocal messages will be sufficient in themselves. If you find yourself holding back on expressing pleasure through sighs and heavy breathing, you may gain more pleasure and sexual freedom by being more open. Furthermore, you provide your partner with added feedback and excitement.

Much of the time you disclose yourself as a sexual person through your touch behaviour – how you hug, kiss and use your hands. You can be playful, sensitive and creative in how you touch your partner. In addition, you can use touch to guide your partner in how to pleasure you.

## Be assertive

With sexual equality, each of you has a right to express sexual likes and dislikes (Alberti and Emmons, 2001). Sometimes you may need assertion skills to resist sexual pressure. For instance, early in a relationship you might respond to a request for sex with 'I find you attractive, but I want to get to know you better first.' You may need to be firm about ensuring use of condoms, stopping sex talk you find distasteful and curtailing physical activities you dislike or find painful. Since the next chapter of this book reviews how to use assertion skills in response to another's negative behaviour, I only mention the topic briefly here.

## Have fun

Woody Allen quips that sex is the most fun he has ever had without laughing. Sex is adult play (Comfort, 1993). As such, it should not be taken with deadly seriousness. However, one person's fun can be another person's idea of stupidity or crassness. There are numerous ways that you can have relaxed fun. Couples need to choose what works best for them. You can use humour to joke about sex both inside and outside the bedroom. You can be playful and frolic as you make love. In addition, you may choose to act out harmless fantasies. Regarding adult playtime, Comfort (1993: 131) writes: 'The rules are only those of childplay – if it gets nasty or spiteful or unhappy, stop the game: while it stays wild and exciting, it has a climax children's games lack; that is the privilege of play when you are an adult.'

## Discuss issues

As well as each of you revealing your sexual likes and dislikes, undoubtedly together you will need to discuss and negotiate many issues connected with your sex life. Sometimes you will have common goals: for instance, how to obtain more privacy for sex or get fun out of it. However, there may be times when you and your partner differ on what, where and when you like to have sex. In such instances, goodwill, willingness to understand one another's positions, negotiation and compromise are useful attributes and skills. On occasion, you and your partner will need to discuss, in a climate of trust and mutual support, sexual doubts, fears and feelings of vulnerability. In addition, you can protect your sex life by, where necessary, making time both to have sex and also to talk about it. Lastly, many issues connected with your relationship and lives outside the bedroom may intrude into your sex life. Relationship skills that you can use to address such issues include those of managing anger and solving relationship problems, the topics of later chapters in this book (see Activity 9.2).

---

**ACTIVITY 9.2**            **Develop my communication skills for relating sexually** |

---

This activity assumes that you are in a relationship. Do Part A on your own and Part B with your partner.

## Part A  My communication skills for a sexual relationship

1. Assess your good and poor skills in each of the following communication skills for a sexual relationship.

   (a) Expressing tenderness and affection
   (b) Tuning into my partner's sexuality
   (c) Disclosing my sexuality
   (d) Being assertive
   (e) Having fun
   (f) Discussing issues.

2. If appropriate identify one or more of your poor communication skills and develop a plan to change how you act. In your plan, specify:

   (a) Your goals, including a time frame
   (b) The steps you intend taking to attain each of your goals
   (c) How you will monitor your progress.

## Part B  Working together

1. Share and discuss your answers to Part A of this activity.
2. If appropriate identify one or more of your joint poor communication skills and develop a plan to work together to change how you act. In your plan, specify:

   (a) Your joint goals, including a time frame
   (b) The steps you as a couple intend taking to attain each of your joint goals
   (c) How you will jointly monitor progress.

---

# SOME MIND SKILLS FOR SEXUAL RELATIONSHIPS

How humans think mediates how well they perform sexually. Masters *et al.* (1986) illustrate this point by stating that inhibitions and guilt, performance anxiety, erotic boredom and blind acceptance of sexual misinformation and myths account for about 80 per cent of the sexual dissatisfaction in American society. The following are some mind skills relevant to sexual relating.

## Creating rules

You and your partner may individually possess unrealistic rules that interfere with your sexual happiness. In addition, you may jointly share unrealistic rules that work against rather than for your sexual relationship. The term Ellis uses to characterize unrealistic rules and beliefs is 'musturbation' (Ellis, 2005). Others use the term 'myths' (for instance, Litvinoff, 1992). The following are some illustrative unrealistic rules, musturbations or myths. The sting of these rules is in the tail. They possess the potential to harm sexual relationships.

How can you overcome your unrealistic rules in regard to sex? First, you can become aware that they exist. For instance, words like 'should', 'ought' and

---

*Body image*

- My/my partner's breasts must be large.
- My/my partner's penis must be long and thick.

*Sex roles*

- Men must take the initiative in sex.
- Women must please men.

*Sexual feelings*

- Men must not show tenderness.
- Women must not show sexual abandonment.

*Sex acts*

- Women must not engage in cunnilingus (mouth-genital contact).
- Intercourse must always be the main sexual activity.

*Sexual performance*

- Men must be two feet long, hard as a steel and able to go all night (Zilbergeld, 1978).
- Women must show pleasure whatever their partner does.

*Approval*

- I must have my partner's approval.
- I must not reveal sexual abuse in childhood.

*Power and control*

- Women must always do what men want.
- Women must never be dominant.

*Change*

- My partner and I must work at sex.
- Change must come quickly.

'must' may signal that you possess unrealistic rules. Also, negative feelings like inhibition and performance anxiety may be cues for underlying unrealistic rules. Acting in negative and self-defeating ways can also indicate rigid rules. Second, you can dispute or challenge how rational the rules are. Either on your own or with your partner you can ask yourself for evidence that supports or negates the rule: for example, 'Where is the evidence that we must always have intercourse when we have sex?' and 'What might be the consequences if sometimes we have sex without having intercourse?' Third, you can restate the unrealistic rule into a more realistic version: for example, 'While we enjoy having intercourse most times we make love, we also enjoy other forms of sexual contact like stimulating each other's genitals and masturbation and do not wish to force ourselves to have intercourse every time we have sex.'

## Creating perceptions

### Perceive sex accurately

Some people perceive sex negatively. Woody Allen jokingly says: 'Is sex dirty? Only if it's done right.' The idea that sex is evil or dirty can contribute to sexual problems and dysfunctions. Masters et al. (1986) observe that such attitudes are forced upon children in certain rigidly religious families. However, they stress that the religious beliefs themselves are not troublesome. An Australian study discovered that, for both male and female subjects, parents' negative attitudes in early childhood both to sex with each other and also towards their children's sexual development were associated with later sexual dysfunction (McCabe, 1994).

Females especially may find it difficult to value their sexuality. The double standard lingers on whereby it is okay for males but less okay for females to be open about their sexuality. In addition, partners may unthinkingly perceive specific sexual acts negatively rather than as part of the range of natural sexual activities. Furthermore, people may be intolerant of homosexual feelings, thoughts and behaviours in themselves and others. Sometimes religious beliefs can contribute to homosexual oppression and self-oppression. Despite an increasingly scientific and less moralistic approach to homosexuality, homophobia is still fairly widespread in Australasia and Britain. Often homophobic people exaggerate the importance of sex in homosexual relationships instead of perceiving its role as similar to that in heterosexual relationships, with the exception of procreation.

### Perceive yourself accurately

You may be prone to negative perceptions about your body: 'Parts of my body are not attractive enough' or 'My body is not sexy enough' (Beck, 1988: 360). Alternatively, you may be narcissistic about your physical attractiveness perceiving yourself as god's gift to women or men. You may have an inadequate perception of yourself as a sexual person and of your unique sexual wishes and preferences. In addition, you may possess considerable misinformation about what effective sexual relating entails and not realize this. Your poor sexual relationship skills may include being demanding and critical of your partner and being excessively interested in your own pleasure. You may possess little insight into your own feelings of vulnerability and needs to prove yourself. People engage in sex with varying degrees of sexual selfishness. For example, Gary, aged 19, spends little time in stimulating his partner Kim, 19, and thinks that lovemaking stops when he has had his orgasm. For her part, Kim strives to please Gary, but inadequately acknowledges the importance of her own sexual pleasure.

For various reasons, you may be poor at owning your strengths. You may be quite skilled at lovemaking, but riddled with doubts about your ability to satisfy your partner. You may expend too much effort in wondering what your partner is thinking and whether or not you will let him or her down. Your 'spectatoring' of how you perform sexually interferes with spontaneity.

## Perceive your partner accurately

At worst, either or both partners can perceive the other as objects for their sexual gratification rather than as persons worthy of respect. You may possess an incomplete or inaccurate picture of how to pleasure your partner. For example, you may perceive that what pleasures you is what pleasures her or him. You may inaccurately mind-read what your partner wants. You may mistakenly believe that you do not need to talk about sex. Furthermore, you may fail to take into account that your partner, not you, is the final arbiter of her or his sexual feelings and wishes. In addition, you may insufficiently attend to your partner's feelings of sexual vulnerability and preferences about the frequency, timing and location of sex.

It is possible to perceive your partner's sexual knowledge and lovemaking skills in too positive a light. By seeing her or him too rosily, you may disparage yourself and insufficiently acknowledge the extent to which your partner fails to fulfil your sexual needs. Some people are good at projecting an image that they are better in bed than they really are – beware of colluding in their self-deceptions.

In addition, partners can misinterpret one another's sexual behaviour. For example, if your partner masturbates or looks at erotic literature, this does not automatically mean that she or he is no longer sexually interested in you. However, if you misinterpret your partner's behaviour, you may feel inferior and find excuses for not having sex. Another example is that of partners who wrongly interpret as rejection or anger one another's not wanting sex at a particular time.

How can you counteract inaccurate perceptions about sex, yourself and your partner? First, you can gather more sexual information through reading, talking to people and, if appropriate, attending courses and workshops. Second, you can reality test the accuracy of your perceptions by challenging them and searching for evidence that confirms or negates them: for example, in your own mind you can test the hypothesis that you know what your partner's sexual wishes are. Third, you and your partner can increase the accuracy with which you perceive yourselves and each other by improving your sexual communication. For example, if you want your nipples caressed better, you can communicate this both verbally and by taking your partner's hand and showing him or her how to maximize your pleasure. Fourth, if necessary, you and your partner can seek counselling or get coached in relating sexually.

## Creating self-talk

You can create self-talk to help you to communicate more effectively in specific sexual relationship situations. For example, Ginny would like her partner Ray to spend more time stroking her clitoris and to do it more gently. Ginny currently inhibits herself by negative self-talk: for instance, 'I'm only being silly wanting more caressing down there from him', 'Ray is going to get annoyed' and 'I'm too nervous to even think of telling him.' Ginny can replace her negative self-talk with coping self-talk in which she uses calming, coaching and affirming self-statements. Sample calming self-statements include: 'Calm down', 'Relax', and 'Breathe slowly and deeply.' With coaching self-statements Ginny reminds herself how to communicate effectively: for example, 'Use tact and diplomacy. Tell Ray how much pleasure he gives me when he strokes my clitoris and ask him to keep doing it, but more gently.' Affirming self-statements Ginny might use include: 'I have a right to sexual fulfillment', 'Ray really wants to please me' and 'I'm capable of making my points when I need to.' Men can also create self-talk to help them to communicate effectively with their partners: for instance, they may feel threatened about asking their partner to try a new position, admitting vulnerability or revealing ignorance.

## Creating visual images

Sexual fantasies are an important part of being a sexual person. Women and men 'are more similar than different in their sexual fantasy patterns' (Masters et al. 1986: 280). Frequently, sexual images are extremely X-rated (Britain) or R-rated (Australia) and incorporate ideas that would seem unusual in everyday discourse. If shared or enacted, the content of your fantasies might land you in jail, get you fired, or lead to your face being slapped. The range of content of sexual fantasies is almost limitless. The imagery can differ in vividness and the action can be explicit or vague. The time can be the past, present or future. Common themes in sexual fantasies include experimentation with different sexual acts and experiences, seduction and conquest, having sex with different partners, participating in group sex, watching others have sex, being a rape victim or victimizer, idyllic encounters and sadomasochism.

Sexual fantasies can have many positive functions. Your sexual fantasies can show what turns you on. You can try out different sexual activities in your mind to see how arousing they are. Before you initiate sexual contact, you can arouse your sexual appetite by tuning into existing fantasies or creating new ones. During sex, you can use fantasy to enhance arousal, increase the attractiveness of your partner and relieve boredom. You can also imagine what it would be like to experiment with different activities here and now. Such fantasies may lead to more creativity, variety, spontaneity and fun. In addition, some people find it arousing if they share and listen to their partner sharing sexual fantasies external to their relationship, including fantasies about having sex with other people (Friday, 1973). Comfort (1993: 141) writes: 'Infantile, symbolic, fetishistic and generally wild fantasies are part of love, and only a problem if they take up too much time and start spoiling the reciprocity of sex.' However, when considering sharing or actually sharing your fantasies, take your partner's feelings and sensitivities into account.

You can use visualizing to help you perform more competently. Lazarus (1984: 73) offers the following basic rule: 'If you wish to accomplish something in reality, first picture yourself achieving it in imagination.' He states that when impotent males and non-orgasmic women imagine engaging in enjoyable and passionate sex, a transfer to real lovemaking soon follows. You can also use visualizing to rehearse and practise engaging in new sexual activities: for example, fellatio or cunnilingus. Other uses of sexual fantasies include aiding masturbation, especially if on your own; acting as a safety valve for non-socially sanctioned impulses; and providing what in many instances is a harmless and pleasant way of passing the time.

Sexual fantasies have the potential for harm as well as good. For instance, you can exist in a world of sexual fantasy, without assuming the risk of real relationships. Even during intercourse, you can imagine having sex with people other than your partner as a way of distancing yourself from working on problems in your relationship. In addition, it is an invasion of your partner's privacy to force her or him to listen to your sexual fantasies unwillingly. An even more serious abuse of fantasy is as a prelude to being sexually violent towards your partner.

## Creating explanations

You require accuracy in how you explain the cause of the adequacy of your sex life. The following are some illustrative explanations that may cause and maintain sexual problems.

- '*Sex is natural.*' You may limit your sexual performance if you rely on the explanation that good sex comes just naturally rather from knowledge and practice as well.
- '*Our relationship is not the cause.*' Sexual problems can result from difficulties and resentments in your non-sexual relationship. Partners differ in the degree to which they can compartmentalize sex from the rest of their relationship. A rule of thumb is 'The better the communication outside the bedroom, the better the sex inside it.'
- '*It's your fault.*' Each partner is responsible for gaining sexual fulfilment in the relationship. Frequently, blaming a partner just increases the difficulties. Overcoming sexual difficulties requires cooperation. Each partner needs to examine and, where necessary, to develop sexual relationship skills.
- '*It's my fault.*' You can assume too much responsibility for your partner's sexual pleasure and orgasms. In addition, you can assume too much responsi-

bility for your own insufficient sexual fulfilment. Good sex is a cooperative activity in which both partners are responsible for successful outcomes.

- *'Improving our sex life is impossible.'* Partners may provide various reasons why improving their sex lives is impossible including 'She/he is only interested in her/his own pleasure', 'She/he never listens', 'I'm naturally frigid', 'My upbringing was too strict' and 'It's against my religious principles.'

When you become aware that you and your partner have become stuck in a less than satisfactory sexual relationship, identify the explanations each of you offers for this state of affairs. Then challenge the explanations by searching for evidence about how true they are. For example, if you think: 'Improving our sex life is impossible because my partner is only interested in her/his own pleasure', search for specific evidence of where your partner has shown interest in promoting your sexual pleasure and not just her or his own. Since partners often reciprocate each other's actions, also look for evidence indicating that you have shown insufficient interest in your partner's pleasure. Furthermore, ask yourself whether you have given your partner adequate feedback of your dissatisfaction with her/his behaviour. Identify specific instances where you gave such feedback and how she or he reacted. You could also ask your partner whether she or he is satisfied with your sexual relationship and is willing to try to improve it. At the end of this process, you may find that your initial explanation for the permanence of your sexual dissatisfaction no longer holds true.

## Creating expectations

In many areas, partners can lessen their sexual fulfilment by inaccurately predicting the consequences of their actions. Expectations about incompetence and rejection can inhibit people from dating, courting and making marriage proposals. Frequently after the initial excitement of courtship and cohabitation partners decrease the amount of non-sexual sensual contact they share. Such behaviour carries two risks that partners may insufficiently acknowledge: first, making their daily relationship less rewarding; second, providing a less affectionate emotional climate for their sexual relationship. As well as ignoring risks, such partners insufficiently acknowledge the gains from maintaining their sensual relationship.

Relaxed sex requires partners to be confident in their ability to attain a satisfactory level of performance. Expecting unsatisfactory performance or failure is a major factor in inhibitions and performance anxieties. For people with low sexual confidence, sexual relationships may be associated with danger and not just pleasure. Unfortunately, expectations of sexual incompetence and failure can turn into self-fulfilling prophecies.

Sharing sexual information and secrets is another area in which partner's erroneous expectations can interfere with sexual fulfilment. Fears about asking for what you want can mean that you never get what you want. Furthermore, harbouring secrets about significant sexual experiences – for instance, sexual abuse, rape, homosexual experience or an affair – can intrude upon the emotional trust and openness desirable for genuine sexual intimacy.

Avoiding unwanted pregnancies and sexually transmitted diseases is an important area where sexual partners need accurately to predict consequences. For example, a study of over 400 female adolescents in the United States found that approximately half underestimated the risk of their sexual behaviour (Kershaw *et al.*, 2003). Often avoiding risks is a matter of predicting the consequences of antecedent behaviours, such as consuming alcohol, that create vulnerability to lapses in sexual judgement.

Partners can systematically assess the realism of their expectations. Such an assessment entails looking at gains as well as risks or losses. For example, you could ask yourself: 'What are the gains of telling my partner what I want sexually?' as well as 'What are the risks of telling her or him?' If you are prone to catastrophic expectations, you can assess your recovery skills when faced with worst-case scenarios. You may be a stronger person than you initially think. Often, the best way to assess an expectation is to act and then assess the consequences: for example, telling your partner what you want sexually and then seeing how she or he reacts. On many occasions, you may need to develop specific skills – for instance, how to pleasure yourself and another person – so that you can feel sexually confident (see Activity 9.3).

## ACTIVITY 9.3      Develop my mind skills for relating sexually

This activity assumes you are in a sexual relationship. Complete Part A on your own and Part B with your partner.

### Part A  My mind skills

Either in relation to a specific sexual problem or to your overall sexual relationship, assess yourself on each of the following mind skills.

*Creating rules*

(a) My strengths
(b) My weaknesses.

*Creating perceptions*

(a) My strengths
(b) My weaknesses.

*Creating self-talk*

(a) My strengths
(b) My weaknesses.

*Creating visual images*

(a) My strengths
(b) My weaknesses.

*Creating explanations*

(a) My strengths
(b) My weaknesses.

*Creating expectations*

(a) My strengths
(b) My weaknesses.

## Part B  Working together

1. Share and discuss your answers to Part A.
2. Focus on your sexual relationship and examine how each of you is influenced by one another's thoughts and actions.
3. Identify the main thinking skills weaknesses, if any, that limit your sexual satisfaction as a couple and specify the steps you intend taking to change it/them.

---

## SEXUAL PROBLEMS

From time to time, every sexual relationship experiences problems. Sexual problems include 'dissatisfaction with sexual frequency, sexual boredom, incompatibility with respect to sexual activities and lack of sexual fulfilment' (Goldsmith, 1988: 31). Sexual problems can also encompass inhibitions and performance anxieties.

Partners differ in when they feel in the mood, get tired, become sick, go through ups and downs in their external relationship and are subject to stresses – for instance, money worries, job pressures, the needs of children and demanding relatives. In attempting to understand any sexual problem, there are at least four relevant contextual questions to ask:

1. 'Do important problems exist in our overall relationship?'
2. 'Are either or both of us having an affair?'
3. 'Are there stresses, possibly external, that interfere with either or both of our energy levels and feelings of well-being?'
4. 'Are there medical considerations that contribute to the sexual problem?'

If you answer any or all of the above questions in the affirmative, your efforts at managing the sexual problem need to address them. For instance, each of these factors could contribute to the common problem of partial loss of desire.

Loss of desire can also be due to erotic boredom. Here, lack of knowledge and poor mind skills can inhibit trying out and enjoying different sexual activities. Also, you can think effectively, but act incompetently. If so, you may need to rehearse and practise becoming more skilled in particular sex acts. Partners enter sexual relationships with different experiences and skill levels. You can share your experiences and help one another to become more skilled. You can also use effective mind skills to overcome your inhibitions, guilt and performance anxieties. Needless to say, this is best done in the context of a mutually supportive emotional relationship.

Another way of looking at sexual problems is from the standpoint of improving what already may be a reasonably satisfactory sex life. The problem is how to make something good even better, without placing unrealistic pressures on either of you. You can cooperate to develop a plan for improving your sexual knowledge, thinking skills, capacity for sexual responsiveness, competence in different sexual activities and communication skills.

Though the terms overlap, sexual dysfunctions can be regarded as more severe and less common than sexual problems (APA, 2000). Those with persistent problems such as insufficient sexual desire, insufficient sexual arousal, orgasmic disorders and sexual pain disorders are advised to seek appropriate medical and counselling attention.

## ACTIVITY 9.4          Group discussion: sexual relationship skills

This is intended as a group activity, though it may be done individually or in pairs. For each part:

1. Spend five to ten minutes answering the question in groups of three or four.
2. Each subgroup shares its answers with the whole group.
3. The whole group ranks the four most important skills from the most important to the least important.

## Part A  Sexual equality

List the four most important skills individuals can use in offering sexual equality to one another.

## Part B  Sexual activity skills

List the four most important physical skills partners can use in their sexual relationship.

## Part C  Sexual communication skills

List the four most important non-physical communication skills partners can use in their sexual relationship.

# 10

# *Assertiveness skills*

**Chapter outcomes**
By studying and doing the activities in this chapter you should:

- know how assertiveness compares with non-assertiveness and aggression
- know some dimensions of communicating assertively
- know some communication skills for assertiveness
- know some mind skills for assertiveness.

A distinction exists between oppositional assertiveness – expressing negative feelings – and affectionate assertiveness – expressing positive feelings (Butler, 1992; Wolpe and Wolpe, 1988). Oppositional assertiveness entails coping with others' negative behaviour whereas affectionate assertiveness means behaving positively towards others. Because positive assertion is so important in relationships, in a preceding chapter I covered skills for intimacy. In this chapter I address how to cope assertively with behaviour you perceive negatively.

## NON-ASSERTIVE, AGGRESSIVE AND ASSERTIVE BEHAVIOUR

In most situations, you may feel, think and act in three main ways: non-assertive, aggressive or assertive. You can also receive another's behaviour non-assertively, aggressively or assertively. In reality, people react to single situations and across different situations with various mixtures of non-assertiveness, aggressiveness and assertiveness. Your degree of non-assertiveness depends not only on the present situation but on your genetic make-up, parental upbringing and the extent to which you have been victimized by peers (Gibb *et al.*, 2004). Nobody is completely assertive.

## Non-assertive

Non-assertive behaviour is passive, compliant, submissive and inhibited. You do not like what is happening to you, but collude in allowing it to continue. You buy peace at the expense of denying your rights. Sometimes, realistically, non-assertive behaviour may be the best option: for instance, for a limited period Anna chooses to put up with her partner Larry's irritability because she realizes that after a back operation he is still weak and in pain. On other occasions though, non-assertive behaviour is 'wimping out'.

## Aggressive

Aggressive behaviour is self-enhancing at the expense of another. You are unfriendly, quarrelsome and unnecessarily hostile. You behave as though you 'have a chip on your shoulder'. You try to get your way through dominating and overpowering rather than by influencing another. Your behaviour is unnecessarily threatening, even to the point of physical violence. Passive aggression is a variation on aggressive behaviour. Here you hurt your partner by withdrawing from meeting his or her needs in some way and playing the victim. Both aggressive and non-assertive behaviour reflect feelings of low self-esteem. Non-assertive behaviour depowers you and aggressive behaviour attempts to depower others.

## Assertive

Assertive behaviour reflects confidence and respect for both yourself and others. It entails responding flexibly and appropriately strongly to different situations. You are in control of yourself and behave in ways that enhance both you and the other. Where possible, you use gentle strength. Colloquially, you 'have your act together'. Alberti and Emmons offer the following working definition of assertiveness:

> Assertive behavior promotes equality in human relationships, enabling us to act in our own best interests, to stand up for ourselves without undue anxiety, to express honest feelings comfortably, to exercise personal rights without denying the rights of others.
>
> (Alberti and Emmons 2001: 36)

The following are some examples of acting non-assertively, aggressively or assertively.

You have cooked a special dinner for your partner who arrives an hour late without contacting you.

*Non-assertive:*     It's all right. Good to see you.

| *Aggressive:* | Damn you. Now the dinner is spoiled. |
| *Assertive:* | I'm concerned at your being so late without contacting me. Was there a reason for this? |

You live with somebody who rarely pulls their weight in cleaning the flat.

| *Non-assertive:* | You say nothing, but resent it deeply. |
| *Aggressive:* | You lazy idiot. Do you think I like acting as your servant all the time. |
| *Assertive:* | I'm unhappy because you almost always leave the cleaning to me. I want us to work out an arrangement so that we share the chores more evenly. |

You may also express positive thoughts and feelings in non-assertive, aggressive and assertive ways to maintain changes in behaviour.

You have been wanting your partner to cut the lawn for some time and she/he finally keep his or her word and does it.

| *Non-assertive:* | Be pleased, but say nothing. |
| *Aggressive:* | That's great. It's about time you kept your word. |
| *Assertive:* | The lawn looks lovely. Thank you. |

The above examples focus non-assertive, aggressive and assertive verbal messages. However, the voice and body messages are also very important. Furthermore, to act assertively you also need to feel and think assertively (see Activity 10.1).

## ACTIVITY 10.1 Assess my assertiveness skills

This activity is in two parts. Complete each part on your own. Then, where appropriate, discuss with your partner, another or others.

## Part A Assess how assertive I am

For each of the items below, indicate with the appropriate code which of the following three options best describes how you either do or might respond.

NA – non-assertively
AG – aggressively
AS – assertively

*You respond*    *Items*

1. _____      The person with whom you live is not doing a fair share of the household chores.
2. _____      You disagree with something your partner says in public.
3. _____      Someone is overdue in paying back money to you.
4. _____      A tradesperson (e.g. plumber, painter) has not done a proper job.
5. _____      You are being pressured to take a drink that you do not want.
6. _____      You do not wish to do a favour for someone.
7. _____      You think your partner has done something to you which is unfair.
8. _____      You want to clarify what someone has said.
9. _____      You are talking with a group of people and want to leave.
10. _____      You want your partner to tidy up the bathroom after he or she uses it.
11. _____      You want your partner to phone you if he or she is going to be late getting home.
12. _____      You want to turn down a social invitation.
13. _____      Your neighbour's dog keeps barking at night.
14. _____      You wait a long time in a restaurant for someone to serve you.
15. _____      You wish to return defective merchandise to a shop.
16. _____      You want to take an unpopular stand on a controversial issue.
17. _____      Someone interrupts when you are talking about something important to you.
18. _____      You think that you have been overcharged for something.
19. _____      You want your partner to spend more time with you.
20. _____      You think that you have been criticized unjustly.

1. Count up the number of times you answered in each category.
2. To what extent do you consider you are assertive, non-assertive, aggressive or a mixture of each and why?

## Part B  Identify specific problem situations

Fill in the personal problem list, by identifying specific situations in which you would like to be more assertive.

*Personal problem list*

1. ...........................................................................................................................................

2. ...........................................................................................................................................

3. ...........................................................................................................................................

4. ............................................................................................................

5. ............................................................................................................

6. ............................................................................................................

7. ............................................................................................................

8. ............................................................................................................

## DIMENSIONS OF COMMUNICATING ASSERTIVELY

Communicating and acting assertively follows from acknowledging significant feelings and thinking assertively. Box 10.1 presents a grid for looking at the choices involved in communicating non-assertively, aggressively or assertively. In assertive behaviour your thinking is disciplined, realistic and goal oriented. Your basic feeling is that of adequacy and you keep in check any self-defeating feelings. Your verbal message is clear. Your vocal and body messages back up your verbal message with an appropriate degree of strength. If necessary, so do your actions. Non-assertive and aggressive behaviour are deficient, to a greater or lesser degree, on each of these dimensions.

---

**Box 10.1    A grid for looking at the choices involved in non-assertive, aggressive and assertive behaviour**

|  | Your thoughts | Your feelings | Your verbal messages | Your vocal messages | Your body messages | Your actions |
|---|---|---|---|---|---|---|
| Non-asssertive behaviour |  |  |  |  |  |  |
| Aggressive behaviour |  |  |  |  |  |  |
| Assertive behaviour |  |  |  |  |  |  |

---

When being assertive, your vocal and body messages can greatly add or detract from your verbal message. For instance, a firm tone of voice may communicate to others that your verbal assertion is to be taken seriously, while a weak tone dilutes it. Assertiveness is not only a matter of presence or desirable verbal, vocal and body messages, but also involves absence of undesirable messages. Be careful not to give messages that put others down. The following are some verbal, vocal and body messages relevant to most instances of assertion.

## Verbal messages

- *Send 'I' messages*. Send 'I' messages that accept responsibility for your thoughts, feelings and actions rather than 'You' messages. For instance, 'I would like you to cooperate in this way (specify)' is preferable to 'You are uncooperative.'
- *Communicate cleanly*. Say what you really mean. Give specific feedback. Do not 'beat about the bush,' make something else the issue, change the subject or hold forth (Litvinoff, 1992).

## Vocal messages

Vocal messages likely to support an assertive verbal message include the following:

- *Volume*. Speak reasonably loudly. Do not put on a 'little girl' or 'little boy' voice.
- *Articulation*. Clearly articulate your words, even if it means speaking slowly.
- *Pitch*. Avoid being shrill.
- *Emphasis*. Emphasize the words that back up your assertive message: for example, 'Please do not phone me again' with an emphasis on the 'do not'.
- *Rate*. Speak at a measured pace. Do not rush your words. Avoid withdrawing into silence.

## Body messages

Body messages likely to support an assertive verbal message include the following:

- *Gaze and eye contact*. Look the other person directly in the eye when delivering your assertive message. Maintain good gaze when your partner responds.
- *Facial expression*. Be genuine, for instance, not smiling when you are serious.
- *Posture*. Stand or sit erect with your chest out and shoulders slightly back. Avoid slouching.
- *Gesture*. Use deliberate and non-threatening hand and arm movements to help express yourself in a constructive fashion. For instance, when you are telling someone that they have gone far enough you can hold up your hand with palm facing outwards.
- *Proximity*. Do not physically avoid your partner. Avoid 'hitting and running', making an assertive statement and leaving before your partner has time to respond.
- *Absence of threatening messages*. Beware of head shaking, door slamming, fist shaking and finger pointing.
- *Absence of distracting messages*. Try to eliminate messages indicating anxiety, such as tugging at your hair, fiddling with your fingers, or shuffling your feet.

*Sam wants to stop his former girlfriend, Rose, from keeping coming around to his flat to try to rekindle their relationship. He decides to use the following assertion skills when she next comes to the door.*

| | |
|---|---|
| *Verbal messages:* | Rose, we've *talked enough* already. I *don't want* you to come around again. Please *go now.* |
| *Vocal messages:* | Firm, reasonably loud, measured pace, emphasis on italicized words. |
| *Body messages:* | Stand erect with chest out, her body facing his, strong eye contact. |

*If Rose does not go, Sam can repeat his assertive message; if she still does not go he can slowly but firmly shut the door.*

## Muscle

How forceful to be so that another 'gets the message' is a consideration relevant to all assertion situations. Muscle refers to the degree of strength of your assertion (Butler, 1992). As a rule of thumb, assertive messages should be at the minimum level of muscle to achieve their objectives. Where possible, assume good intentions, be friendly, use tact and be gentle. Your partner's goodwill is precious to maintaining your relationship, so avoid using a cricket bat where a feather would do. It is better for your partner to feel that they change willingly rather than under duress. The more muscle you use, the greater the risk of eliciting resistance and anger and also leaving a residue of resentment that can surface later.

## Timing

Timing refers to when you deliver assertion messages. Sometimes you have virtually no choice, for instance, if someone makes an unwanted sexual advance. On other occasions, you require assertiveness skills to counter remarks you cannot anticipate. Frequently, however, you can choose when and where to be assertive. It may be easier for you to deliver assertiveness messages when your feelings are back under control, your energy level is good, you have sufficient time to do it properly, and you have thought through what to say and how to say it. Consider when your partner might be most receptive to your assertiveness messages. Though not always possible, try to avoid times when she or he is in a bad mood or concentrating on doing something.

Become aware of your avoidance behaviour. Frequently, you do better to confront another's negative behaviour early on. Keep putting it off can allow the behaviour to continue, if not worsen. However, on other occasions, adopt a wait-and-see approach to avoid delivering premature assertion messages.

## A six-step framework for communicating assertively

The following is a six-step framework for communicating assertively in specific situations in your relationship.

1. *Be aware.* Become aware of where you may be communicating either submissively or aggressively. Listen to feedback from your partner as well as to your own thoughts and feelings.
2. *Specify goals.* You may fail to be assertive through lack of clarity concerning your goals. Be specific as to what you want and assess whether it is in the best interests of your relationship. During this process you may generate and evaluate many goals prior to deciding which is best.
3. *Develop a plan.* Develop a plan to attain your goals. Your plan is likely to focus on how to change your thinking as well as your behaviour. Take into account appropriate verbal, vocal, body and action messages.
4. *Rehearse and practise.* Practice may not make perfect, but it can increase competence. Especially if you anticipate finding your assertiveness difficult, rehearse and practise it in advance. You may role play with another how you want to behave. Alternatively you can use visualized rehearsal and practice. Remember to anticipate setbacks and difficulties in your practice.
5. *Implement your assertiveness.* Pick an appropriate time to give your assertive message and go ahead and do it.
6. *Evaluate.* Evaluate how well you used assertiveness skills and their positive and negative consequences for yourself, your partner and your relationship. Learn from both successes and mistakes. Be prepared to persist in building skills.

When developing assertiveness skills, you can work on easier problems before moving on to more difficult ones. Success in being assertive in the 'shallow end' can provide confidence to move on to the 'deep end'.

## SOME COMMUNICATION SKILLS FOR ASSERTIVENESS

The following are some areas for communicating assertively.

## Disagree

In equal relationships, each partner feels free to disagree. You do not think that you have to be in total harmony with each other all the time. You can add spice to your relationship and broaden your horizons through difference as well as through agreement. However, you can disagree without being unnecessarily dis-agreeable. Disagreements can range from minor differences of opinion to major upheavals. Skills of assertively disagreeing can help you prevent the former turning into the latter.

When conversing, one approach to disagreeing is to counter another's idea by directly stating your opinion: for example, you counter 'I want us to go swimming' with 'I want us to go to the movies.' You can soften this by reflecting the other's opinion to show that you have clearly heard them, before stating your own: for example, 'You want us to go swimming, but I want us to go to the movies.' In addition to 'I want to', following are words that show you disagree without first signalling disagreement:

- I'd prefer to
- I'd like to
- I think that
- I feel.

Another approach to disagreeing is first to state your disagreement and then make an 'I' statement about your position: for instance, 'I disagree. I want us to go to the movies.' In addition to 'I disagree', following are words you can use to start such statements:

- I beg to differ.
- I see things differently.
- I'm not comfortable with that.
- I'd prefer that we didn't.

When disagreeing, support your verbal messages with appropriate vocal and body messages. In addition, listen carefully to your partner's reactions. You can prevent your relationship from becoming unnecessarily negative if you also show your partner when you agree with all or part of what they say or do.

## Say no

You may need to learn to say no assertively. Part of this is learning not to feel afraid or guilty about saying no. Another part of this is actually saying no backed up by vocal, body and, if necessary, action messages that show you mean what you say. Below is an example of someone saying no and not fully meaning it.

> Carol, 23, wanted to end her relationship with Al. She told him she did not want him coming around to her flat anymore. However, when he came, she would talk to him at the entry door for a while and then let him in and give him a coffee. Sometimes they would also have sex.

In this example, Al knows that Carol does not mean what she says. Her words say no but her actions say yes and reward exactly the kind of behaviour she wants to discourage. It is preferable to say no firmly and, if necessary, calmly to reinforce this message with appropriate actions. In this case, appropriate actions for Carol include not talking at the entry door and shutting the door if Al does not go away.

## Set limits

In this book, saying no means refusing another's behaviour altogether, whereas setting limits means placing restrictions on its amount. In setting limits, you require clarity regarding your goals. For example, Monika and Stefan, a couple in their thirties, have a mutual friend called Harriet who lives in a nearby town and keeps phoning them up two or three times a week to talk about her problems. Monika and Stefan like Harriet and want to help her. However, they also value their privacy and increasingly resent Harriet's intrusions on it. Reviewing their own behaviour, Monika and Stefan realize that they have been rewarding Harriet's dependency on them by taking all her calls and allowing her to go on at length. Together, Monika and Stefan establish a goal of allowing Harriet to phone them once a week at a mutually convenient time. Having established their goal, Monika and Stefan decide to let Harriet know next time she calls that they value her friendship, are interested in her and happy to talk, but would prefer just one good conversation a week. Monika and Stefan decide that if Harriet asks for a reason to state that they both lead busy lives and need more space for themselves. If Harriet persists in phoning them twice or thrice weekly, they can remind her of their request and ask her to think about it. If Harriet still does not get the message, Monika and Stefan can consider saying no more phone calls.

Often, as in the above example, setting limits involves not colluding in another's dependency on you. If your partner has a tendency to offload responsibility for their problems and decisions onto you, following are some verbal messages that can help you hand back responsibility to him or her:

- What are your choices?
- How is your current behaviour helping you?
- What are your goals in the situation?
- What are your options?
- What skills do you require?

## Request changes in behaviour

People in relationships build up patterns of behaviour. When you request a change in your partner's behaviour you may have one of three goals: getting him or her (a) to do something that they are not already doing; (b) to do something that they are already doing either more and/or better; (c) lessening or stopping an unwanted behaviour. You may be non-assertive, aggressive or assertive in each of these three areas. Below are some examples.

*Requesting a new behaviour*

Kim wants Matt to bring her flowers on birthdays and anniversaries.

| | |
|---|---|
| *Non-assertive:* | Keep commenting on how other people bring their partners flowers on birthdays and anniversaries. |
| *Aggressive:* | 'You've got no imagination. Don't you know that a woman likes flowers on birthdays and anniversaries?' |
| *Assertive:* | 'I'd really appreciate it if you would bring me flowers on birthdays and anniversaries.' |

*Requesting more of an existing behaviour*

Nigel wishes that Brittany would show more interest in his job.

| | |
|---|---|
| *Non-assertive:* | Say, nothing, but feel bad. |
| *Aggressive:* | 'You only seem interested in your own job. Why don't you take more interest in mine?' |
| *Assertive:* | 'I value your opinion and want to talk with you more about my job.' |

*Requesting less or the stopping of an existing behaviour*

You are studying for an exam tomorrow and your partner is playing a CD very loudly.

| | |
|---|---|
| *Non-assertive:* | You thump the table and curse to yourself. |
| *Aggressive:* | 'Turn that bloody CD player down. Don't you realize that I have work to do.' |
| *Assertive:* | 'When you're playing a CD so loud, I can't concentrate on revising for my exam tomorrow. Please turn the volume down.' |

When requesting a behaviour change, consider giving honest positive feedback as well. It is very easy to initiate a negative cycle. Where possible, emphasize the positive by stating what you want rather than what you do not want. In addition, remember your partner is more likely to maintain a behaviour change if you show appreciation for it.

## Handle defensiveness

Bolton (1986: 158) comments on the human tendency to be defensive and how, as part of sending an assertive message, you may need to handle the 'push–push back phenomenon'. There are internal and external agendas when faced with another's defensiveness. The internal agenda concerns how you handle your own thoughts and feelings. Defensiveness is a common initial reaction to assertive messages. It does not necessarily indicate either that you have asserted yourself poorly or that you may not ultimately be successful. Even if unsuccessful, you can only be responsible for your own behaviour. The expectation that your partner will always do what you want is unrealistic and can only contribute to you denigrating yourself when she or he does not.

The external agenda concerns how you behave towards your partner. Beware of reacting defensively to another's defensiveness. You risk getting sucked into an upward spiral of defensiveness in which the real topic of your assertive message may become lost in accusation and counter-accusation.

Assuming you decide to persist in assertiveness you have a number of options. First, you may pause after the negative response and then calmly yet firmly repeat your behaviour change request. Second, you may reflect your partner's feelings before repeating your request.

> *Partner A:*  When you play a compact disc so loud, I can't concentrate on revising for my exam tomorrow. Please turn the volume down.
>
> *Partner B:*  Why the hell are you complaining?
>
> *Partner A:*  I realize your angry at my request, but I badly need to concentrate on my revision and would be grateful if you could turn the CD player down.
>
> *Partner B:*  [still not too pleased] OK.

A third option is to use more muscle. For instance, you may both use a firmer voice and also strengthen your verbal message by saving 'I'm serious, please turn the CD player down.' A fourth option is to try to negotiate a mutually acceptable solution – for instance, negotiating times when your partner can play the CD player loudly and times when you can revise without it. The skills of solving relationship problems are covered later in the book.

## Deal with power plays

Power plays are attempts by others to get you do what they want rather than what you want. An important way another can power play you is to define situations on their terms. Anxious people can become very skilled at manipulating others. In close relationships, this can become the tyranny of the weak in that the more vulnerable partner controls the more adequate partner by playing on guilt feelings, wishes for a peaceful life and tendencies to collude. Trev uses anger to get what he wants. Moira obscures the issue to avoid dealing with her partner directly. Joan finds that tears are very effective in getting her partner to bend to her wishes. Vince withdraws affection if his partner does not give him the feedback he wants. In all the above instances people use power plays – anger, mystification, tears and withdrawal of affection – to get what they want at their partner's expense. Sometimes a whole relationship has underlying assumptions that place one of the partners at a disadvantage. This may be the case where, on the basis of traditional sex-role assumptions, men discourage women from pursuing careers.

Becoming aware of others' attempts to operate on your self-definition and to manipulate you is the first step in being able to handle their power plays. You then have a number of options:

- Being non-assertive and at least tacitly acquiescing in their false definitions and manipulations.
- Being aggressive and perhaps escalating the tension and emotional temperature by counterattacking.
- Being assertive by quickly yet firmly persisting in your definition of yourself and the situation. This option may also include working on your own tendencies towards acquiescence or escalation.

In addition, you may confront your partner with how they behave and invite discussion of it. Finally, if you are relating to a highly manipulative person, you can get out of the relationship. Ending a relationship can also be an assertive option.

## Encourage one another's assertion

In a close relationships based on assumptions of teamwork and equality, you feel responsible for the happiness and fulfilment of one another and not constantly absorbed with securing your own rights. Assertion for 'us' rather than just either for 'me' or for 'you' is motivated by your positive feelings for each other. This can involve both of you demonstrating daily quiet strength, caring and vigilance. Following are some of the many ways you can encourage one another's assertion for the sake of your relationship:

- *Possess realistic relationship goals and rules.* You can openly discuss the goals of your relationship: for example, a commitment to honest and open communication on the basis of equality. You can also try to clarify the relationship rules most likely to attain them: for example, 'Each of us cares enough about the other to be considerate in the way we assert ourselves and to allow time and attention to process the implications of our assertive remarks.' In short, you give each other permission to be assertive.
- *Provide rewarding consequences.* The consequences you provide for each other's assertiveness can either encourage or discourage it. You can provide rewards for assertive messages by treating them with respect and concern. You can show respect and concern by the quality of your listening and understanding. At times, you can even praise each other for having the courage to be assertive in difficult areas.
- *Demonstrate thinking and acting assertively.* Thinking and acting assertively can be contagious. If you are open and honest, it generally makes it easier

for your partner to be the same way. Your joint openness protects your relationship against destructive cycles of mutual inhibition or aggression.

- *Provide openers and confront.* You can show that you care for each other's views by asking about them. If you think that your partner holds back and requires encouragement to be assertive, offer that encouragement. If necessary, you can confront your partner with the need to be assertive.
- *Show understanding.* If either of you thinks that you have a problem with being assertive, the other can be there to offer assistance and support as you explore how to build your skills. Sometimes this assistance and support involves help in working through painful past experiences contributing to present difficulties.
- *Be assertive outside of your relationship.* If each of you adopts assertiveness as a way of life outside your relationship, this may make it easier to be assertive within it. You can support each other in your attempts to be assertive in your outside contacts.

Assertiveness for 'us' requires constant vigilance. It is easy to settle for less than your relationship's full potential for happiness and fulfilment. Working together as a team you are more likely to attain the potential than if each of you is bound up with your own assertiveness agendas (see Activity 10.2).

---

| **ACTIVITY 10.2** | **Develop my communication skills for being assertive** |

---

First do Part A on your own, before discussing with your partner, another or others. Do Part B with your partner or someone else.

## Part A  Assessment

Take a relationship that is important to you and assess your good and poor skills in each of the following assertion areas.

(a) Disagreeing
(b) Saying 'no'
(c) Setting limits
(d) Requesting a new behaviour
(e) Requesting more of an existing behaviour
(f) Requesting less of or the stopping of an existing behaviour
(g) Handling defensiveness
(h) Dealing with power plays
(i) Encouraging your partner's assertion.

## Part B  Communication

Select a personal problem situation in which you need to behave more assertively and:

1. Specify your communication skills goals.
2. Develop a plan to attain your goals, taking into account appropriate verbal, vocal, body and action messages.
3. Rehearse and practise, both with a partner and using visualized rehearsal.
4. Implement your assertiveness skills.
5. Evaluate how well you used your assertiveness skills and their positive and negative consequences for yourself and others.
6. If necessary, alter/improve your assertive behaviour.

---

## SOME MIND SKILLS FOR ASSERTIVENESS

Alberti and Emmons (2001: 81) observe: 'Right *thinking* about assertiveness is crucial. Thoughts, beliefs, attitudes and feelings set the stage for behavior.' A number of key mind skills can release you to behave more assertively.

### Creating rules

When growing up, you may have been subject to many pressures not to be assertive. You may have lived with parents who demonstrated non-assertiveness or aggression. There are many sources from which, rightly or wrongly, you may have internalized faulty assertiveness rules. Below I mention some sources for learning to become non-assertive and also illustrate unrealistic rules that can interfere with open communication:

- *Your family.* 'You must avoid conflict and commenting on unusual behaviour.' 'You must not openly talk about sex.'
- *Your religion.* 'You should care for others rather than look after your needs.' 'You should always be gentle and self-effacing.'
- *Your gender.* 'Women should not be strong and independent.' 'Men should cover up their feelings.'
- *Your culture.* (Asian) 'You must be very conscious of saving people's face.' (Anglo-Saxon) 'You should not express emotions too openly.'
- *Your race.* 'Whites are better than blacks.' 'Whites are less smart than Asians.'
- *Your peer group.* 'You must conform to group norms.' 'You must be popular.'
- *Your age.* 'Children should be seen and not heard.' 'Parents know better than children.'

- *Your schooling.* 'Teachers know better than pupils.' 'Older children know better than younger children.'

Probably everyone possesses some unrealistic rules that interfere with assertiveness. These reflect musturbatory demands on yourself and your partner. Following are some rules that either are or possess the potential to be unrealistic:

- I/my partner must be nice.
- I/my partner must avoid conflict.
- I/my partner must be liked.
- I/my partner must be feminine.
- I/my partner must be masculine.
- I/my partner must not wear the pants.
- I/my partner must not have wishes of my own.
- I/my partner must never hurt each other.
- I/my partner must not seem vulnerable.
- I/my partner must not show anger.
- I/my partner must not make a mistake.
- I/my partner must not admit a mistake.

The first step in overcoming unrealistic rules that hinder assertiveness is to become aware that you possess them. Next you can logically analyse how realistic they are and what their positive and negative consequences are for you. Then, you can restate them into flexible rules that work better for you. Below is an example.

> *Unrealistic rule:*   'I/my partner must never hurt each other.'
> *Realistic rule:*   'While I prefer not to hurt my partner, I think it is important to our relationship to confront significant issues between us, even though sometimes this may cause pain.'

It is important that you and your partner develop and adhere to assertiveness rules that support your relationship. For instance, assuming both partners agree, the above personal rule regarding hurt could be extended to become the following relationship rule: 'While we prefer not to hurt each other, we think it is important to our relationship to confront significant issues between us, even though sometimes this may cause pain.' Below I suggest some additional relationship rules regarding assertion:

1. It is important to let each other know where we are emotionally.
2. Each of us cares sufficiently about the other to want to know their thoughts and feelings.
3. Each of us wants to meet the legitimate preferences of the other.
4. Each of us cares enough about the other to be considerate in the way we assert ourselves and to allow time and attention to process together the implications of our assertions.

# Creating perceptions

## *Perceive yourself accurately*

Assertiveness requires you to perceive that you have rights and responsibilities. Furthermore, assertiveness requires giving yourself permission to pursue your rights. You may inhibit your assertiveness by negatively labelling yourself: for instance, as 'selfish', 'domineering' and 'bossy'. In addition, others may encourage you to perceive your assertiveness negatively. Among adjectives attached to assertiveness by women are 'unfeminine', 'bitchy' and 'castrating' (Butler, 1981, 1992).

Alternatively, you may label your behaviour too positively. You may perceive yourself as assertive when your actions are either non-assertive or aggressive. If you are non-assertive, the perception of being assertive and doing all you can may be a convenient defence against actually being assertive and facing its consequences. If you are aggressive, the perception of assertiveness provides an acceptable mask for your hostility.

When considering being assertive, you also need to perceive your options rather than do the first thing that comes into your mind. Sometimes you may do nothing. If you decide to proceed, you can generate a range of assertive options and then choose the one most likely to attain your goals.

## *Perceive your partner accurately*

Assertiveness requires you to perceive your partner accurately. You may underreact or overreact because you perceive her or him as more vulnerable or stronger than in reality. You may wrongly transfer feelings and thoughts from previous relationships – for instance, with your parents or a previous lover – onto her or him and then act accordingly. Furthermore, you may exaggerate the symbolic meaning of your partner's actions. For instance, Beck (1988: 30) gives the example of Ken's statement 'I've decided that we need a new boiler' possessing the symbolic meaning 'You underestimate me' to his wife Marjorie. Marjorie thinks 'Why didn't he consult me first before he decided?' Because of her hypersensitivity to indications of lack of respect, Marjorie will now find it difficult to behave assertively.

In addition, you may fail to perceive the impact of your assertive behaviour on your partner. You may have come on too strong or too weak. If you came on too strong, you can attempt to repair the damage. If you came on too weak, you can be firmer next time. If you inaccurately perceive your partner's reactions, you lose flexibility in knowing how best to continue being assertive.

What skills can you use to perceive more accurately? You can question the evidence for your perceptions: for instance, 'Where is the evidence that, if I stand up for my rights, I am castrating?' 'Where is the evidence that my partner underestimates me?' or 'Where is the evidence concerning the effectiveness of my being assertive?' As part of this process, you can generate and consider alternative perceptions. You can then choose the perception that best fits the available facts.

## Creating self-talk

Many people interfere with their effectiveness in asserting themselves by negative self-talk. Illustrative negative self-talk statements include: 'I'm no good', 'I'm a failure', 'I'm going to stuff it up', 'I'll only make matters worse', 'Why bother?', 'What's the use?' and 'She/he never takes any notice of me.' If you engage in negative self-talk, you can counteract it with coping self-talk. As mentioned already, coping self-talk consists of calming, coaching and affirming self-statements.

Let's take the earlier example of having cooked a special dinner for your partner who arrives an hour late without contacting you. Your negative self-talk statements might be: 'She/he doesn't love me', 'She/he never considers my feelings' and 'After all the trouble I've been to, then she/he does this to me.' You identify your negative self-talk as inaccurate or at least decide to give your partner the benefit of the doubt. You counteract your negative self-talk with coping self-talk. Your calming self-statements include: 'Relax' and 'Take it easy.' Your coaching self-statements include: 'Smile and seem pleased to see her/him' and 'Give her/him the opportunity to explain why she/he is late.' Your affirming self-statements include: 'I can handle this' and 'I know she/he cares for me.'

Above I illustrated using coping self-talk in relation to a specific situation requiring assertiveness. You can also use self-talk to develop a more general capacity to be assertive. For example, you can rehearse and practise the following self-statements that encourage and legitimize assertion: 'I have a right to say/do that', 'I have a responsibility to stand up for myself', 'I believe in equality in my relationships', 'My opinions count' and 'I am important'.

## Creating visual images

You can use many visualizing skills to enhance your assertiveness. First, you can use imagery to help select assertiveness goals. Second, you can stop imagining the dire consequences of being assertive. When you catch yourself indulging in negative images, you can imagine a large neon sign flashing 'STOP' off and on. You can also vigorously shout 'STOP' to yourself at the same time as visualizing the image. Then, switch to more positive or congenial images (Kwee and Lazarus, 1986; Lazarus, 1989).

Third, you can use mental rehearsal that focuses on your enacting competent verbal, voice and body messages in a specific situation. Start by getting a real picture of the scene in your imagination as if in a photograph and then turn it into a moving picture that contains your assertive behaviour (Lewinsohn et al., 1986). You can enhance your motivation by imagining the positive outcomes for yourself and others of your assertiveness. You may also imagine ways of coping with different responses from your partner to your assertiveness. Before, during and after your mental rehearsals you can use calming, coaching and affirming self-talk, as appropriate. Many people do not rehearse scenes thoroughly enough and then find themselves at a loss for words in real situations (Lazarus, 1984). Fourth, you can use mental relaxation, in which you picture yourself in a restful scene, to calm you down before and possibly after your assertiveness.

## Creating explanations

If you are non-assertive in situations, there are many explanations of varying degrees of accuracy. Some explanations focus on yourself: for instance, you are submissive and lacking in confidence because of your nature or upbringing. You may see yourself as the helpless victim of circumstances. You may also think that your partner should know what bothers you without being told. In addition, you may have tried unsuccessfully to assert yourself in the past and concluded that it is no use trying again. You may consider your partner's behaviour is so deeply ingrained that it is no use trying to change her or him.

You might like your partner to become more assertive, but think that he or she should be able to do this without your help. Furthermore, if your partner reacts negatively to your attempts at assertiveness, you may automatically blame him or her for being defensive or bloody-minded rather than search for alternative explanations.

The danger of all these potentially faulty explanations for how you and your partner behave is that they are dead ends. You need to become aware both of your faulty explanations and of their consequences for you and your relationship. You can then distinguish between fact and inference and form explanations that are more conducive to acting assertively. Such explanations make two assumptions: first, that each of you is responsible for your own thoughts, feelings and communications; second, that you are jointly responsible for constructively developing your relationship.

## Creating expectations

Sometimes being assertive in close relationships seems much more risky than in relationships with less to lose. You may find that you are testing the limits of your partner's commitment to your relationship. You may catastrophize the consequences of being assertive and greatly overestimate the probability of negative outcomes. Furthermore, you may minimize your resources for coping with negative consequences.

However, you can fail to be assertive because you underestimate the positive consequences of assertiveness. Minimization of the potential for reward rather than maximization of the potential for loss holds you back. Because you inadequately perceive the gain side of the loss/gain ledger balance, you are unwilling to take risks that might have a high chance of bringing genuine gains to your relationship.

Awareness of any tendency you may have to either overestimate the negative or underestimate the positive consequences of assertiveness is the starting point for working on these mind skills weaknesses. Then challenge your existing thinking by realistically appraising both potential gains and losses. If you tend to underestimate the gains, you can work hard to generate and assess the realistic benefits of being assertive both in general and in specific situations. You can also become more aware of your strengths and of any support factors, for instance, your partner or friends, that can help you become more assertive (see Activity 10.3).

## ACTIVITY 10.3          Develop my mind skills for being assertive |

Answer the following questions on your own. Then, if appropriate, discuss with your partner, another or others.

1.  In relation to one of the situations in which you would like to be more assertive on your personal problem list in Activity 10.1, assess your strengths and weaknesses in each of the following mind skills areas:

    (a) Creating rules
    (b) Creating perceptions
    (c) Creating self-talk
    (d) Creating visual images
    (e) Creating explanations
    (f) Creating expectations.

2.  Specify how your current mind skills interfere with your acting assertively?
3.  Identify one or more of your main poor mind skills and develop a plan to change how you think. In your plan specify:

    (a) Your goals, including a time frame
    (b) The steps you intend taking to attain each of your goals
    (c) How you will monitor your progress.

## ACTIVITY 10.4            Group discussion: assertiveness skills |

This is intended as a group exercise, though it may be done individually or in pairs. For each part:

1.  Spend five to ten minutes answering the question in groups of three or four.
2.  Each subgroup shares its findings with the whole group.
3.  The whole group ranks the four most important skills from the most important to the least important.

## Part A  Sending assertive messages

List the four most important skills people can use in sending assertive messages to a partner.

## Part B  Receiving assertive messages

List the four most important skills people can use in receiving assertive messages from a partner.

## Part C  Encouraging one another's assertion

List the four most important skills partners can use to encourage one another's assertion.

# 11

## *Manage anger skills*

**Chapter outcomes**
By studying and doing the activities in this chapter you should:

- be able to define anger
- know about some positive functions of anger
- know about some communication skills for managing anger
- know about some mind skills for managing anger.

Angie is under a lot of stress at work. She is also very irritable at home. When her boyfriend Jock draws her irritability to her attention and asks her what is wrong, Angie gets even angrier and tells him that he just can't understand what she is going through.

Toby resents his partner Anita spending so much time talking to her mother, Tania, on the phone. Toby angrily tells Anita, 'I'm pissed off with the way you let yourself be controlled by that demanding bitch.'

As in the above examples, anger can feature prominently in close relationships. This chapter focuses on how you can manage your own anger, whereas the next chapter reviews joint approaches to solving relationship problems.

## DEFINING ANGER

Dictionary definitions of anger include extreme or passionate displeasure and hostile feelings because of opposition. Anger can range from mild, for instance, slight irritation, up to extreme rage. It can be short term or go on over a long period of time. It can also be acknowledged by the angry person or be denied in some measure.

Angry feelings can be demonstrated by verbal, vocal, body, touch and taking action messages. Verbal messages can vary from assertive expressions of anger to aggressive put-downs such as 'You stupid bitch/bastard', 'Fool', 'You clumsy oaf', 'You worthless fraud', 'You've got it all wrong again' and 'You always screw up.' Vocal messages range from shouting and emphasizing attacking comments to giving your partner the silent treatment. Body messages include scowling, glaring, flushing, fist clenching, finger stabbing, and stomping out of the room. Touch messages include anything from a mild push to murder. Taking action messages include withdrawal of desirable actions, for instance, not giving a birthday gift, and sending blunt messages, such as angry letters or a legal writ. In addition, your body may experience anger through physiological reactions such as heightened blood pressure, hypertension, ulcers and insomnia.

Research in North America shows that men and women are angered by similar things, experience anger equally strongly and tend to express anger in similar ways (Deffenbacher *et al.*, 2002). However, in close relationships, expression of anger does not take place on a 'level playing field' between the sexes since men tend to be stronger and control more resources. Easteal (1994) argues that violence against women is well entrenched in Australian society. She sees many women and children as hostages in their homes and asserts that domestic violence is underreported because many women subscribe to the following three rules: 'Don't talk', 'Don't trust' and 'Don't feel.' Psychological violence always accompanies physical violence. Psychological violence used on its own by partners of both sexes with poor managing anger skills is far too common in close relationships.

## Positive uses of anger

Anger can also have positive outcomes in relationships. Angry feelings do not in themselves destroy relationships, but handling them poorly may do so. Anger can be a *guide* to a clearer definition of yourself. Both sexes can use anger to become more expert at knowing who they are and what they want. In addition, anger can be a *signal* for you and your partner that something is wrong in your relationship and requires attention. This should be a cue to examine your own thoughts, feelings and actions and not just those of your partner. Anger can also be a *motivater* leading to identifying problems, expressing important feelings and redressing concerns (Deffenbacher *et al.*, 2002).

A controversial issue is the use of anger as a *purge* so that afterwards you and your partner calm down and become more rational. An improved emotional climate does not always follow angry outbursts. Lazarus and colleagues consider that 'blowing off steam' is self-defeating and that it is better to express emotions assertively (Lazarus *et al.*, 1993). Nevertheless, in close relationships the partners can establish rules and develop skills that allow anger to be ventilated and then used constructively rather than for tearing each other apart (see Activity 11.1).

## ACTIVITY 11.1                    Assess my angry feelings |

Answer the following questions on your own. Then, if appropriate, discuss with your partner, another or others.

1.  To what extent is managing anger a problem for you?
2.  To what extent do you get angry with yourself rather than with your partner (or another)?
3.  How good are you at tuning into your angry feelings?
4.  What are the other feelings, for instance, hurt or anxiety, that you experience when you are angry?
5.  What physical reactions, for instance, tension, do you experience when angry?
6.  How confident a person are you and to what extent does this affect your proneness to anger?
7.  To what extent do you consider you are less of a person because you have angry feelings? If so, please explain.
8.  How good are you at tuning into positive feelings about your partner (or another) that might prevent or soften your anger?
9.  What messages do you send when you feel angry?
    *   verbal messages
    *   vocal messages
    *   body messages
    *   touch messages
    *   taking action messages.
10. Have you ever been or do you consider you have the potential to be physically violent when angry? If so, please elaborate.

---

# SOME COMMUNICATION SKILLS FOR MANAGING ANGER

The following are some suggestions for what you can actually do to prevent, express, manage and repair damage from your anger.

## Keep your temper

In addition to using mind skills described later, there are a number of things you can do when you tune into your early warning systems that you are in danger of losing your temper. For example, you can breathe slowly and regularly. You can delay your response until less agitated: for instance, by using counting to 10 or to a 100. You can remove yourself from the situation and take time out. You can engage in 'cooling off' activities like going for a walk or taking a bath, or 'letting off steam activities' like running or playing a competitive sport.

## Express anger assertively

Alberti and Emmons (2001: 143) observe: 'Remember that anger and aggression are not the same thing! Aggression is a style of behavior. Anger can be expressed assertively – aggression is not the only alternative.' Assuming you decide it is worth conveying anger, how do you go about it? Though not always easy, try to use tact and diplomacy in your verbal messages. You can give specific feedback about what bothers you, state your feeling as an 'I' message and let your partner know what you want. Beware of put-downs, defensiveness and playing the victim. Below are examples of expressing anger aggressively and assertively.

*Martha to Sven*
> *Aggressive anger:*   'You're doing it again. What's wrong with you? My father is much smarter than you. Shut your bloody gob.'
>
> *Assertive anger:*   'When you call my father an interfering bastard, I get angry. Please stop it.'

You can accompany your assertive verbal messages with appropriate vocal and body messages. For instance, speak in a firm voice without shouting and emphasize words like 'angry' and 'stop'. In addition, make good eye contact and avoid threatening gestures.

## Relax yourself

Later in this chapter I mention how you can try to counteract angry feelings by visualizing the tension leaving your body and creating a restful scene. In addition, focusing on your breathing and taking a series of regular slow deep breaths can often help you to become more relaxed. If anything, emphasize exhaling: for instance, 'Breathe in . . . out . . . out . . . in . . . out . . . out.'

Progressive muscular relaxation is another method by which you can work to dissipate your anger. The term 'progressive relaxation' refers to the progressive cultivation of the relaxation response. You may use progressive muscular relaxation in conjunction with visualized relaxation and other mind skills, for example, coping self-talk. Relaxation skills can help you to deal with unpleasant and counterproductive aspects of heightened emotional arousal. The desired consequences of this are that you think and act more rationally.

The first step in relaxing yourself physically is to find a quiet space where you will be uninterrupted. You may use a mattress, recliner chair or comfortable chair with a headrest. If possible wear loose-fitting, comfortable clothing and remove items such as glasses and shoes. Your arms should be either by your sides if you are lying down or on the arms of your chair if seated. Your legs should be uncrossed and your eyes shut.

Progressive muscular relaxation involves tensing and relaxing various muscle groups. There is a five-point tension–relax cycle that you go through for each muscle group (Bernstein and Borkovec, 1973):

1. *Focus*. Focus attention on a particular muscle group.
2. *Tense*. Tense the muscle group.
3. *Hold*. Maintain the tension for five to seven seconds.
4. *Release*. Release the tension in the muscle group.
5. *Relax*. Spend 20 to 30 seconds focusing attention on the letting go of tension and further relaxing of the muscle group.

Following are 16 muscle groups for progressive muscular relaxation: right hand and forearm; right biceps; left hand and forearm; left biceps; forehead; eyes, nose and upper cheeks; jaws and lower cheeks; neck and throat; chest and shoulders; stomach; right thigh; right calf; right foot; left thigh; left calf; and left foot. Progressive muscular relaxation requires regular practice to gain its full benefits. When learning the technique, you should practise for at least 15 minutes daily for a week.

At times brief muscular relaxation approaches may assist you to manage anger. For example, you can tense and relax four composite muscle groupings: arms and hands; face and neck; chest and trunk of body; and legs and feet. Another option is to tense and then relax all your muscles simultaneously, accompanied by inhaling and then exhaling a deep breath.

## Manage stress

Stress can come from both within and without. Both sources can contribute to anger. Develop awareness of your early warning signals of stress and listen to them. In addition, become more aware of what stresses you. Such awareness may help you not only to prevent and manage your anger but also to avoid taking it out on other people.

Each of you has an optimal level of stress or a particular level of stimulation at which you feel most comfortable. At this level you experience stress without distress (Selye, 1974). Beneath this level you may be insufficiently stimulated or bored. Above this level you are likely to experience physiological and psychological distress. Body reactions include hypertension and proneness to heart attacks and ulcers. Feelings of distress may include shock, depression, frustration, anger, disorientation and fears of insanity or nervous breakdown. If the heightened stress is prolonged or perceived as extremely severe, you may feel you are in a state of excessive stress or crisis.

Below are two examples of people whose stresses make them more prone to anger. Kent has allowed himself to develop an excessively stressful lifestyle. Tracey is reacting to external pressures. However, in both examples there is an interaction between internal and external sources of stress.

> Kent is a high-pressure foreign exchange dealer. He is always on the go both professionally and personally. He lives on his nerves and burns the candle at both ends. When things go wrong, he gets tense and irritable. He is like a tightly stretched rubber band just waiting to break out in anger.

Tracey has just received a promotion at work. She now has to supervise 15 people. While pleased at the promotion Tracey still needs to develop the skills of being a good supervisor. She feels under pressure because of her promotion and is very irritable when she gets home. Tracey does not sleep well and her appetite is poorer than usual.

Some of the skills of managing stress are peculiar to the specific situations in which people find themselves. For example, as Tracey develops supervisory skills she is likely to feel less under stress. Other skills are more general: for example, possessing good mind skills. Further skills of managing stress include muscular and visualized relaxation, developing adequate recreational outlets, staying physically fit, keeping in touch with nature (my favourite!), developing your support network of helpful people, and improving your managing problems skills. Sometimes the most effective way to manage anger is to analyse the broader context of stresses in which it occurs. There may be choices that you can make and skills that you can develop for dealing with stresses outside a relationship that will free you to be less angry, more relaxed and happier within the relationship.

## Handle aggressive criticism

Below are five verbal strategies for dealing with aggressive criticism. You need to accompany your verbal messages with appropriate vocal and body messages. Use self-talk that assists you to stay calm and in control of your emotions. You are a person in your own right who does not allow herself or himself to be overwhelmed by another's criticisms and feelings. The strategies may be used in combination as well as singly.

1. *Reflective strategy*. This strategy allows your partner to vent their strong feelings and shows you have understood both their feelings and their reasons: for example, 'You feel mad at me because you think I am not pulling my weight in doing the household chores.' Often people stay stuck in anger like broken records because, rightly or wrongly, they consider they are not being heard. Reflecting another's anger does not mean that you automatically agree with them.
2. *Deflective strategy*. The object here is to blunt the thrust of aggressive criticism by agreeing with part of it. This strategy is especially useful where you actually do agree with part of the criticism. Examples of this are: 'You have a point, I am rather untidy at times' or 'I'm not always as considerate as I would like to be.'
3. *Enquiry strategy*. Following on from either a reflective or deflective response or from both responses, you may then use an enquiry: 'Please be more specific about what I've done to upset you.' The enquiry may defuse the aggressiveness of the criticism since it shows you are willing to allow your

partner to elaborate their position. However, sometimes an enquiry ignites rather than defuses anger. People can become threatened when asked reasons for their anger.

4. *Feedback strategy.* After showing that you have heard your partner's criticism you may choose to give feedback both about the criticism and the manner in which it was given: for example, 'I feel very uncomfortable when you criticize me so harshly. The reason that I am so late in picking you up was that I was in a traffic jam on the way over.' Sometimes when another person attempts to talk you down, calmly and firmly repeat your position at the same time as acknowledging that they feel differently.

5. *Deferral strategy.* Often you have a choice as to whether to back off now and react to criticism at a later date. Backing off does not mean backing down. Rather you husband your resources for when you can be most effective. You may say something like 'I've heard what you say (if necessary specify). I would like some time to think about it.' Alternatively, if it becomes clear that you disagree, you might say 'It's obvious that we disagree. I think we both need some time to think about it. Could we fix a time to discuss it again?' Deferral strategies are not intended to avoid issues. Rather they allow either or both parties to cool down and then deal more rationally with the matter.

## Apologize and take corrective action

Defensiveness is posssibly more dangerous than anger in close relationships. If you are defensive you risk fanning the flames of one another's anger. However, if you are open, capable of acknowledging hurtful behaviours when pointed out and willing to change them, you not only defuse those situations but also make it easier for your partner to behave likewise. By your honesty and actions ill-will can get transformed into goodwill.

If you have been unreasonably aggressive, you will likely have hurt your partner and diminished their self-esteem. When cooler, you may feel genuine remorse and shame. In addition, you may wish to diminish the suffering and pain you have caused. A skill of repairing your relationship is to make a genuine apology. A good verbal apology restores balance by acknowledging that you have broken a norm or relationship rule: for example, 'I'm sorry that I was so rude about your father last night.' You may add an explanation for being so aggressive: for instance, 'I had drunk too much' or 'I've been overworking.' Your partner may perceive a good verbal apology as a pseudo-apology unless your vocal and body messages also indicate genuine regret. Before, during or after an apology you can physically reach out to your partner by touching his or her hand, arm or shoulder.

You are likely to damage rather than restore your relationship if you apologize and then repeat the same aggressive behaviour. Corrective actions speak louder than crocodile tears.

## Forgive and move on

After an angry outburst, your partner may apologize to you. Assuming the apology is genuine, she or he is attempting to restore the damage done to your self-esteem. By offering an apology your partner acknowledges wrongdoing and places herself or himself in a vulnerable position. Assuming you choose to accept the apology, you can still acknowledge your pain: for example, 'I felt very hurt by your remarks about my father, but I accept your apology.' If you do not accept genuine apologies and forgive, you risk alienating your partner. Your failure to reward honesty may cause your partner to be defensive in future. In addition, you risk torturing yourself by holding longstanding grudges. Sometimes your partner may not have the inner strength to verbally apologize, but will take corrective action. Again, the best policy may be to forgive and move on in your relationship.

On occasion you may decide to move beyond anger and forgive your partner even if no apology has been received (Worthington and Scherer, 2004). Emotions leading to such forgiveness include empathy, sympathy, compassion and love. Appropriate forgiveness may have positive benefits for both partners, for instance better physical health and a less stressful relationship (Macaskill, 2005) (see Activity 11.2).

---

**ACTIVITY 11.2**                    **Develop my communication skills for managing anger**

---

First complete this activity on your own. Then, if appropriate, discuss and practise with your partner, another or others.

1. Assess your good skills and poor skills in each of the following communication skills of managing anger.

    (a) Keeping your temper
    (b) Using preventive assertion
    (c) Expressing anger assertively
    (d) Relaxing yourself
    (e) Managing stress
    (f) Handling aggressive criticism
    (g) Apologizing and taking corrective action
    (h) Forgiving and moving on.

2. If appropriate, identify one or more of your poor managing anger communication skills and develop a plan to change how you act. In your plan, specify:

    (a) Your goals, including a time frame
    (b) The steps you intend taking to attain each of your goals
    (c) How you will monitor your progress.

---

## SOME MIND SKILLS FOR MANAGING ANGER

A one-word amendment to Shakespeare's saying 'Love's best habit is a soothing tongue' is to substitute mind for tongue. A soothing *mind* is the precondition for a soothing *tongue*. Mental cultivation to manage your anger is essential for effective relating. On the one hand you can choose to think yourself into hatred, aggressive blaming, nursing resentments, wanting to cause psychological pain and communicating violently. On the other hand you can choose to think yourself into a calmer, more rational and more problem-solving frame of mind.

### Creating rules

Ellis considers that the main cause of anger is people being unwilling to relinquish childish demandingness (1977). An important way you can control anger is to dispute and replace unrealistic rules, based on absolutistic and demanding thinking, with more realistic rules, based on rational and preferential thinking (Ellis, 2005). Often, in close relationships, people make unrealistic role-related claims on one another: for instance, 'You're my wife and I expect you to act that way' (Butler, 1981: 141). In long-term relationships submerged unrealistic rules have time later on to emerge. You can create your anger by possessing unrealistic musturbatory rules about how you, your partner, your relationship and life should be. Box 11.1 shows some examples.

When you find yourself getting angry, it helps if you do not act impulsively. Instead stop and think whether any of your unrealistic rules contribute to it. You can develop the skill of backtracking from your angry feelings or actions to the thoughts that generate and sustain them. Then you evaluate how realistic are your rules. You can dispute your rules by asking questions like: 'Where is the evidence to confirm or negate their realism?' 'Do I expect the same of other people's relationships?' 'What are the positive and negative consequences of maintaining my rule(s)?' Often you will find that your rules are partially true, but you have made them too rigid: for instance, a rule might be 70 per cent realistic and 30 per cent unrealistic.

A final step is to restate your unrealistic anger-evoking rules into more realistic rules. The following are some guidelines for stating realistic rules: (a) express preferences rather than demands; (b) emphasize coping rather than perfectionism; (c) base them on your own valuing process; (d) allow flexibility so they are amenable to change in light of new information; and (e) word them so that they lead to a functional rating of specific characteristics and not to a global self-rating of your or your partner's personhood. The following are some examples of restating anger-evoking rules into more realistic rules.

| | |
|---|---|
| *Unrealistic rule:* | 'I must always get my revenge.' |
| *Realistic rule:* | 'My interests are not best served by thinking in terms of revenge. I can work out more appropriate strategies for gaining my preferences and keeping our relationship intact.' |

---

### Box 11.1   Unrealistic musturbatory rules

*About yourself*

- I must never make mistakes.
- I must always be right.
- I must punish my partner for wrongdoings.
- I must never forgive and forget.
- I must never apologize.

*About your partner*

- A wife/husband must always ...
- My partner must approve of me all the time.
- My partner must never make me angry.
- My partner must never criticize me.
- Where cultural differences exist, my partner must always adjust to my culture.

*About our relationship*

- Our relationship must never have conflict in it.
- Our relationship must seem conflict free to outsiders.
- We must compete rather than collaborate with each other.

*About life*

- Life must be fair.
- Life must be free of hassles.

---

| *Unrealistic rule*: | 'My partner must never criticize me.' |
|---|---|
| *Realistic rule*: | 'Feedback is important in our relationship. However, I prefer my partner using tact and diplomacy when giving feedback.' |

## Creating perceptions

An important skill for partners wishing to avoid the slide from fusion to fission is that of, wherever possible, perceiving one another through kind rather than unkind eyes. Beck (1988: 61) observes that marital conflict 'fosters and exaggerates egocentric perspectives'. Partners systematically bias their perceptions by 'framing' one another negatively: for instance, 'He likes to see me suffer' and 'She is so manipulative.' Once this framing process starts, partners misinterpret positive or neutral acts as negative and perceive negative acts even more negatively. Clearly such negative framing fans and sustains anger.

## Identify tricks of the mind

Beck observes that distressed couples can fall prey to a number of cognitive distortions or tricks of the mind that interfere with perceiving themselves and their partner accurately. If you can identify your characteristic ways of mis-interpreting, you are in a stronger position to correct them. The following are some common tricks of the mind (Beck, 1988; Beck and Weishaar, 2005):

- *Tunnel vision*. Partners focus only on that part of the overall picture that they want to see: for example, continually finding fault with one another.
- *Arbitrary inference*. Drawing a specific conclusion about yourself or your partner without supporting evidence. For example, you wrongly perceive your partner's silence as anger.
- *Mind-reading*. Ascribing thoughts and intentions to your partner either without checking with him or her or, if you've checked, thinking you know better. For instance, you can erroneously mind-read that your partner wishes to hurt you.
- *Overgeneralization*. Using imprecise language that is far too global: for example, 'She/he *never* does anything round the house' or 'She/he *always* keeps me waiting.'
- *Magnification*. Making your partner and events out to be worse than they really are. Exaggerating negative consequences.
- *Negative labelling*. Placing negative labels on your partner and then reacting to them as though they were the whole truth: for instance, 'She/he's impos-sible', 'She/he doesn't give a damn', 'She's a castrating bitch' and 'He's a narcissistic bully.'
- *Polarized thinking*. Thinking in black-and-white terms: for instance, 'She/he either loves me or she/he doesn't' or 'Either we get on really well or we don't get on at all.'

## Reality test your perceptions

This section focuses on not being unnecessarily hard in the way you judge others' behaviour. This also can be a way of not being too hard on yourself.

> Libby and Andy had been living together for six months. Libby was becoming extremely uptight because Andy was not more openly affectionate. She concluded that he did not love her any more.

You can jump to conclusions that trigger anger. Let us assume that the interpret-ation of her partner's behaviour that Libby chose to give herself was erroneous. This may have been partly due to her own insecurity and partly because she had insufficiently developed skills of propositional thinking. Propositional thinking means treating your thoughts as hypotheses and then using the process of scientific enquiry to generate and review evidence that confirms or negates your hypotheses (Beck, 1988; Beck and Weishaar, 2005). The outcome of Libby's misinterpretation was that she felt angry with her partner.

An obvious but often overlooked skill of trying to interpret your partner's behaviour is to ask them about it. You check out their reasons before jumping to conclusions. Another skill is to generate alternative interpretations and then choose one or more that best fits the factual evidence. The following are alternative interpretations that Libby might have for Andy's behaviour:

- He never has been openly affectionate, but he has always been there for me when I want him.
- Andy is good at showing affection. It's just that I am very demanding.
- Andy came from a family where his parents were not openly affectionate and he needs help in becoming more expressive.

If you become aware that you have a tendency to become unnecessarily aggressive, a useful skill for curbing your 'knee-jerk' reactions to perceived provocations is to search for alternative and better ways of interpreting them. As part of reality testing your perceptions, you can ask the following questions:

- Stop . . . think . . . am I jumping to conclusions?
- Are my perceptions based on fact or inference?
- Am I distorting the evidence through one or more tricks of the mind?
- If based on inference, are there alternative interpretations more closely related to the facts?
- If necessary, what further information do I need to collect?
- What is the interpretation I choose because it best fits the facts?

## Creating self-talk

If you tend to be impulsive when angry and 'shoot' your mouth, consider using coping self-talk. Anger-evoking situations may be viewed as challenging you to respond in task-oriented rather than in impulsive and self-defeating ways. Simple self-instructions like 'Calm down', 'Cool it', 'Count to ten' and 'Take it easy' can often give you the time and space to get your feelings more under control. Once this takes place you have considerably more choice concerning whether or not and how to express your anger.

Pete is angry with Cindy because she said she could collect him from work and has kept him waiting for half an hour. When she finally arrives looking tired and rushed he tells himself, 'Take it easy. Count to ten. She is obviously tired and this is no time for either of us to have a row.' Cindy apologizes and says that she was delayed by having to change a flat tire.

In many relationships provocations are relatively predictable. You know that your partner may tease you, leave their clothes around, not do a domestic chore or some other thing that you dislike. Here you can use coping self-talk to help achieve your goal of managing a specific provocation better. This entails making choices that increase your sense of mastery and lessen the likelihood of your anger being both unpleasant for yourself and counterproductive in your relationship (Meichenbaum, 1983). Remember, using coping self-talk involves calming self-statements: for instance, 'Stay calm'; coaching self-statements about how you can best perform the task at hand; and affirming self-statements that enhance your confidence. The following are examples of coping self-talk statements you can use before, during and after provocations and fights:

> *Before*
> 'Remember, stick to the issues and avoid put-downs.'
>
> 'I can handle this situation if I don't let my stupid pride get in the way.'
>
> *During*
> 'Stay cool. I'm not going to let her/him have the satisfaction of getting to me.'
>
> 'Relax. My anger is a signal telling me to calm down and keep by goal in mind.'
>
> *After*
> 'Even though the situation is unresolved, I'm glad I didn't come on strong.'
>
> 'Using my coping self-talk prevents me from feeling powerless and overwhelmed.'

## Creating visual images

You can use visualizing, or consciously changing the images in your mind, to help you manage anger better. Ways that you can use visualizing include the following.

### Visualized rehearsal

When preparing how to handle anger-evoking provocations you can visually go through the various steps in how you want to behave. Once you have worked this out you can repeatedly imagine yourself handling the provocation competently. You can accompany these 'movies in your mind' with a soundtrack of coping self-talk.

### Visualized relaxation

Visualization is best achieved by sitting or lying in a quiet and comfortable place, shutting your eyes and having no distractions. Here I describe two skills of visualized relaxation: visualizing the tension leaving your body and visualizing a restful scene.

### VISUALIZING THE TENSION LEAVE YOUR BODY

The following is some self-talk you can use for visualizing the tension leave your body. Talk to yourself in a soft, dreamy voice:

> I'm going to count to ten in groups of two, and after each group of two relax a different muscle grouping. It's as though I'm going to be turning out the different lights in a house at night. One, two . . . focus on the tension leaving my legs and feet . . . the upper part of my legs, my knees, the lower part of my legs, my feet and my toes. I'm enjoying the peaceful calm sensations of relaxation as the tension leaves my legs and feet. Three, four . . . focus on the tension leaving the trunk of my body . . . the upper part of my back, the lower part of my back, my sides, my chest/breasts, my stomach, my buttocks. My relaxation is getting deeper and deeper and deeper. Five, six . . . focus on the tension leaving my arms and hands . . . the upper part of my arms, my biceps, my elbows, the lower part of my arms, my hands, and my fingers. My arms and hands feel warm and relaxed, warm and relaxed, warm and relaxed. Seven, eight . . . focus on the tension leaving my head and face . . . my forehead, the area around my eyes, my nose, my cheeks, my mouth, my jaw, my neck, my ears, the back of my head and the top of my head. My head feels drowsier and drowsier and drowsier. Nine, ten . . . focus on the tension leaving the whole of my body . . . my head and face, my arms and hands, the trunk of my body, and my legs and feet. I enjoy the sensations of peace and calm, peace and calm, peace and calm as the tension flows from the whole of my body and my relaxation becomes deeper and deeper and deeper.

### VISUALIZING A RESTFUL SCENE

You may visualize restful scenes not only as a prelude to other forms of visualization, for example, visualized rehearsal, but also as a way of calming yourself down when angry. Visualizing a restful scene may follow either visualizing the tension leaving your muscles or progressive muscular relaxation, which was described earlier in this chapter. Each of you probably has one or more special scenes where you feel relaxed, for instance, looking at a valley with lush green meadows or sitting in a favourite chair at home. The following is an example of a visual relaxation scene:

> I'm lying on an uncrowded beach on a sunny day enjoying the pleasant sensations of warmth on my body. I feel the caressing of a gentle breeze. I can hear the peaceful noise of the sea lapping against the shore nearby. I'm enjoying the soft touch of my towel and the sand. Also, I'm enjoying the salty smell of the sea and the fresh air. I haven't a care in the world. I experience feelings of peace and calm, peace and calm, peace and calm as

my sensations of relaxation and well-being get deeper and deeper and deeper.

## Creating explanations

Blaming is probably the most common way that you can anger yourself by explaining cause wrongly. Lazarus and his colleagues write: 'Blaming, accusing, condemning, chiding or reproaching others or yourself is destructive. In fact, these actions hinder constructive, creative solutions to conflicts' (1993: 69). Though you can blame yourself, most commonly in close relationships blaming involves externalizing the cause of your problems and anger outside of yourself. Blaming is a mind skills weakness for many reasons. First, you fail to acknowledge your own contribution to problems. Almost invariably, the causes of relationship problems are neither black nor white. Usually when blaming you explain the cause defensively. Either unintentionally or intentionally you tell yourself stories intended to make you seem totally right and the other person totally wrong. Second, when you blame you may make your partner not only responsible for the problem but for your angry reactions as well: for instance, by thinking and possibly saying 'It's all your fault. Look how angry you've made me.' Third, blaming can have unwanted negative consequences: for instance, your partner reacts defensively and counterattacks. Fourth, blaming mainly addresses the past rather than the future. You can stay stuck because first you blame your partner for creating a problem and then you blame him or her for not solving it. Fifth, blaming contributes to feelings of powerlessness. For instance, Ewan explains to his coach that he keeps abusing his wife Joanne because her nagging makes him so furious. Rather than collude, the coach replies: 'Well, you're not going to let her keep controlling you like that are you?'

How can you explain the cause of your anger more accurately? You can become more mindful of the risks of blaming. You can monitor the frequency, duration and intensity of your blaming thoughts. Whenever you catch yourself blaming, ask yourself the following questions:

1. 'How have I contributed to the creation of the problem?'
2. 'How am I contributing to the maintenance of the problem?'
3. 'What is the outcome I would really like for myself and for our relationship?'
4. 'What can I do to achieve that outcome?'

## Creating expectations

Consequential thinking involves thinking through the consequences for yourself and others of your thoughts, feelings and actions. Frequently, anger blinds people from accurately predicting the consequences of their actions. You can sow the seeds of anger in relationships if you underestimate the gains from showing caring and kindness to your partner. You can also underestimate the gains from assertive expressions of anger that provide specific feedback and invite discussion. In addition, you may underestimate your ability to show anger effectively: for instance, your fears of getting out of control may be groundless. Furthermore, if you have become more in control of your anger, you risk back-sliding when you start underestimating the gains from maintaining self-control.

> Neil was a married man with three children, who came for counsel-ling having hit his 16-year-old daughter, Elsa, when she came home from a date two hours later than agreed. Neil's wife, Hazel, was fed up with his angry outbursts and their marriage was head-ing for the rocks. After a couple of months of counselling in which Neil acquired and used anger management skills, he thought he had lost some influence in the family by adopting a more reason-able approach to provocations. Using a whiteboard, Neil's counsel-lor, Marion, developed with him a balance sheet of the positive and negative consequences of using his skills. As a result, Neil saw the balance was heavily in favour of continuing to use his anger management skills.

Perhaps most often partners underestimate the losses from anger displays and, consequently, fail to exert sufficient self-discipline. You can insufficiently take into account the pain your behaviour causes and how it may create, sustain and escalate problems. You can come on too strong and too frequently. You can fail to give your partner the benefit of the doubt by predicting that if you give an inch she or he will take a mile. In addition, you may underestimate the losses from staying the same. For instance, you may think 'Once a victim, always a victim'. As a result, you continue your painful martyrdom (see Activity 11.3).

---

**ACTIVITY 11.3        Develop my mind skills for managing anger  ❙**

---

First do this activity on your own. Then, as appropriate, discuss with a partner or others.

Think of a situation in your relationship with your partner where you have got or still feel very angry. Look at your role in creating and, possibly, sustaining your anger in relation to each of the following mind skills:

- creating rules
- creating perceptions
- creating self-talk
- creating visual images
- creating explanations
- creating expectations.

Where necessary, work to correct the poor mind skills that contribute to your anger.

---

**ACTIVITY 11.4** **Group discussion: managing anger skills** |

---

This is intended as a group exercise, though it may be done individually or in pairs.

For each part:

1. Spend five to ten minutes answering the question in groups of three or four.
2. Each subgroup shares its answers with the whole group.
3. The whole group lists the four most important points or skills from most important to least important.

## Part A Feelings associated with anger

Examine your own feelings and list the four most important feelings people in the group have that are associated with or underlie anger in close relationships.

## Part B Identify anger-engendering thoughts

Examine your own thoughts and list the four most important kinds of thoughts people in the group use to fuel anger in close relationships.

## Part C Skills weaknesses for managing anger

Examine how you communicate and list the four most important communication skills weaknesses people in the group use to manage anger in close relationships.

## Part D Skills strengths for managing anger

List the four most important communication skills strengths that people can use to manage anger in close relationships.

---

# 12

# Manage relationship problems skills

**Chapter outcomes**
By studying and doing the activities in this chapter you should:

- have some idea of the association between relationship conflict and satisfaction
- know about some interactive patterns that sustain relationship problems
- understand the importance of acceptance in managing problems
- know how partners can increase the exchange of rewarding behaviours
- know about cooperatively solving relationship problems
- understand some ways to stay in touch.

Conflicts and problems are inevitable in ongoing relationships. This chapter focuses on managing conflict in relationships by using acceptance, behaviour exchange and cooperative problem-solving skills. Partners can use the relationship skills described so far in this book to create emotional climates where problems are less likely to flare up in the first place and more likely to be solved amicably in the second place. However, partners may find some problems more difficult to solve and hence become in conflict. The word conflict comes from the Latin roots *com-* together and *fligere* to strike. Dictionary definitions of conflict emphasize words like fight, struggle, antagonism and sharp disagreement. These dictionary definitions have three elements: first, a difference or disagreement; second, the disagreement is severe; and third, there is ill-will.

Problems are perplexing or difficult questions that require some form of solution or resolution. Relationship problems can vary in severity, duration and frequency. They have the potential to generate more heat than light. In addition, what may seem minor issues from outside may possess symbolic meanings to either or both partners that can create huge rows. Consequently problems are not just matters of difference but of perceptions and interpretations.

The negative effects of conflict stemming from relationship problems scarcely need cataloguing. Conflicts can cause immense psychological pain that can last well after relationships end. Relationships that offered promising opportunities for both partners can founder because partners possess insufficient skills to surmount their problems. In Chapter 1, I provided statistics on the high level of breakdown and distress in British and Australian marriages.

Are conflict and relationship satisfaction incompatible? Arguing is one of the activities most characteristic of marriage and more conflict is found in marriages than any other kind of relationship (Argyle, 1991). However, some couples report high levels of both satisfaction and conflict. Avoiding conflict by 'sweeping problems under the carpet' and emotional withdrawal either indicate dissatisfaction or, possibly, a brittle pseudo-satisfaction. Perhaps the critical consideration is how skilled partners are at managing their relationship problems rather than whether or not they have them in the first place. The results of an Australian study investigating 33 couples in the early years of marriage support this proposition. Partners high in relationship satisfaction after two years of marriage were less likely to manipulate one another, avoid dealing with conflict, behave coercively and engage in destructive patterns such as demand–withdraw than couples low in relationship satisfaction (Noller *et al*, 1994).

## INTERACTIVE PATTERNS

Many who write about relationship problems view the maintenance of conflicts in terms of interactive patterns. Interactive patterns between partners can be viewed as systems. A system is a set or arrangement of connected parts to form a whole. Family discord is frequently viewed in systems terms (Goldenberg and Goldenberg, 2005). It is possible to view discord between marital or cohabiting partners likewise: for instance, collusive and competitive joint problem-solving styles may be seen in systems terms. In such systems partners are mutually trapped by their characteristic responses to one another's differences – each partner's behaviour being related to the other partner's behaviour. A cooperative joint problem-solving style is harder to view in rigid systems terms, since this style assumes that partners are rational choosers.

Though there are many couple interactive patterns or systems, two common ones are closeness–distance and control and responsibility (Christensen and Jacobson, 2000; Jacobson and Christensen, 1996). In closeness–distance, the more a partner demands emotional closeness, the more the other partner withdraws. Demand–withdraw is another way of describing this pattern. In general, women are more demanding and men more withdrawing, a sex difference found to be more likely than the reverse in non-distressed couples, clinic couples prior to therapy, divorcing couples and dating couples. In about 70 per cent of heterosexual closeness–distance patterns women want more closeness, and in the other 30 per cent men want more closeness. Although anxiety plays a large part, there can be something empowering about being the distancer. You have the power over the person wanting closeness. Male and female homosexual couples are more likely to have issues around distance and closeness respectively. The withdraw role in a closeness–distance pattern can either be collusive, in the interests of keeping the peace, competitive, demonstrating passive aggression, or possibly both.

In the control and responsibility interaction pattern, controlling behaviour ignites the power struggle. Couples feel increasingly powerless as their efforts are thwarted again and again with any attempt to generate more responsibility by one partner just resulting in more creative ways of shirking responsibility by the other.

## ACCEPTANCE IN INTIMATE RELATIONSHIPS

One of the *Concise Oxford Dictionary of Current English*'s definitions of acceptance is willingness or ability to tolerate (Thompson, 1995). Acceptance can have connotations of resignation or preservation of the status quo, which may be of differing levels of positive or negative from the viewpoint of partners in intimate relationships. More positive ways of viewing acceptance are provided by Jacobson and Christensen (1996) who see acceptance as having two dimensions. One dimension is an attempt to convert relationship problems into vehicles for intimacy. The other dimension is derived from assisting partners to let go of the struggle to change each other. This is partly a matter of letting go of both the premise that the differences between them are intolerable and also of the struggle to change their partner in terms of an idealized image of a husband or wife. These authors make no assumptions about what behaviours should be accepted. Effective couples therapy generates a context where both accepting and changing occur. Acceptance does not mean that particular behaviours, for instance, battering, cannot be rejected for moral, legal or ethical reasons.

Acceptance is such an important way of managing conflict that some mind skills relevant to implementing it are examined below. Thinking, feeling and acting accepting is a process which may be very difficult in some cases and not be desirable in others.

### Creating rules

Possibly more than in the past, many people hold more stringent or perfectionist standards about what is acceptable behaviour in a close relationship. Partners can perceive each other's behaviour as lapses, faults, hostile and uncaring, when such views may be either false or unhelpful to the relationship or both. In close relationships, partners are confronted by genuine differences, some of which are hard and sometimes impossible to change. Furthermore, accepting some differences may make partners more likely to change than when they feel they are being forced to change.

## Creating perceptions

In relationship conflicts, partners can have inaccurate perceptions both about the cause of the conflict and their behaviour in relation to it. Furthermore, they may be unable to accept the fact that serious conflict exists in their relationship. Conflicts can move towards being solved where either or both partners perceives the other's behaviour with more acceptance. For example, Jo may gain more insight into her tendency to react unnecessarily harshly to her partner Jason's behaviour. Jason, then, might become more accepting of Jo's criticism of his behaviour, even though he still may not agree with all of it. In addition, partners may be able to work on conflicts better when they acknowledge and accept the fact of their conflicts rather than try to deny them.

## Creating self-talk

Partners can use coping self-talk to become more accepting of the fact that there are differences in their relationship and also about specific differences. For example, it may sometimes be helpful to remind yourself that 'Differences are a normal part of all relationships' and 'Even though we have a serious difference on this issue, there are a lot of important things that we agree on.' Partners can calm themselves down and coach themselves in showing more acceptance of their partner's position on specific issues, even if they do not agree with them: for instance, 'I may become more accepting if I listen and try to understand my partner's position on this issue rather than just condemn her/him for disagreeing with me.' On occasion, you might decide to accept a behaviour of your partner that you find troublesome because the behaviour is important to them and difficult to change, for instance, smoking. You may then need to use self-talk to remind yourself of your decision and the reasons for it.

## Creating visual images

Partners who use calming self-talk to become more accepting can accompany this with calming visual images. These visual images may concern themselves, their partner or some neutral calming scene. For example, you might visualize yourself being calm, try to visualize your partner's behaviour in realistic rather than exaggerated terms, or make visual images of lying on a beach and tension flowing from your body. Before addressing an issue with your partner, you can accompany coaching self-talk with visualizing yourself communicating in ways that are accepting rather than antagonistic to your partner. For example, you can identify aggressive body messages that you may send and visualize yourself with more accepting behaviour. You can also visualize some positive outcomes of behaving less aggressively towards your partner, or at least imagine yourself not getting aroused when they do not behave as you would like.

## Creating explanations

In the last chapter I addressed the way blaming was a way of explaining cause wrongly. If you can view your problem as an 'it' rather than in 'you–me' terms, you may view your differences in a more dispassionate way. You can accept your partner's right to have opinions and do things that are different to what you would like. You may also become more accepting if you see your differences in the larger context of differences in your sex, age, upbringing, culture, and so on. Furthermore, if you can accept responsibility for your behaviour independent of how your partner behaves, you are likely to be more accepting since you do not feel that you are being controlled by them.

## Creating expectations

You can become more accepting if you realize the consequences of aggressive behaviour towards your partner. You can learn to build your expectations on the principles of unconditional self-acceptance (USA), unconditional acceptance of others (UAO) and unconditional acceptance of life (UAL) with its immense problems and difficulties (Ellis, 2003). By gaining more realistic expectations, you should become better able to focus on what you and your partner can change in an area of disagreement and accept that you will not get everything you want. Furthermore, sometimes you may not be able to change an aspect of your partner's behaviour at all (see Activity 12.1).

---

**ACTIVITY 12.1**        **Become more accepting** |

---

This activity assumes that you are in a relationship. First each partner starts by doing the activity on their own. Then partners can discuss their answers together.

1. Look at how you might be more accepting in your relationship in each of the following mind skills areas. Be specific about how you might change your thinking.
   - creating rules
   - creating perceptions
   - creating self-talk
   - creating visual images
   - creating explanations
   - creating expectations.
2. Where appropriate, practise your more accepting thinking in real life.
3. Summarize what you have learned from doing this activity.

---

## EXCHANGING REWARDING BEHAVIOURS

Partners in distressed relationships reciprocate more unrewarding behaviours than those in satisfied relationships. Successful couples keep their relationships rewarding both by maintaining existing caring behaviours and by initiating new ones. They also enhance their relationship in other ways: for instance, by livening up sex and developing common interests. Exchanging a high number of rewarding behaviours both prevents and contains conflicts: preventing them, because happy people are less likely to pick unnecessary fights, and containing them by creating goodwill. However, increasing your exchange of rewarding behaviours is definitely not a substitute for developing communication skills for cooperatively solving relationship problems.

Partners in unhappy relationships may be well advised to take a systematic approach to increasing their exchange of rewarding behaviours. Partners can become habituated to one another's caring behaviours so that they lose their reward value. Couples who start with a narrow initial range of caring behaviours are especially vulnerable to erosion of mutual rewardingness. Partners may also take for granted and not show appreciation for caring actions and rewarding behaviours that they still value.

Increasing the exchange of rewarding behaviours can be viewed in six steps (see Box 12.1). These steps are heavily influenced by the behaviour exchange approach of Jacobson and Christensen (1996).

---

**Box 12.1    Six steps in exchanging rewarding behaviours**

1. Become aware of the importance of exchanging rewarding behaviours.
2. Make independent lists of rewarding behaviours to offer your partner.
3. Each partner enacts items from their lists for an agreed upon period.
4. Hold a review session on what worked. Recipients have a chance to comment on and add to the giver's list.
5. Engage in a revised enactment of rewarding behaviours.
6. Review progress and make further agreements.

---

## Become aware of the importance of exchanging rewarding behaviours

Though it may seem obvious, you may need to become more aware that partners are more attractive to one another if they exchange rewarding behaviours than if they appear as uncaring. This basic point can easily get lost in the heat of a conflict. You may also need to remind yourself that how you act influences how your partner reacts. Stuart (1980:194) observes that a basic principle of social interaction is that: 'Positive actions are likely to induce positive reactions, first in the attitudes of others, and then in their behaviors.'

Humans tend to reciprocate negative or unrewarding behaviours more quickly than positive or rewarding ones, on a tit-for-tat theory. Nevertheless, if you can maintain rewarding behaviours, you improve your chances of softening your partner's attitude. In turn, this softening of attitude both increases their rewarding behaviours and decreases their unrewarding ones towards you. Furthermore, if you both agree that insufficient exchange of rewarding behaviours is a problem in your relationship, the fact that each of you now makes an effort to please can help rebuild trust.

## Make independent lists of rewarding behaviours to offer your partner

Once partners have agreed to try to be more rewarding to each other, the next step is for each independently to think of what they might do to make their partner happier and to write this down. This is different from making a list of what they want from their partner. Partners generate wish-lists for pleasing each other. The very act of agreeing to do this task gives the message that both partners have the power unilaterally to affect the quality of the relationship. They may now begin to realize that, instead of seeing themselves as victims of the other's oppression, they can focus on their own role in improving the relationship. Partners should agree on a suitable period of time to develop their lists, say one week, and not attempt to put anything into practice during this period. They should attempt to make their lists as comprehensive as possible.

When making lists, it is important that partners focus on actual communications. For instance, it is not good enough to write: 'She would like it if I were to become more loving.' Instead, the particular items in becoming more loving require identification: for instance, taking her out to dinner weekly or each day kissing her before you both go to work.

## Each partner enacts items from their lists for an agreed upon period

At an agreed upon time, partners can start a specified period of undertaking the task of increasing each other's satisfaction with and happiness in the relationship. Specifically, each goes through their list and picks one or more items that they choose to increase within, say, the next week. It is also possible to choose items that are unrewarding to your partner that you will decrease. Jacobson and Christensen (1996) recommend that partners do not discuss their lists with one another at this stage. You should observe the effects of enacting these behaviours on your partner's relationship satisfaction and she/he should do the same.

Note that the giver suggests the rewards that she/he will provide rather than provides rewards in response to requests. One reason for this is that because the requests did not come from the recipient, this eases the burden on the giver and so increases the chances of compliance and success. Another reason is that because the giver chooses the rewarding behaviours without suggestion or coercion from their partner, it makes it more likely that the behaviours will be well received by the recipient. It is important that each of you only focuses on giving those items on your lists that will not detract from your own relationship satisfaction.

A skill in helping one another at this stage is to acknowledge and reward the other's attempts by showing that you notice and saying 'Thank you', 'That's great', 'I like that' or 'I appreciate your saying/doing that.' A fundamental psychological principle is that people are more likely to repeat actions which rewarded than those that go unrewarded. Possibly in the past each of you may receive fewer rewards because you did not apply this principle adequately.

## Hold a review session on what worked

At the end of your stipulated period in which you each enact positive behaviours – and possibly reduce negative ones as well – you hold a review session. Assuming that the assignment has been successful and relationship satisfaction has been enhanced, you should take turns in describing which items from your list you attempted and note whether or not each one contributed to increasing the other's satisfaction. This is the first time that the receiver provides input on the giver's behaviour. Resulting from this feedback, the giver should know which behaviours are likely to maintain the enhanced relationship satisfaction.

After the initial enquiry about what worked and what did not, recipients take turns in giving systematic input to givers. The recipient can comment on each item on the giver's list and designate it as 'keep', 'minor, but still keep' and 'delete'. This feedback should not be interpreted as a prescription, but just as information that the giver may or may not want to take into account in improving the relationship in subsequent weeks. Finally, each receiver can also suggest items that they regard as useful additions to the giver's list.

## Engage a revised enactment of rewarding behaviours

Partners who now know more about each other's reactions to their behaviours and what each wants can specify a further period of time for enacting rewarding behaviours. The responsibility is still with the giving partner as to which reward-ing behaviours they provide. However, the giving partner has now received feed-back and consequently should be able to behave in even more rewarding ways than previously. If the process is successful, the result of each partner's increase in rewarding behaviours should make it easier for the other to reciprocate with appropriate pleasing behaviours.

## Review progress and make further agreements

Again monitor your own and your partner's efforts to become more rewarding and acknowledge what each of you achieves. When your time period expires, hold another joint review session in which each of you goes through everything you tried. Questions to ask in such sessions include: 'Was it noticed?', 'Was it appreciated?', 'How valuable was it to the recipient?', 'What was it like for the giver?' and 'Could you do it in future?' Fine-tune your agreement or make it a stepping stone to another. Partners can add or subtract items from their wish-lists. Furthermore, you can indicate the importance of items, if you've not done so already (see Activity 12.2).

---

**ACTIVITY 12.2**        **Exchange rewarding behaviours**

---

This activity assumes that you are in a relationship. Whether or not your relationship is troubled, go through the following six steps in exchanging rewarding behaviours. As appropriate, partners do the steps on their own or together.

1. Become aware of the importance of exchanging rewarding behaviours.
2. Make independent lists of rewarding behaviours to offer your partner.
3. Each partner enacts items from their lists for an agreed upon period.
4. Hold a review session on what worked. Recipients have a chance to comment on and add to the giver's list.
5. Engage in a revised enactment of rewarding behaviours.
6. Review progress and make further agreements.

---

It is possible that your partner will not agree to participate in such a formal procedure as exchanging rewarding behaviours. Even without agreements, you can develop skills of monitoring and reviewing how rewarding you are toward your partner and taking corrective action, if necessary. In addition, develop the skills of helping your partner to be more rewarding towards you: for instance, by making specific, tactful requests for caring actions and by saying thank you. Avoid sabotaging an increase in the exchange of rewarding actions by denying that your partner can do anything right.

## COOPERATIVELY SOLVING RELATIONSHIP PROBLEMS

Winston Churchill said that 'to jaw-jaw is better than to war-war'. Couples may already use good caring companionship and intimacy skills with one another and still have problems. Such couples are likely to have a credit balance of goodwill in their relationship bank account to draw on when problems occur. Other partners may need to increase their exchange of rewarding behaviours to reduce ill-will debit balances and increase goodwill credit balances before addressing major longstanding problems. Since relationship problems are inevitable, couples inevitably require good skills for solving them.

I now present CUDSA, a five-step model for cooperatively solving relationship problems (see Box 12.2). Each of the CUDSA steps represents a cluster of skills. In fact, implementing the model involves almost all the sender and receiver skills described in this book. The model represents a framework of skills that partners can strive to use when difficulties and disagreements occur between them.

---

**Box 12.2    A cooperative problem-solving model (CUDSA)**

1. **C**onfront the problem.
2. **U**nderstand one another's perspective.
3. **D**efine the problem.
4. **S**earch for and assess solutions.
5. **A**gree upon the preferred solution.

---

CUDSA provides an easily comprehensible and memorized model for solving relationship problems. Frequently, the five steps of this confront–understand–define–search–agree model overlap. Sometimes conflicts can be handled in a more informal way. However, on other occasions you need to be systematic. Even when only one of you starts by adhering to the model, you may influence the conflict management process constructively. Unfortunately, in conflicts, some partners are so prone to defensive thinking that a model that assumes you are both fairly rational can have limited practicality.

## Confront the problem

Joanna is dissatisfied because Jake spends so much time drinking with his friends. She has avoided talking directly about this problem for fear of hurting and then losing him.

Ross was getting increasingly annoyed because Pam was not doing her share of cleaning the flat. He largely kept his resentment to himself until one evening he blew up and said a whole lot of things he later regretted.

Some of you, like Joanna, may find it easier to avoid than to confront relationship problems. Others, like Ross, may collect trading stamps and one day cash them in by going for their partner's jugular vein. There are many skills of confronting relationship problems in ways that are likely to initiate rational rather than destructive processes.

When you become aware of a problem, you may still choose whether or not to confront it openly. Considerations here include what will be gained and whether the problem is important enough to either or both of you to bring it out into the open. Tavris (1989: 248) observes: 'Couples who are not defeated by rage and the conflicts that cause it know two things: when to keep quiet about trivial angers for the sake of civility, and how to argue about important ones, for the sake of personal autonomy and change.' Assuming that the conflict is not so obvious that your partner cannot ignore it and also that you decide to bring it into the open, the following skills may help:

1. *Keep calm.* Even if you have had a flare-up, use anger management skills to calm yourself down. While you want your partner to take notice of you, you wish to avoid being unnecessarily threatening. Shouting and screaming is likely to alienate your partner and consolidate her or his unwanted behaviours.

2. *Pick a proper time and place.* Choose a proper time to raise the issue that there is a problem between you. It is probably not a good time to initiate problem solving when either of you is rushing off to work, when you have visitors, or when you have both arrived home tired after a hard day. A good time may be after a meal when both of you have more energy. Agree on a suitable place to discuss your problems that is quiet and comfortable and free from interruptions and distractions. Probably kitchens and lounges are better locations than bedrooms for raising and solving problems.

3. *Assert that a problem exists.* Confronting a relationship problem involves assertion. Use 'I' messages and clearly state the existence of the problem. Jacobson and Christensen say that the way a problem is stated can set the tone for the entire discussion and suggest trying to begin with something positive: for example, 'I like it when you hold me when we watch TV, but I feel rejected when you aren't affectionate in other situations' (1996: 186). You can get the problem-solving process off to a good start by using tact and diplomacy rather than off to a bad start by using sarcasm and blaming. You can also neutrally state the problem as a difference – 'You want to see more of your mother and I want us to spend more time together' – rather than personalize it – 'There you are, off to your wonderful mother again.' If your partner still resists owning up that the problem exists, you can persist in your assertion until your partner recognizes that this is a problem for her or him as well as for you. For instance, look at your partner directly and use repetition and emphasis to make your point.

4. *Invite cooperation in problem solving.* Some differences may be resolved quickly and amicably once they are out in the open and discussed. If this is not the case, try to enlist your partner in cooperating to solve the problem. In essence you say: 'We have a problem in our relationship. Let's see if we can cooperate to solve it for our mutual benefit.' Both of you then need to set aside sufficient time and energy for dealing with it.

## Understand one another's perspective

Ron and Janis are unhappy in their marriage. When they argue neither of them closely listens to the other. Instead they shout, finger point and make comments like 'You *never* think of anyone but yourself' and 'You have *always* been selfish.'

Partners can agree that, at the start of discussing a problem, each of you takes turns in having uninterrupted 'air time' to state your perspective. During your air time the only talking that your partner should do is to reflect and ask you to clarify your perspective. Each of you is more likely to listen once safe in the knowledge that you will have your turn. If your partner interrupts, you have a number of choices: pausing; saying something like 'Please let me finish, you have had (will have) your turn'; and putting out your arm with your palm facing them – a standard body message requesting silence.

Making the effort to try to understand each other's perspective is critical to solving relationship problems for a number of reasons. First, you may discover that your so-called problem is only based on misunderstandings and misperceptions. It need not exist in future. Second, making the effort to listen indicates one another's commitment to solving your problem cooperatively. You show respect for one another. Third, trying to understand one another may take some of the emotional steam out of the conflict. Often, when partners feel they have been heard and understood, they calm down and become less aggressive, thus helping one another to think more rationally. Finally, trying to understand one another's perspective helps both of you to start identifying the real issues in the conflict, rather than focusing on imaginary issues. The following are some sender skills of understanding one another's perspective:

1.  *Express feelings, reasons and requests assertively.* Focus on stating your perspective rather than analysing your partner. Beck (1988: 325) writes: 'As your problem-solving sessions unfold, you will make more progress if you focus on what it is that you want to achieve, rather than on what your partner does wrong.' Share your feelings in an open yet tactful way. Use reason to support your points.

2.  *Be specific.* Provide specific feedback so that your partner knows what actions you would like changed. Avoid sending general negative messages that poison the atmosphere and lead nowhere: for instance, 'You're a fool' or giving dirty looks. In addition, try and avoid vague complaints such as 'You're not affectionate enough' into specific requests, such as 'I would appreciate it if you initiated sex sometimes.' If necessary, turn back to the section on assertively requesting changes in behaviour in Chapter 10. Do not expect your partner to read your mind and avoid communicating as though you have a monopoly on the truth and wish to impose your definition of the problem on your partner.

3.  *Be brief.* Stating your position is the entry point to getting your partner to help solve the problem in your relationship. You may lose your partner's

attention and create ill-will if you go on too long: for instance, by giving a whole list of examples of the problem or getting diverted into discussing the causes of the problem.

4. *Discuss only one problem at a time*. It is best to focus on only one problem at a time in a given session. It is easy to sidetrack dealing with problems by bringing other problems into the discussion. This does not mean that other problems cannot be discussed later, but stops partners getting into a fruitless listing and complaining about problems rather than attempting to deal with one directly.

5. *Own responsibility for your contribution*. When partners become mad at each other, they both view themselves as victims of each other's behaviour. However, if you can communicate some insight into how you may have contributed to the problem, you may help your partner to become less defensive and aggressive. An example of a conciliatory statement might be: 'It's true that I have been irritable lately.' Owning responsibility for your contribution can contribute to problem solving in a collaborative rather than a competitive way.

6. *Stick to the issues*. Focus on a current issue. Avoid dragging in irrelevant past history and indulging in personal attacks. Do not put your partner down by means of hurtful vocal and body messages. Relationship problems are often over highly sensitive issues. Your partner is more likely to tune out to you if your vocal and body messages belittle her or him.

The following are some receiver skills of understanding one another's perspective.

1. *Use listening and showing understanding skills*. Use good attending behaviour. Sometimes you can lessen emotional distance by putting your arm around your partner or holding hands. Listen to and observe vocal and body as well as verbal messages. Help your partner to share their perceptions of the conflict. Use restatements and reflections to show that you have understood. Pay particular attention to tuning in accurately to your partner's feelings: this, above all, may help her or him to feel understood by you. When something your partner says is unclear, tactfully request clarification – for instance, 'I think I hear you saying . . ., but I'm not altogether certain.' Where appropriate, show your support and agreement. At the end of your partner's initial statement of his or her perspective, you can summarize to check you have understood it properly. Using checking and summarizing skills prevents you making unwarranted assumptions and inferences.

2. *Turn a deaf ear to negative statements*. Reputedly Admiral Horatio Nelson used to turn his blind eye toward anything he did not want to see. Similarly, when listening to your partner's perspective you may be wise to turn a deaf ear to some less than flattering remarks about you. See negative remarks as symptoms of hurt and anger and strive for the inner strength neither to 'tune out' to your partner nor to retaliate. Where possible, focus on the cause of the relationship problem rather than choosing to become upset by your partner's personal attacks. However, look after yourself. If the abuse

persists, you can change your tactics by challenging it or by leaving the situation.

3. *Admit to and alter misperceptions.* In light of any significant new information, update your perspective of your partner and the problem. Where you have misunderstood your partner's actions and intentions, let her or him know this. If you have been wrong, consider apologizing.

## Define the problem

When the last of her three children started primary school, Irene wanted to return to the workforce. Her husband Rich was unhappy about Irene going back to work because he was already under pressure with his job and did not want any extra work at home. Once they became calmer, they both agreed to define the problem as how to get the housework and childcare done. Rich admitted he had changed his position from not wanting Irene to have a job once they agreed to define the problem in a way that allowed the preferences of both of them to be met.

In step two each partner may offer his or her own definition of the relationship problem. Conflicts can become extremely destructive when partners compete to define the problem on their terms. Both of you risk repetitively stating your positions and getting increasingly frustrated and resentful. The task of step three is to try and arrive at a mutually acceptable definition of your problem. In step three, the sender and receiver roles that partners adopt are less clear than in step two. Consequently, the risk of destructive arguing is greater. The following are some skills for defining problems:

1. *Avoid unfair fight tactics.* Unfair fight tactics are competitive put-downs that show a lack of respect for your partner. Such tactics are manipulative and coercive power plays designed to influence another's definition of you, themselves and the problems between you. Unfair fight tactics include:
   - mind-reading and ascribing negative motives
   - unnecessarily attacking psychologically vulnerable spots
   - engaging in overkill and coming on far too strong
   - dominating the conversation
   - using threats that engender insecurity
   - unnecessarily dragging in third parties' opinions to support your own
   - using guilt-engendering tactics such as playing the victim and tears
   - playing games, such as feigning cooperation yet always frustrating the search for mutually acceptable definitions of your problem.
2. *Identify common ground.* Even where relationship problems are not based on misunderstandings, partners may still have considerable common ground. Avoid polarizing problems into a simple 'good guy–bad guy' format which obscures areas of agreement. Identify and acknowledge any common

ground. An important way you can both acknowledge common ground and defuse emotions is to acknowledge your own mistakes and hurtful behaviours.

3. *Identifying hidden agendas.* Try and deal with the real rather than the surface agendas. For instance, if a spouse suspects her or his partner is having an affair, picking on her or him in a whole range of other issues is not the best way of trying to define and solve the problem. Ideally both of you should be able to communicate your needs, including those that are unmet, simply and clearly. Being allowed to say 'I want', 'I need' and 'I prefer' without recrimination can contribute to identifying the real agendas in a conflict.

4. *Identify specific communications and actions that sustain the problem.* Focus on the specific actions of yourself and your partner that maintain the conflict. In short, focus more on *how* the problem is being sustained rather than on *who* started it or *why* it arose.

5. *State the problem clearly and simply.* The end product of step three is a simple statement of the problem. Avoid personalizing the problem unnecessarily. Where possible, move from defining the problem in 'you–me' terms to defining the problem as an 'it'. You and your partner may find it easier to address a relationship problem with some detachment if you define it neutrally as a shared problem. Irene and Rich at the start of this section provide an example of how to do this.

## Search for and assess solutions

Again take the example of Irene and Rich given in the last section. Having defined the problem as an 'it', they can now cooperate to search for mutually acceptable solutions. Such solutions might include Irene going to work part-time, getting less expensive accommodation, paying someone to clean the house, paying for some childcare, arranging with other parents for childcare, eating out more, getting more take-away meals, and so on. Searching for alternative solutions is often best done in two distinct stages: first, generating solutions; second, assessing them rationally. Generating solutions is a creative process that can be inhibited by prematurely assessing emerging solutions. The following are some skills of step four:

1. *Generate solutions.* Generating solutions is a creative process. The objective is to generate a range of options, among which there may be some effective ones. Sometimes it helps to brainstorm. The object of brainstorming is to discover ideas. The rules for a brainstorming period include avoiding criticism and evaluation of ideas and coming up with the greatest quantity possible. Whether you brainstorm or not, offer solutions constructively and tactfully: for instance, 'One solution might be to . . .' as contrasted with 'I think we should . . .' – the latter wording setting up a potential conflict.

2. *Assess solutions rationally.* Assess solutions on the basis of what is best for both of you. If you have brainstormed, agree on which solutions seem feasible and assess the possible consequences of each of them. You both

need to state your reactions to possible solutions as preferences rather than demands (Ellis, 2005). Provide logical reasons for your preferences. Be prepared to acknowledge if some of your reasons are more emotional than logical – such reasons may still be important. If necessary, ask your partner for her or his preferences among proposed solutions and the reasons for them.

### Agree upon the preferred solution

Craig and Janet both hated doing the dishes. Also, they disliked their kitchen sink being full of dirty dishes. After reviewing other solutions, they agreed that they would buy a dishwashing machine. Their agreement included details of how they would share the dishwashing until the machine arrived, how they would go about purchasing the dishwasher, and how they would share the dishwashing once the machine was installed.

Agreeing upon a preferred solution to a relationship problem involves two stages: reaching the agreement; stating it clearly. The following are some skills of step five:

1.  *Make concessions and compromises.* If you ask many couples what makes for a successful relationship, they often answer 'give and take'. Some relationship problems, such as the example of Irene and Rich given earlier, lend themselves to 'win–win' solutions for both partners. However, many relationship problems are not so straightforward. Sometimes, as with Janet and Craig, the best you can achieve in a 'no-lose' solution where neither party feels violated. When assessing solutions, you may be faced with choices as to whether or not to modify your position. In such circumstances, making realistic trade-offs and compromises can be a useful skill. Acknowledge and show appreciation of any concessions made by your partner and, if necessary, remind her or him of any concessions that you make.

2.  *State agreements clearly.* Unclear agreements are more likely to be broken than clear ones, if only through misunderstanding. Agreements vary according to the nature of the conflict. For instance, if like Janet and Craig your conflict has been about household chores, your agreement will include *who* is to do *what* and *when*. Often it is desirable to put agreements in writing. Writing out your agreements helps you to verify that they are clearly understood and to avoid future conflicts over the terms of the agreement. Written agreements can also be posted in places where they serve as reminders to implement them. Some agreements involve planning how to implement them. Craig and Janet's agreement specified who was responsible for purchasing the dishwasher and how this task was to be performed.

## Implementing and reviewing agreements

The five stages discussed so far suggest how couples might make agreements. Relationship problems are not solved unless agreements are kept. It is critical to back up your agreements by your actions. Never agree to do anything unless you have sufficient commitment to keep your word. If partners do not keep their sides of agreements, the anger and hurt attached to the initial relationship problem may be rekindled and possibly worsened. In addition, couples can ignite problems if either or both of them keep agreements with bad grace – obeying the letter of the agreement but not its spirit.

If for some reason your partner does not keep her or his side of an agreement, try and find out why. She or he may still think the agreement is a good one and want to stick to it. There may have been unexpected complications that have made adhering to the agreement difficult. Assuming your partner wants to adhere to the agreement, your goal is to achieve willing adherence rather than to alienate her or him. If, for whatever reason, you cannot live within an agreement, renegotiate rather than break it. Breaking your agreement is a breach of trust. Furthermore, your partner may consider this gives her or him similar rights. This may further damage your relationship.

Agreements are not meant to be set in concrete, but to work in the best interests of both partners. Some solutions may turn out to be inadequate when they are implemented. Frequently, only fine-tuning of initial agreements is necessary. However, on other occasions, either or both of you may discover that the preferred solution has major weaknesses. Possibly you have another reasonable solution available from your earlier search for alternatives. Otherwise you need to generate and assess further solutions. Sometimes partners find that another problem emerges in addition to or instead of the original one. In such instances you can return to the earlier steps of the CUDSA problem-solving model (see Activity 12.3).

| ACTIVITY 12.3 | Use the CUDSA model for solving a relationship problem |
|---|---|

This exercise assumes you are in a relationship. Complete Part A on your own and Parts B and C with your partner.

### Part A  Assess my own and my partner's skills in solving relationship problems

For each of the CUDSA model's five steps assess

1. Your good and poor skills.
2. Your partner's good and poor skills.

## Part B  Share and discuss

1. You and your partner share and discuss your answers to Part A of this exercise.
2. What skills do you need to develop, both as individuals and as a couple, to improve how you solve relationship problems cooperatively?

## Part C Use the CUDSA model

1. Choose a problem in your relationship that both of you wish to solve.
2. What have been your attempted solutions to the problem to date? What have been the consequences of your attempted solutions? So far what have been your skills strengths and weaknesses in trying to solve the problem?
3. Pick a good time and place for a problem-solving session. During your problem-solving session systematically proceed through the following steps of the CUDSA model:
   - Step 2    Understand one another's perspective
   - Step 3    Define the problem
   - Step 4    Search for and assess solutions
   - Step 5    Agree upon the preferred solution.
5. Review how well you, individually and as a couple have used the skills of each step of the CUDSA model.
6. After your problem-solving session, implement your solution and review how you got on.

---

## STAYING IN TOUCH

The occurrence of conflict can be lessened and softened if couples are good at staying in touch with one another on an everyday basis. Gottman and Silver (1999) followed up numerous partners who had attended their relationship workshops. Based on the answers, they make the following suggestions that involve spending five hours a week for how to keep your relationship alive. Partners can have their own style of staying in touch and the times given for each activity are only suggestive:

1. *Partings.* Each working day spend two minutes making sure that, before you part in the morning, you know about one thing that is happening in your partner's life that day – for example, having lunch with someone. Total time: 10 minutes.
2. *Reunions.* At the end of each working day, ensure that you hold a 20-minute stress-reducing conversation. Total time: 1 hour 40 minutes.

3. *Admiration and appreciation.* Every day of the week, find some way of communicating genuine affection and appreciation towards your partner. Total time: 35 minutes.
4. *Affection.* During each day show affection by kissing, holding and touching during the time you are together. Furthermore, make sure to kiss each other with fondness and tenderness before going to sleep. Total time: 35 minutes.
5. *Weekly date.* Have a weekly date in which you stay connected by talking with one another, updating information and, if necessary, working through issues in your relationship. Total time: 2 hours once a week.

I end this chapter on cooperatively solving relationship problems with some words of wisdom from theologian Reinhold Niebuhr:

> God, give us the serenity to accept what cannot be changed,
> the courage to change what should be changed,
> and the wisdom to distinguish one from the other.

See Activity 12.4.

---

**ACTIVITY 12.4**                                   **Stay in touch**

This activity assumes that you are in a relationship.

1. For a week, spend a minimum of five hours engaging in the following activities with your partner (the timings are for the week are only suggestive). Of course, you can spend more time on such activities if you want.
   - partings (total time 10 minutes)
   - reunions (total time 1 hour 40 minutes)
   - admiration and appreciation (total time 35 minutes)
   - affection (total time 35 minutes)
   - weekly date (total time 2 hours)
2. At the end of the week, discuss with your partner how you got on and if necessary set yourselves a similar task for the following week.

---

**ACTIVITY 12.5**            **Group discussion: manage relationship problem skills**

This is intended as a group activity, though it may be done individually or in pairs:

For each part:

1. Spend five to ten minutes answering the question in groups of three or four.
2. Each subgroup shares its answers with the whole group.
3. The whole group ranks the four most important problems, mistakes or skills from the most important to the least important.

## Part A Relationship problems

List the four most common kinds of relationship problems that partners encounter.

## Part B  Mistakes in managing relationship problems

Examine your own skills for managing relationship problems, and list the four most important mistakes you make when trying to manage relationship problems.

## Part C  Managing relationship problems skills

List the four most important skills that partners can use for managing relationship problems.

# 13

## End a relationship skills

**Chapter outcomes**
By studying and doing the activities in this chapter you should:

- view ending relationships as a learning process
- know about ending in different kinds of relationships
- know about some communication skills for ending relationships
- know about some mind skills for ending relationships
- know about some starting up again skills.

In Chapter 6 on choosing a relationship skills, I mentioned that you are likely to end a number of relationships in your quest for a stable long-term partnership. Especially when you are young, ending relationships can be viewed as part of a learning process. You are developing a sense of both yourself and of others as partners. You are finding out how you are with different kinds of people, what characteristics you like in yourself and what characteristics you like in a partner.

Some relationships end almost before they get started: for instance, one person does not accept even a first date. Other relationships may last for a short time, but one or both of you may decide that you do not have enough in common to continue spending time together. If you share some commitment, you may start going steady and, possibly, going out only with each other. Then, if and when your commitment is greater, you may decide to live together. Nowadays, living together generally comes before getting married. Ultimately, most people still get married, but there is a growing minority of partners who decide to continue living together without tying the marital knot. Around half of all long-term relationships break up.

The major emphasis in this book is on starting and maintaining happy and successful human relationships. Nevertheless, whatever their length, partners can end relationships for good and poor reasons and with varying levels of skill.

# COMMUNICATION SKILLS FOR ENDING RELATIONSHIPS

Ending a relationship can vary from being quite easy to very difficult. For example, Emma and Dave, both 18, go out on three dates, but soon discover that each does not want to continue the relationship. They thank each other for the time they have spent together, but agree to go their separate ways. Even ending long-term relationships may be relatively easy where both partners have reached the stage of no longer feeling committed to one another and decide to split up.

At the other extreme are extremely bitter endings to relationships where either or both partners feel that they have been emotionally damaged by their partner's wrongdoing. Sometimes short-term relationships end with great animosity. In longer term relationships, partners who have lived with one another for months or years may store up great resentment that makes it hard to end without hurting each other even more. Though not emphasized in this book, the endings of such relationships can get even more complicated and difficult where the couple has responsibility for children.

Assuming that you are considering ending a relationship, the following are some communication skills that you might consider.

## Assertiveness skills

There are many different reasons for ending relationships and many different stages at which relationships end. Consequently, there is a wide variety of situations for being assertive about raising the issue of ending or wanting to end a relationship. Box 13.1 shows three examples of people or couples about to end a relationship. In the first example, one partner is submissive or non-assertive; in the second, both are aggressive; in the third, both are assertive.

In the aggressive and assertive examples of Box 13.1, both partners were either aggressive or assertive. This is not always the case and, often, one partner may be more assertive and the other partner more aggressive. Here it is important for you to keep your goal of ending the relationship with as little damage as possible clearly in mind. The more you can consistently use assertiveness skills, the more likely you are to work through your partner's aggression, though this is not always the case. In the final analysis, you can only take responsibility for your own behaviour. Readers wanting to refresh their memories on assertiveness skills can review Chapter 10.

## Manage anger skills

Sometimes it is possible to end relationships with little hostility and, possibly, with relief. On other occasions you may be faced with dealing with your own anger and that of your partner. Inasmuch as possible, try to express your anger assertively, give specific feedback about what bothers you, state your feelings as an 'I' message, and let your partner clearly know your position. In addition, try

---

### Box 13.1    Ending relationships with varying levels of assertiveness

**Non-assertive**

Rod and Alice are a couple in their early twenties who have been living together for seven months. Rod strongly feels that Alice does not appreciate him, spends too much time at work and he suspects her of having sex outside their relationship. Alice just tends to get on with her life and shows little interest in Rod. Rod has great difficulty raising his resentment with Alice. In the end, Alice comes home one day and finds that Rod has moved out.

**Aggressive**

Shelia, 23, and Ray, 27, used to get on really well and liked the fact that they differed in many respects. However, gradually Shelia has been spending more time at work and Ray has been going out with his mates in the evenings when Shelia is not back for dinner. Each resents the other's behaviour. They have got beyond trying to sort out their difficulties calmly. Now they justify their own behaviour and condemn the other's. Neither of them is prepared to compromise and they shout and act aggressively towards one another. They are both getting to the stage where they are completely fed up with one another and the relationship.

**Assertive**

Doreen, 24, and Liam, 26, have been living together for three years. They used to get on very well together even though they argued quite frequently. Though they still like each other, the spark has gone out of their relationship. They have tried to rekindle their affection and have worked together on the problems in their relationship, but are still not able to feel real love for each other. Doreen and Liam honestly share their feelings. They discuss ending the relationship, going their separate ways, but remaining as friends.

---

to help your partner express anger assertively and acknowledge any points where you agree.

When ending relationships, you can also use the other communication skills for managing anger mentioned in Chapter 11. For example, you can use skills of keeping your temper, such as breathing slowly and regularly, delaying responding until less agitated, and engaging in 'cooling off' activities like going for a walk. Some people help themselves by using relaxation skills, both muscular and mental. In addition, you can use skills of managing stress in other areas of your life so you have more energy to devote to ending your relationship successfully. It may also help in ending relationships if you can apologize where you have spoken or acted wrongly, though do not expect that this will always be appreciated. Ultimately, you want to get yourself to the point where you can forgive your partner and move on.

## Solve relationship problems skills

The following discussion does not get into legal aspects of divorce. Whether you are married or not, especially if you have been living together, you and your partner are going to have to solve numerous problems connected with your splitting up. You may both have calmly and rationally made the decision to break up. However, this frequently is not the case. You and your partner may still be raising issues in ways that are negative and accusatory, showing contempt, being critical and being defensive (Gottman and Silver, 1999). You may feel hostile and alienated from one another and feel that you have been wronged. More often than not there is so much bad feeling in the relationship that one or both of you want to end it. You may have tried to take a cooperative problem-solving approach to the issues in your relationship and been unsuccessful in resolving them.

However badly you may feel about one another, it will likely be easier to break up if it is a joint decision. Then you can together try to solve all the problems connected with breaking up, for instance, when and how do you divide your property. If one of you decides to end the relationship, you require skills of getting your partner to acknowledge this fact. Though you may be faced with resentment, you need to let your partner know that you really mean it. Hopefully, your partner will get to the stage where she or he accepts the fact that the relationship is over and can move on to issues connected with ending it reasonably smoothly. However, even when agreeing to end a relationship, partners may still mistrust and resent one another. You then have to calm your anger as much as possible and try to deal with the breaking up issues as rationally as you can. Keep your goal of ending the relationship in mind and try not to get sidetracked into personal attacks and spending time on being defensive.

Two issues for partners who break up are how to let other people know and what to do about your property. Your friends and relations may have known that your relationship was in trouble and when you let them know your break-up may come as no surprise. When thinking of splitting up, there is a risk of letting yourself be unduly influenced by others: for instance, you may only listen to people who agree with you. Though it may be all right to get others' opinions, it is important that you independently decide rather than manipulate others to take your position.

Property issues can range from relatively easy to very difficult. If you are renting, it is probably easier when breaking up than if you have purchased a

property. Inasmuch as possible try to solve division of property issues cooperatively. On many occasions, especially if the relationship has not lasted a long
time, it is fairly obvious which property belongs to whom. Partners may be able
to apply the CUDSA cooperative problem-solving model to remaining
decisions about property. On other occasions, there can be nasty fights about
property in which either or both partners use poor skills. In such instances, the
outcomes may be both acrimonious and, possibly, unfair (see Activity 13.1).

## ACTIVITY 13.1    Communication skills for ending a relationship

Please do those parts of this activity that have meaning for you.

1. If you are in a relationship, how confident are you that it will continue
   and, if necessary, what can you do to repair it?
2. Assuming that you want to end your relationship, how can you best use:
   - assertiveness skills
   - manage anger skills
   - solve relationship problems skills?
3. Where necessary, set yourself specific goals for improving your
   communication skills connected with ending your relationship.

## MIND SKILLS FOR ENDING RELATIONSHIPS

When you are looking for a long-term partner, it is likely that you will be in a
number of relationships of varying degrees of seriousness. Sometimes it may be
obvious to both of you that you do not have a future together. On other
occasions, you may differ in your opinions, but it only takes one of you to
discontinue the relationship. Your use of mind skills is relevant both to whether
you stay together and whether you decide to end a relationship. Some relationships end prematurely and others continue to the dissatisfaction of both parties
because people did not use good enough mind skills.

### Creating rules

You need to have realistic rules about ending relationships. For instance, partners with the rule 'I must stay in a close relationship' would be well advised to
turn this into a preferential rule 'I would prefer to stay in a close relationship,
but sometimes circumstances make this inadvisable.' Both men and women can
be vulnerable to ending relationships if they want ideal relationships and are
unwilling to examine the assumptions that they bring to them. Each sex can also
have unrealistic rules about how the other sex should behave. Nowadays in a

climate of greater gender equality than previously, rules that restrict the role of women to playing a supportive role to the man's career are obvious candidates for examination. This does not mean that the man may not have the primary role as breadwinner, especially when there are young children, but partners who agree to a preferential rule have negotiated this outcome. In short, relationships can end because either or both partners have demanding rather than preferential rules. Furthermore, ending is likely to be much more bitter when partners have demanding rules about the process: for instance, 'You must admit that you were wrong' or 'You must let me take what I want.'

## Creating perceptions

Ending a relationship can be based on the accurate perception that one or both of you and your partner would be happier out of it. Though often painful, it may be in your best interests. This can be part of the process of picking the right person with whom to have a long-term relationship in the first place (Hamburg, 2000).

Often relationships end because as partners you get increasingly negative feelings and perceptions about one another and lose sight of your own and one another's positive qualities. Each of you can hold on to distorted perceptions of what your relationship, yourselves and each other are like. Initially, these distortions may have worked in favour of the relationship, but as time goes by reciprocal negativity sets into many relationships. Partners who stay together are more likely than those who drift apart to make sure that they hold on to some positive perceptions about one another, even in times of distress. They do not let negative perceptions take hold and develop a momentum that inevitably causes the relationship to end.

## Creating self-talk

When ending relationships, you need to avoid negative self-talk. You can unnecessarily make remarks to yourself like 'I'm going to mess it up', 'Things will only get worse if I bring the subject of ending up' and 'The situation is hopeless.' Instead, you can try to use the skills of coping self-talk. For example, before, during and after raising the issue of ending the relationship with your partner, you can make calming statements like 'Calm down' and 'Relax'. Even when your partner is the one to initiate the ending, you can make similar statements. You can coach yourself in how to handle the conversation and the subsequent ending of the relationship in the best and least hurtful way for you and your partner. For example, you can tell yourself 'Do not raise my voice' and 'Try and stick to the issues.' You can also tell yourself that 'It is not an easy situation for my partner either' and try to understand her or his position with self-talk like 'Listen carefully' and 'Don't just give my view of the situation.' When your partner seems unreasonable, you can tell yourself that 'She/he is entitled to his/her view of the situation, I do not have to agree with everything, and there is no use my attacking her/him.' Your goal is to end the relationship by not generating any unnecessary bitterness and by dealing with the issues that require facing as directly as possible. If necessary, you can also use affirming self-talk like 'I'm pleased that I managed not to lose my cool and that was a great help.'

## Creating visual images

Before ending a relationship you can use visualizing skills. To help make the decision as to whether or not to end, you can visualize both what it would be like to stay in the relationship and what the future might hold if you were out of it. For instance, you can imagine what life might be like six months from now under both circumstances. Where you view yourself having difficulties after ending, you can visualize yourself using good skills to cope with the pain of ending and then to start rebuilding your life.

You can also use visualizing skills to help you actually end a relationship. You can challenge the realism of any negative images you may have about the process and outcomes of ending. In addition, you can accompany your calming self-talk with calming visual images. You can coach yourself, using your imagination, as to how you are going to end the relationship, what you are going to say and how you are going to say it. You can imagine different ways in which your partner might respond and visualize how you might handle them. After talking with your partner about ending, you can use calming visual images to relax again, imagine how things went and visualize how you might act in future.

## Creating explanations

When you are choosing a long-term partner, you are likely to end many relationships along the way. Some of these will probably be very short term. You may not have invested heavily in them emotionally. Other relationships may have lasted longer and your emotional investment may have been greater. In all relationships, you create explanations for the time you spend in them and for whether you stay in them or get out. For example, you may end many relationships quickly because your explanation is that you have insufficient in common with the others. However, in longer term relationships often explanations of wanting to end become more negative. Goodwill can go out of the relationship and get replaced by mutual blaming. When you decide to end a relationship, you can make things much worse by fighting old battles and blaming. You need to assume responsibility for ending the relationship as cleanly as possible, despite how badly you perceive your partner may have behaved and may still be behaving. You may have to struggle hard to control yourself in order to keep your goal of ending the relationship with as little unnecessary animosity as possible. This process can be helped if you are willing to see, and possibly openly acknowledge, some of your own faults.

## Creating expectations

When you initiate ending a relationship, you expect that your future outside of the relationship will be happier than your present. Some of you may end a relationship too soon and might be better off staying in it and improving your skills at relating. Others of you may stay in unproductive relationships too long hoping that things will get better, but having little evidence that they will. On occasion, the choice to end will be taken by your partner whose expectations about your future together may be less hopeful, or at least clearer than yours. Where possible, it is best that both partners are agreed on ending a relationship, thus lessening the likelihood of either partner feeling excessively rejected.

Partners may put off ending relationships because they are afraid that the process of ending will be acrimonious. You may also anticipate difficulties about adjusting to living alone or, if changing partners, living with someone else. When you decide to end a relationship, you can make it easier on yourself if, at the same as focusing on the present, your expectations about your future are realistic. For example, despite current difficulties, you are likely to manage in the short term and may well be happier in the longer term. However, it pays to have realistic expectations about how good your relationship skills are. Unless they improve, those with poor skills can expect to be ending relationships again and, possibly, again (see Activity 13.2).

---

**ACTIVITY 13.2**        **Mind skills for ending a relationship** |

---

Please do those parts of this activity that have meaning for you.

1. If you are considering ending a relationship, how can you use each of the following skills:
   - creating rules
   - creating perceptions
   - creating self-talk
   - creating visual images
   - creating explanations
   - creating expectations?
2. Where necessary, set yourself specific goals for improving your mind skills connected with ending your relationship.

---

## STARTING UP AGAIN SKILLS

There are numerous factors connected with the ending of relationships: for instance, their length, the degree of commitment of each partner, whether or not a third party was involved and how good the relationship skills of both partners were.

You may have many relationships of varying lengths before settling down with a long-term partner. As mentioned, approximately half of long-term relationships in Britain and Australia end by breaking up.

Especially when you are young and getting to know what you want out of a relationship, you are likely to spend time with a number of partners. Often there is no real expectation that the relationship will continue. You both are finding companionship and learning about relating closely to another.

When you and your partner have been committed to a relationship and spent considerable time in it, including living together, ending can be much more difficult. When breaking up, you may wonder about your adequacy and whether you will ever meet anyone again. While not dwelling on the past, you may try to learn from it. Many relationships break up because partners have not chosen wisely in the first place. Did you rush into living together and not take sufficient time before doing so? If so, this is something you can try to avoid in future. Has your relationship taught you anything about what you really value in a partner and what you want to avoid? Again, you may have some ideas about this. What good and poor relationship skills do you think that you used? Here, you may strengthen your good skills and try and correct your poor skills. While it is important that you do not carry around a sense of failure, it is nevertheless useful if you can learn from your mistakes.

Some partners leave because they have found someone who appeals to them more. For example, if you are in a clearly unsatisfactory relationship and someone who seems genuinely suitable happens to be interested in you, you may take this as the reason for ending your current relationship. Whether you then immediately live together with the other person is another decision. There is much to be said for getting to know your new partner better before living together. Living with someone on the rebound has obvious risks attached to it: for instance, you may infer similarity when what you are getting is availability. Many ex-partners feel that they do not want to rush into another relationship. Rather they need to work through the pain of the last relationship, get to know themselves better as independent persons, and then start looking for a partner again.

When you decide to seek another partner, you will probably have to use the sort of search and find skills that are described near the beginning of Chapter 6. Rather than repeat this discussion, you are referred back to it. Inevitably, your search for a new partner will be influenced by your experience of your last partner. This can be desirable, so long as you learn from negative aspects of your experience and do not just set yourself up for repeating them again.

**ACTIVITY 13.3**          **Group activity: ending a relationship and starting again skills**

This is intended as a group activity, though it may be done individually or in pairs.

For each part:

1. Spend five to ten minutes answering the question in groups of three or four.
2. Each subgroup shares its answers with the whole group.
3. The whole group ranks the four most important problems, mistakes or skills from the most important to the least important.

## Part A Ending a relationship: communication skills

List the four most important communication skills partners can use when ending a relationship.

## Part B Ending a relationship: mind skills

List the four most important mind skills partners can use when ending a relationship.

## Part C Starting again: communication skills

When starting again, list the four most important communication skills a person can use when finding a new relationship.

## Part D Starting again: mind skills

When starting again, list the four most important mind skills a person can use when finding a new relationship.

# Coach yourself

**Chapter outcomes**
By studying and doing the activities in this chapter you should:

- understand the importance of coaching yourself
- be able to monitor your relationship skills
- possess some skills for coaching yourself
- know about some sources of assistance in maintaining and developing your skills.

Many readers are using this book in conjunction with taking a course on relationship skills. Ultimately the success of any relationship skills course rests on how good you have become at coaching yourself in the skills in which you were trained. Whether or not you have taken a course, all readers are left with the problem of how to maintain and improve your skills on your own. Thus, you must learn to become good at coaching yourself in relationship skills. By providing descriptions of the main skills, this book has given you a framework for being able to coach yourself more systematically.

You need to keep seeing the need for your role as a coach in maintaining and developing your relationship skills. Hopefully, you have used many skills to the point where they become habitual and you do not think about them that much. Nevertheless, since it is easy to revert to using poor skills, you need to check every now and then that you are using good skills. You can also strengthen your motivation if sometimes you reward yourself when you do use a good skill. Even a simple statement like 'I'm pleased that I did that (specify the skill)' may be enough. When in a relationship, partners can also help one another to keep using good skills. For example, you can admit mistakes and also appreciate it when the other tries hard to think and communicate skilfully.

# SKILLS OF BEING YOUR OWN COACH

Let's now look at some of the ways you can successfully enact a lifelong choice to be your own relationship skills coach.

## Commit yourself

This book attempts to provide you with a framework for coaching yourself. Most of the important relationship skills are described and activities are provided for improving your skills. Each of you is personally responsible for using and, where necessary, improving your relationship skills. You need to commit yourself to carrying out this responsibility. Hopefully, your partner will commit herself or himself too, but you cannot guarantee this. Consequently, you need to make a unilateral commitment to working to improve your relationship skills (Ellis and Crawford, 2000). Even if there is a mutual commitment, each one makes a unilateral commitment of responsibility to learn and use the relationship skills, regardless of what the other does.

## Assess yourself

Coaches usually start by getting a feel for the skills of the person or people they are to coach. As someone who is going to take on the task of systematically coaching yourself, you can monitor your relationship skills. While I am asking you to do Activity 14.1 now, it is a task that you can undertake at regular intervals in future. Once you can become aware of relationship areas on which you need to work, you are in a strong position to start coaching yourself in them.

There is nothing weak in wanting to assess and work on your relationship skills. You work at other skills – academic, work and sporting – that bring you happiness, so why not work at these most important skills of all. You can adopt a positive attitude and learn to be honest in evaluating yourself. Though frequently people leave it until their relationships are distressed before they work on their skills, you may be able to prevent this from happening.

You may have a partner who also wants to maintain and improve your relationship. If so, you can each assess yourselves and then, possibly with your partner's help, set yourself goals. Some of these goals may be skills that you can enact on your own, but others may be best enacted jointly, for instance, spending more free time together.

---

**ACTIVITY 14.1**　　　　　　　　　　**Monitor my relationship skills**　|

---

If you are in a relationship, answer this activity in respect of how you relate to your partner. If not currently in a relationship, answer the questions as best you can. Answer the questions on your own first, then discuss with your partner, another or others.

1. What do you consider are your strengths and weaknesses in each of the following relationship skills areas:
   - listening skills
   - showing understanding skills
   - managing shyness skills
   - choosing a relationship skills
   - intimacy skills
   - companionship skills
   - sexual relationship skills
   - assertiveness skills
   - manage anger skills
   - manage relationship problems skills.
2. Make a list of the relationship skills weaknesses on which you most need to work.

---

## Develop self-instruction skills

Much of this book has been written as though you are the recipient of coaching. However, though this may still happen, for much of your life you will be on your own. Therefore, you need to develop self-instruction skills. Instead of a coach telling you, here are some things that you may need to tell yourself:

- the reasons for working on one or more skills
- the component parts of a skill
- how and if you can watch demonstrations of the skill(s)
- how to rehearse the skill(s)
- how to enact the skill(s) in real life
- how to evaluate your enactment(s)
- how to do homework.

You need to be clear about the content of any skill that you are using. If necessary, you can go back and check what is written about the skill in the chapters of this book. Describe the skill to yourself simply and clearly. You may practise doing this either silently or aloud. Speak to yourself with messages that hold your attention and are encouraging. You can also think through and coach yourself in what might be appropriate body messages for any skill you intend using.

## Look out for demonstrations

When you coach yourself, there may be a problem finding adequate demonstrations of a skill. Observing live demonstration is often the best way to learn how to enact a skill. You can keep an eye out and watch people whom you know who use good skills. If you are working with your partner, she or he may be able to demonstrate a skill that you want to improve. Failing that, you may have access to watching videotapes or listening to cassettes. You may also find written demonstration an especially good way for learning mind skills. It is preferable if you can observe and learn from repeated demonstrations of a skill in a variety of situations rather than just be content with one observation. If you watch or observe demonstrations, try to summarize for yourself the main points that are relevant to your situation.

## Rehearse and practise

You may often be in positions to rehearse the communication skills and mind skills components of a relationship skill. Remember to concentrate on your verbal, vocal and bodily communication. Think through how to apply the skills you intend to use and then practise them. With or without their knowledge and permission, you will end up practising many of the relationship skills with your partner. Again, as with demonstration, repeated rehearsals are desirable. Whether they are real-life or simulated, you can process your rehearsals. For instance, you can ask yourself: 'How well did I use my skills in that rehearsal?' and 'How might I have reacted better to different ways my partner might respond?' Then, if necessary, amend the way you behave. You can also congratulate yourself if you used good skills and tried hard.

As part of coaching yourself, you may set homework. Keep your homework assignments manageable and, if relevant, graduate their difficulty by starting with the easier tasks. In every circumstance, to improve your skills and maintain your gains 'Remember that the road to Carnegie Hall is paved with practice, practice, practice!' (Ellis and Crawford, 2000: 142). The same holds true for the roads to London's Albert Hall and to the Sydney Opera House.

## HELP IN COACHING YOURSELF

The following are some sources of assistance as a coach for your relationship skills.

## Relationship skills reading

Though needing to be supplemented by practice, relevant reading is a way to develop your relationship skills. A leading text that covers a variety of relationship skills is Johnson's *Reaching Out: Interpersonal Effectiveness and*

*Self-Actualization* (2003). Prominent originators of therapeutic approaches have also written books on relationship skills for ordinary people: for instance, Beck's (1988) *Love is Never Enough: How Couples Can Overcome Misunderstandings, Resolve Conflicts, and Solve Relationship Problems Through Cognitive Therapy*; Ellis and Crawford's (2000) *Making Intimate Connections: 7 Guidelines for Great Relationships and Better Communication*; Rogers's (1973) *Becoming Partners: Marriage and Its Alternatives*. Other leading self-help books include Gottman and Silver's (1999) *The Seven Principles for Making Marriage Work* and Alberti and Emmons's *Your Perfect Right: Assertiveness and Equality in Your Life and Relationships* (2001). Relate in Britain has also published a number of relationship guides: for instance, Litvinoff's (1991) *The Relate Guide to Better Relationships*.

Some of these books, such as *Reaching Out* (Johnson, 2003), include activities that you might find useful to perform. A further suggestion is to re-read this book and possibly redo some of the activities. One approach is to go through the whole book every now and then as a refresher. Another approach is to focus on specific chapters when you feel you need to make a further effort to maintain or to develop a skill. Often, it can help to work in conjunction with your partner, another or others.

## Work with your partner

As above, I have emphasized the importance of partners working together in various relationship skills areas, for instance, facilitating intimacy, encouraging one another's assertion and managing anger. When you use relationship skills strengths, your example encourages your partner to reciprocate. By helping one another to work through specific difficulties, either in your lives as individuals or as a couple, you show active concern for each other's welfare. By using relationship skills daily, you raise your chances of staying rewarding to one another – you increase the good times and decrease the bad times. Furthermore, you help one another stay out of destructive cycles of blame and recrimination.

You can set aside a special weekly or monthly time to discuss your relationship. Your relationship session need not be a grim affair. Rather a 'you–me' talk session provides a chance to catch up with one another. You can sort out problems and misunderstandings as they emerge rather than later, by which time they may have become more serious.

## Co-coach

Co-coaching is an approach to working together. You can co-coach either with your partner or with someone else. The latter has risks if your partner disapproves of sensitive material being discussed with third parties. In co-coaching you have joint coaching sessions on a regular basis. You decide who starts as 'coach' and 'client'. The 'coach' gives the 'client' air time to examine his or her relationship concerns and skills, supports this exploration by showing active understanding and then coaches the client. It is probably best if the focus is on just one skills area. The first person's air time may last for 15 or 20 minutes, longer if necessary. Afterwards you reverse roles. When you have both had your individual turns as 'client', together hold a sharing and discussion session. Co-coaching with a spouse or partner has much to recommend it. It can help maintain communication as well as provide a regular opportunity to use and improve your relationship skills.

## Develop your support network

People, as individuals and as couples, exist in support networks of varying degrees of adequacy: family, friends, work colleagues, clubs, church, and so on. In addition, you can have access to voluntary or professional helpers. Develop a support network that contains people who use and reward the relationship skills you wish to maintain and develop. Specific networking skills include identifying suitable people and organizations to partake in your support network, knowing how best to access them, using them when necessary and being prepared to contribute so the flow of support is two way.

You may choose to meet on a regular basis with a group of other people to work on your relationship skills. Being in a support group has the advantage of enabling you to practise your skills, observe others' skills and obtain feedback. Peer support groups can be specifically focused on discussing relationships and helping one another with problems in them. Alternatively, within the context of another focus – for instance, either a women's group, a men's group or a bereavement group – you can work on the relationship skills pertinent to that group's main task.

## Attend workshops and training courses

No hard and fast distinctions exist between training courses and workshops. However, training courses are usually spread over a longer period, say a month or more, whereas workshops are relatively intense experiences lasting from a day to a week. Means of finding out about relationship skills workshops and training courses include contacting counselling services: for instance, the local branch of Relate in Britain or of Relationships Australia, seeking information from professional associations in psychology, counselling and social work, and looking in newspapers, relevant journals and newsletters. In all instances, look before you leap. Since acquiring good relationship skills requires much work and practice, avoid courses and workshops offering miracle cures. Box 14.1 provides a checklist for assessing training courses and workshops.

## Undergo professional coaching and counselling

Either individually or as a couple, you may decide that you need the services of a professional coach, or possibly a counsellor, to help improve your relationship

---

**Box 14.1    Checklist for assessing training courses and workshops**

1.  What are the goals of the course or workshop?
2.  What are the training methods that may be employed during the course or workshop?
3.  What is the pertinent training and experience of the trainer or trainers?
4.  What is the size of the course or workshop and is there a screening process prior to entry?
5.  When does the course or workshop start? How long is each session? Over what period will the course or workshop continue? Where will it be held? Are the facilities adequate?
6.  What, if any, is the fee for the course or workshop and are there any additional expenses that may be incurred?

---

skills. Usually, on training courses or workshops, there is little chance for trainers to spend much time on individual problems. You may be so lacking in confidence that you prefer a safer environment. Group counselling may be desirable either instead of, concurrently with, or after individual counselling. Counselling groups tend to be comprised of a leader and around six to ten members. They provide a more sheltered environment for working on emotional and relationship issues than that found in many training groups and workshops. All the items on the Box 14.1 checklist are relevant to assessing counselling groups.

Choosing a coach or a counsellor can be a difficult process. They differ greatly in their personalities, knowledge, skills and theoretical orientations. Someone reflecting this book's approach would be one combining existential-humanistic and cognitive-behavioural theoretical orientations. Put in lay person's language, this would be a coach or a counsellor who believes in the concept of relationship skills, coaches mind skills and communication skills as well as focuses on feelings, and consistently encourages personal responsibility and self-help. Look for someone with whom you feel comfortable and who both supports and challenges you to attain more of your potential. If dissatisfied, be prepared to change.

You may not be immediately aware of a suitable coach or counsellor. You may find the name of someone appropriate by asking a helping service professional: for instance, a psychologist, social worker, doctor or priest. You could look up the relevant occupational listings in the phone book. You could contact a citizen's advice bureau. In addition, you could make enquiries to relevant local, regional and national associations such as Relate (Britain) and Relationships Australia (see Activity 14.2).

**ACTIVITY 14.2**                    **Coach myself in a relationship skill** |

This activity may be done on your own or together with a partner. If working with your partner, you may alter the activity to a co-coaching format.

1. Commit yourself to being your own coach, whether or not your partner does as well.
2. Choose a particular relationship skills area that you want to improve and assess your communication skills and mind skills strengths and weaknesses in it.
3. Decide on:

   (a) A particular situation in which you want to use your improved skill
   (b) How you can handle the situation more skilfully.

4. If possible, look out for or remember a person or people who demonstrate the skill on which you focus.
5. Rehearse your improved skill.
6. Enact your improved skill in real life.
7. Evaluate your use of skill.
8. Set yourself homework for keeping using and improving your skill.

---

## CULTIVATING HAPPY RELATIONSHIPS

The late Mother Teresa said: 'To keep a lamp burning we have to keep putting oil on it.' Relationships, like gardens, require constant cultivation. Instead of keeping on tilling the soil, removing the weeds and applying fertilizers, you have to take care not to allow the beauty, love and happiness in your relationship gardens to deteriorate. In this book, I have outlined the communication skills and mind skills that you can develop and use not only to create, but to keep recreating and sustaining your happiness, be it as a couple or as an individual. I sincerely wish you the strength and the skills to keep creating, cultivating and sharing much happiness and warmth in your relationships.

# References

Alberti, R. and Emmons, M. (2001) *Your Perfect Right: Assertiveness and Equality in Your Life and Relationships*, 8th edn. Atascadero, CA: Impact.

Alden, L. E. and Wallace, S. T. (1995) Social phobia and social appraisal in successful and unsuccessful social interactions. *Behaviour Research and Therapy*, 33, 497–505.

American Psychiatric Association (2000) *Diagnostic and Statistical Manual of Mental Disorders DSM-IV-TR*. Washington, DC: American Psychiatric Association.

Argyle, M. (1991) *Cooperation: The Basis of Sociability*. London: Routledge.

—— (1992) *The Social Psychology of Everyday Life*. London: Routledge.

—— (1994) *The Psychology of Interpersonal Behaviour*, 5th edn. Harmondsworth: Penguin.

Argyle, M. and Henderson, M. (1985) *The Anatomy of Relationships*. Harmondsworth: Penguin.

Australian Institute of Family Studies (1993) Divorce trends. *Family Matters*, 35, 28–29.

Bandura, A. (1986) *Social Foundations of Thought and Action: A Social Cognitive Theory*. Englewood Cliffs, NJ: Prentice-Hall.

Beck, A. T. (1988) *Love Is Never Enough: How Couples Can Overcome Misunderstandings, Resolve Conflicts, and Solve Relationship Problems Through Cognitive Therapy*. New York: Harper & Row.

—— (1999) *Prisoners of Hate: The Cognitive Basis of Anger, Hostility, and Violence*. New York: HarperCollins.

Beck, A. T. and Weishaar, M. E. (2005) Cognitive therapy, in R. Corsini and D. Wedding (eds) *Current Psychotherapies*, 7th edn, pp. 238–68. Belmont, CA: Thomson Brooks/Cole.

Bem, S. L. (1974) The measurement of psychological androgyny. *Journal of Consulting and Clinical Psychology*, 42, 155–162.

—— (1981) Gender schema theory: a cognitive account of sex typing. *Psychological Review*, 88, 354–364.

Benedict, R. (1942) Unpublished lectures on synergy in society, Bryn Mawr, USA.

Berg, J. H. and Derlega, V. J. (1987) Themes in the study of self-disclosure, in

V. J. Derlega and J. H. Berg (eds) *Self-disclosure: Theory, Research and Therapy*, pp. 1–8. New York: Plenum.

Berne, E. (1964) *Games People Play: The Psychology of Human Relationships*. New York: Grove Press.

—— (1972) *What Do You Say After You Say Hello?* London: Corgi.

Bernstein, D. A. and Borkovec, T. D. (1973) *Progressive Relaxation Training: A Manual for the Helping Professions*. Champaign, IL: Research Press.

Blatner, A. (2005) Psychodrama, in R. J. Corsini and D. Wedding (eds) *Current Psychotherapies*, 7th ed, pp. 405–438. Belmont, CA: Thomson Brooks/Cole.

Bolton, R. (1986) *People Skills: How to Assert Yourself, Listen to Others, and Resolve Conflicts*. Sydney: Simon & Schuster.

Bradley, P. (2002) Relationship education: helping couples live happy, full lives. *InPsych*, 24, 3, 14–16.

Bruch, M. A. and Pearl, L. (1995) Attributional style and symptoms of shyness in a heterosexual interaction. *Cognitive Therapy and Research*, 19, 91–107.

Buber, M. (1970) *I and Thou*. New York: Charles Scribner.

Butler, P. E. (1981) *Talking to Yourself: Learning the Language of Self-Support*. San Francisco, CA: Harper & Row.

—— (1992) *Self-assertion for Women*. San Francisco, CA: HarperCollins.

Buunk, B. P. (1995) Sex, self-esteem, dependency and extradyadic sexual experience as related to jealousy responses. *Journal of Social and Personal Relationships*, 12, 147–153.

Carroll, M. (2003) The new kid on the block. *Counselling Psychology Journal*, 14, 10, 28–31.

Christensen, A. and Jacobson, N. S. (2000) *Reconcilable Differences*. New York: Guilford Press.

Clarkson, P. (2003) No sex please, we're counsellors. *Counselling and Psychotherapy Journal*, 14, 2, 7–11.

Colliver, A. (1992) *Choosing to Love: Creating Trust and Commitment in Your Relationship*. Sydney: Random House Australia.

Comfort, A. (1993) *The New Joy of Sex*. London: Mitchell Beazley.

Dalai Lama, His Holiness, and Cutler, H. C. (1998) *The Art of Happiness: A Handbook for Living*. Sydney: Hodder.

Deffenbacher, J. L., Oetting, E. R. and DiGuiseppe, R. A. (2002) Principles of empirically supported interventions applied to anger management. *The Counseling Psychologist*, 30, 262–280.

Derlega, V. J. and Chaikin, A. L. (1975) *Sharing Intimacy: What We Reveal to Others and Why*. Englewood Cliffs, NJ: Prentice-Hall.

De Vaus, D. (2002) Marriage and mental health. *Family Matters*, 62, 26–32.

De Vaus, D., Qu, L. and Weston, R. (2003) Premarital cohabitation and subsequent marital stability. *Family Matters*, 65, 34–39.

Diener, E. and Seligman, M. E. P. (2002) Very happy people. *Psychological Science*, 13, 81–84.

Drever, P. (2002) The psychology of coaching. *InPsych*, 24, 2, 24–25.

Easteal, P. (1994) Violence against women in the home: How far have we come? How far do we have to go? *Family Matters*, 37, 86–93.

Egan, G. (1977) *You and Me: The Skills of Communicating and Relating to Others*. Monterey, CA: Brooks/Cole.

—— (2002) *The Skilled Helper: A Problem-Management and Opportunity-Development Approach to Helping*, 7th edn. Pacific Grove, CA: Brooks/Cole.

Ekman, P. and Friesen, W. (1971) Constants across cultures in the face and emotion. *Journal of Personality and Social Psychology*, 17, 124–129.

Elliott, R. (2004) Personal correspondence, 20 May.

Ellis, A. (1977) *Anger. How to Live With and Without It*. Melbourne: Sun Macmillan.

—— (1987) The impossibility of achieving consistently good mental health. *American Psychologist*, 42, 364–375.

—— (2003) *Ask Albert Ellis? Straight Answers and Sound Advice from America's Best-Known Psychologist*. Atascadero, CA: Impact.

—— (2005) Rational emotive behavior therapy, in R. J. Corsini and D. Wedding (eds) *Current Psychotherapies*, 7th edn, pp. 166–201. Belmont, CA: Thomson Brooks/Cole.

Ellis, A. and Crawford, T. (2000) *Making Intimate Connections: Seven Guidelines for Great Relationships and Better Communication*. Atascadero, CA: Impact.

Fischer, R. L. (1972) *Speak to Communicate: An Introduction to Speech*. Encino, CA: Dickenson.

Freud, S. (1949) *An Outline of Psychoanalysis*. New York: Norton.

Friday, N. (1973) *My Secret Garden: Women's Sexual Fantasies*. London: Quartet.

Fromm, E. (1957) *The Art of Loving*. London: Unwin.

Gibb, B. E., Abramson, L. and Alloy, L. B. (2004) Emotional maltreatment from parents, verbal peer victimization, and cognitive vulnerability to depression. *Cognitive Therapy and Research*, 28, 1–21.

Glasser, W. (1995) *Staying Together: A Control Theory Guide to a Lasting Marriage*. New York: HarperCollins.

Goldenberg, H. and Goldenberg, I. (1990) *Counseling Today's Families*. Pacific Grove, CA: Brooks/Cole.

—— (2005) Family therapy, in R. J. Corsini and D. Wedding (eds) *Current Psychotherapies*, 7th edn, pp. 372–404. Belmont, CA: Thomson Brooks/Cole.

Goldsmith, S. (1988) Treatment of sexual dysfunction, in E. Weinstein and E. Rosen (eds) *Sexuality Counseling: Issues and Implications*, pp. 16–34. Pacific Grove, CA: Brooks/Cole.

Gordon, T. (1970) *Parent Effectiveness Training: The Tested New Way to Raise Responsible Children*. New York: Wyden.

Gottman, J. M. and Silver, N. (1999) *The Seven Principles for Making Marriage Work*. New York: Three Rivers Press.

Hackmann, A., Surawy, C. and Clark, D. M. (1998) Seeing yourself through others' eyes: a study of spontaneously occurring images in social phobia. *Behavioural and Cognitive Psychotherapy*, 26, 3–12.

Hamburg, S. R. (2000) *Will Our Love Last?: A Couple's Road Map*. New York: Scribner.

Haskey, J. (1995) Trends in marriage and cohabitation: the decline in marriage and the changing patterns of living in partnerships. *Population Trends*, 80, 5–15.

Haworth, J. and Lewis, S. (2005) Work, leisure and well-being. *British Journal of Guidance & Counselling*, 33, 67–79.

Hermans, H. J. M. and Kempen, H. J. G. (1998) Moving cultures: the perilous problems of cultural dichotomies in a globalizing society. *American Psychologist*, 53, 1111–1120.

Ivey, A. E. and Ivey, M. B. (2002) *Intentional Interviewing and Counseling: Facilitating Client Development in a Multicultural Society*. Belmont, CA: Wadsworth.

Jacobson, N. and Christensen, A. (1996) *Acceptance and Change in Couple Therapy: A Therapist's Guide to Transforming Relationships*. New York: Norton.

Johnson, D. W. (2003) *Reaching Out: Interpersonal Effectiveness and Self-Actualization*, 8th edn. Boston, MA: Allyn & Bacon.

Kassorla, I. C. (1980) *Nice Girls Do*. New York: Berkley.

—— (1984) *Go For It!* New York: Dell.

Kershaw, T. S., Ethier, K. A., Niccolai, L. M., Lewis, J. B. and Ickovics, J. R. (2003) Misperceived risk among female adolescents: social and psychological factors associated with sexual risk activity. *Health Psychology*, 22, 523–532.

Kwee, M. G. T. and Lazarus, A. A. (1986) Multimodal therapy: the cognitive-behavioural tradition and beyond, in W. Dryden and W. Golden (eds) *Cognitive-Behavioural Approaches to Psychotherapy*, pp. 320–355. London: Harper & Row.

Lazarus, A. A. (1984) *In the Mind's Eye*. New York: Guilford Press.

—— (1985) *Marital Myths: Two Dozen Beliefs that can Ruin a Marriage (or Make a Bad One Worse)*. San Luis Obispo, CA: Impact.

—— (1989) *The Practice of Multimodal Therapy: Systematic, Comprehensive and Effective Psychotherapy*. Baltimore, MA: Johns Hopkins University Press.

—— (1992) Multimodal therapy: technical eclecticism with minimal integration, in J. R. Norcross and M. R. Goldfried (eds) *Handbook of Psychotherapy Integration*, pp. 261–263. New York: Basic Books.

—— (2005) Multimodal therapy, in R. J. Corsini and D. Wedding (eds) *Current Psychotherapies*, 7th edn, pp. 337–371. Belmont, CA: Thomson Brooks/Cole.

Lazarus, A. A., Lazarus, C. N. and Fay, A. (1993) *Don't Believe It For A Minute! Forty Toxic Ideas that are Driving You Crazy*. San Luis Obispo, CA: Impact.

Lewinsohn, P. M., Munoz, R. F., Youngren, M. A. and Zeiss, A. M. (1986) *Control Your Depression*. New York: Prentice-Hall.

Litvinoff, S. (1992) *The Relate Guide to Sex in Loving Relationships*. London: Vermilion.

—— (1993) *The Relate Guide to Starting Again: How To Learn From the Past To Give You A Better Future*. London: Vermilion.

Macaskill, A. (2005) The treatment of forgiveness in counselling and therapy. *Counselling Psychology Review*, 20, 26–32.

McCabe, M. P. (1994) Childhood, adolescent and current psychological factors associated with sexual dysfunction. *Sexual and Marital Therapy*, 9, 267–276.

McKay, M., Fanning, P. and Paleg, K. (1994) *Couple Skills: Making Your Relationship Work*. Oakland, CA: New Harbinger.

Maslow, A. H. (1970) *Motivation and Personality*, 2nd edn. New York: Harper & Row.

—— (1971) *The Farther Reaches of Human Nature*. Harmondsworth: Penguin.

Masters, W. H. and Johnson, V. E. (1970) *The Pleasure Bond*. New York: Bantam.

Masters, W. H., Johnson, V. E. and Kolodny, R. C. (1986) *Masters and Johnson on Sex and Human Loving*. London: Pan Macmillan.

Meichenbaum, D. H. (1983) *Coping with Stress*. London: Century.

—— (1985) *Stress Inoculation Training*. New York: Pergamon.

Meichenbaum, D. H. and Deffenbacher, J. L. (1988) Stress inoculation training. *The Counseling Psychologist*, 16, 69–90.

Moreno, Z. T. (1959) A survey of psychodramatic techniques. *Group Psychotherapy*, 12, 5–14.

Muehlenhard, C. L., Koralewski, M. A., Andrews, S. L. and Burdick, C. A. (1986) Verbal and non-verbal cues that convey interest in dating: two studies. *Behavior Therapy*, 17, 404–419.

Neenan, M. and Dryden, W. (2002) *Life Coaching: A Cognitive-Behavioural Approach*. Hove: Brunner-Routledge.

Nelson-Jones, R. (2002) Are there universal human being skills? *Counselling Psychology Quarterly*, 15, 115–119.

—— (2004) *Cognitive Humanistic Therapy: Buddhism, Christianity and Being Fully Human*. London: Sage.

Noller, P., Feeney, J. A., Bonnell, D. and Callan, V. J. (1994) A longitudinal study of conflict early in marriage. *Journal of Personal and Social Relationships*, 11, 233–252.

Norcross, J. C. (2000) Here comes the self-help revolution in mental health. *Psychotherapy*, 37, 370–377.

Office for National Statistics (2003a) *Population Trends, Winter*. London: Office for National Statistics.

—— (2003b) *Population Trends, Autumn*. London: Office for National Statistics.

Perry, M. A. and Furukawa, M. J. (1986) Modeling methods, in F. H. Kanfer and A. P. Goldstein (eds) *Helping People Change: A Textbook of Methods*, 3rd edn, pp. 66–110. New York: Pergamon.

Pietromomaco, P. R. and Rook, K. A. (1987) Decision style in depression: the contribution of perceived risks versus benefits. *Journal of Personality and Social Psychology*, 52, 399–408.

Pistole, M. C. (1995) College students' ended love relationships: attachment style and emotion. *Journal of College Student Personnel*, 12, 417–438.

Powell, J. J. (1969) *Why Am I Afraid to Tell You Who I Am?* London: Fontana.

Previti, D. and Amato, P. R. (2004) Is infidelity a cause or a consequence of poor marital quality? *Journal of Personal and Social Relationships*, 21, 217–230.

Prior, D. M. (2003) *Professional coaching language for greater public understanding*. www.coach-federation.org.

Rachman, S., Gruter-Andrew, J. and Shafran, R. (2000) Post-event processing in social anxiety. *Behaviour Research and Therapy*, 38, 611–617.

Rapee, R. M. (1993) Recent advances in the treatment of social phobia. *Australian Psychologist*, 28, 168–171.

Rogers, C. R. (1951) *Client-Centered Therapy*. Boston: Houghton Mifflin.

—— (1973) *Becoming Partners: Marriage and its Alternatives*. London: Constable.

—— (1975) Empathic: an unappreciated way of being. *The Counseling Psychologist*, 5, 2, 2–10.

Schwartz, S. H. (1992) Universals in the content and structure of values: theoretical advances and empirical tests in 20 countries, in M. Zanna (ed.) *Advances in Experimental Social Psychology*. New York: Academic Press.

Segrin, C., Taylor, M. E. and Altman, J. (2005) Social cognitive mediators and relational outcomes associated with parental divorce. *Journal of Social and Personal Relationships*, 22, 361–77.

Seligman, M. E. P. (1991) *Learned Optimism*. Milsons Point, NSW: Random House Australia.

Seligman, M. E. P. (2002) *Authentic Happiness: Using the New Positive Psychology to Realize Your Potential for Lasting Fulfillment*. New York: Free Press.

Seligman, M. E. P. (2003) Positive psychology: Fundamental assumptions. *The Psychologist*, 16, 126–127.

Selye, H. (1974) *Stress Without Distress*. Sevenoaks: Hodder & Stoughton.

Stuart, R.B. (1980) *Helping Couples Change: A Social Learning Approach to Marital Therapy*. New York: Guilford Press.

Sullivan, H. S. (1953) *The Interpersonal Theory of Psychiatry*. New York: Norton.

Tavris, C. (1989) *Anger: The Misunderstood Emotion*. New York: Simon and Schuster.

Teasdale, J. D. and Dent, J. (1987) Cognitive vulnerability to depression: an investigation of two hypotheses. *British Journal of Clinical Psychology*, 26, 113–126.

Thompson, D. (ed.) (1995) *The Concise Oxford Dictionary of Current English*. Oxford: Oxford University Press.

Trewin, D. (2004) *Yearbook Australia 2004*. Canberra: Australian Bureau of Statistics.

Trotter, R. J. (1986) The three faces of love. *Psychology Today*, September, 46–50, 54.

Wellings, K., Field, J., Johnson, A. M. and Wadsworth, J. (1994) *Sexual Behaviour in Britain: The National Survey of Sexual Attitudes and Lifestyles*. Harmondsworth: Penguin.

Williams, P. and Davis, D. C. (2002) *Therapist as Life Coach: Transforming Your Practice*. New York: Norton.

Wolpe, J. and Wolpe, D. (1988) *Life Without Fear: Anxiety and its Cure*. Oakland, CA: New Harbinger.

Worthington, E. L. and Scherer, M. (2004) Forgiveness is an emotion-focused coping strategy that can reduce health risks and promote health resilience: theory, review and hypotheses. *Psychology and Health*, 19, 385–405.

Yalom, I. D. (1980) *Existential Therapy*. New York: Basic Books.

Zilbergeld, B. (1978) *Male Sexuality*. New York: Bantam.

Zimbardo, P. G. (1977) *Shyness: What It Is, What to Do About It*. Reading, MA: Addison-Wesley.

# Name index